The Resume.com Guide to Writing Unbeatable Resumes

The Resume.com Guide to Writing Unbeatable Resumes

ROSE CURTIS, CPRW

WARREN SIMONS, CPRW

McGraw-Hill

New York   Chicago   San Francisco
Lisbon   London   Madrid   Mexico City   Milan
New Delhi   San Juan   Seoul   Singapore
Sydney   Toronto

9 0 QPD/QPD 0

ISBN 0-07-141105-4

McGraw-Hill books are available at special discounts to use as premiums and sales promotions, or for use in corporate training programs. For more information, please write to the Director of Special Sales, Professional Publishing, McGraw-Hill, Two Penn Plaza, New York, NY 10121-2298. Or contact your local bookstore.

This book is printed on acid-free paper.

Contents

List of Resumes by Industry/Job Title

Preface

Whether you've been in the workforce for 20 years or are applying for your first job, a powerful resume will set you apart from the competition and introduce your name with the air of professionalism employers crave. Your resume is your handshake, your agent, and your marketing department rolled into one, and this vital document is an indispensable asset that will expedite your job search and make a prospective employer pick up the phone.

The cornerstone of a winning job search is a great resume, and the Certified Professional Resume Writers and Editors at Resume.com have created this book to help you understand what does and doesn't work in today's job market. Our proven techniques and industry secrets will help ensure that your next job search will be a fruitful one. Resume.com has written thousands of effective resumes for job applicants in every industry, and we know exactly what employers look for—from creating a marketing strategy to applying for the position, following up, interviewing, and ultimately accepting a new position.

Our diverse network of professional resume writers has a fluent understanding of what makes a resume work. This book will walk you step by step through our methodology, teaching you how to create a professionally written resume that will give you the competitive advantage you need in a crowded job market.

We'll also explore the fundamental changes that have taken place in the hiring process over the last five years as a result of innovations in technology and the ways those changes probably will affect your job search. In today's market one job opening can attract a thousand resumes, and only the best will stand out. Resume.com has built its reputation by making sure that professionals find success every step of the way. Writing your own resume can be difficult and frustrating, but we'll show you the formats and requirements that our network of Certified Professional Resume Writers and career consultants have used to turn job seekers from every industry into career professionals.

From choosing the format that is best for you to giving you industry secrets, this is the most comprehensive resource for resume writing available today. Our resume writers and career consultants have worked closely with thousands of job seekers around the world, collecting valuable insider information to demonstrate what hirers are looking for and how this information can work for you.

WHAT IS RESUME.COM?

Resume.com is a career-services company with over 100 resume writers and career consultants nationwide. With our fingers directly on the pulse of the job market, we are dedicated to providing the highest quality of service to all job applicants looking for the best source of career advice. Resume.com has been an industry leader since its founding in March 2000, and its blue-chip partners include the *New York Times* and Yahoo!, two of the most recognized and respected sources of industry news in the world. Resume.com has appeared on CNN and in numerous profiles in the *New York Times*, the *Los Angeles Times*, and the *Miami Herald*.

WHY THIS BOOK IS UNIQUE

The goal of Resume.com is to arm you with every competitive advantage available. This book will guide you through every phase of your job search—what we call the four steps: **career planning, resume writing, marketing,** and **interviewing**. If you already know what you want to do, you've already completed your preplanning. If you do not, jump to Appendix B, where you'll find helpful worksheets that will organize your interests and experience and help you determine the direction in which you want to go.

The majority of this book is focused on helping you create your own professional resume, Step 2 of the process. In addition, we'll show you how hirers will review your resume, when and how you should follow up after submitting a resume, and every step necessary to get effective responses from employers, including the **cover letter**, **resume**, and **follow-up letter**.

Once you've completed this step, review Chapter 9 to get the inside scoop on marketing yourself by using mass marketing methods such as Internet job boards, associations, newspapers, and more. This is Step 3.

The purpose of a resume is to get interviews, which is Step 4 in the job search process. Writing your resume will prepare you to organize your thoughts and remind you of your responsibilities and accomplishments. To help you navigate Step 4 of your job search, we've included detailed instructions on how to develop a **list of references**, **letter of recommendation**, and a postinterview **thank you letter**.

Unlike other books on the market, this book gives you the opportunity to speak with a career specialist. A career consultation with a Resume.com career specialist is available to you at www.resume.com to ensure that you receive the support and career advice you need every step of the way.

The Resume.com Guide to Writing Unbeatable Resumes

1

An Introduction to Professional Resumes

Whether you're applying for your first position or are a senior executive with over 20 years of experience, your resume consists of more than a list of your previous jobs, your name, and your phone number. A good resume is your handshake and a promise of the professionalism that you'll bring to a new job. Understanding how a potential employer will judge your resume is an important element of the job search, and exploiting this knowledge to your advantage can result in greater success in less time.

Before you begin reviewing the step-by-step tips and industry secrets we'll share with you, it's important to understand *how* most hiring managers will evaluate your resume.

Practically all hiring managers are overworked and understaffed, and after a job ad is placed on the Internet or in a newspaper, an employer has to review hundreds, if not thousands, of resumes before narrowing the field to a select few. Additionally, openings have to be filled in a timely manner, and although we'd like to believe that every resume will be reviewed carefully, that's usually far from the case. **Most resumes will be reviewed for only 10 seconds before being eliminated**. Picture a stack of 1500 resumes in front of you and a one-week deadline to get several qualified candidates in the door for an interview and you'll start to see how ferocious the competition is and how quickly the evaluating takes place.

After the initial round of review and elimination, a hirer usually will spend a few minutes looking over the 10 to 15 resumes that have made the cut. It's here where the resume has to glow. Correct formatting, spelling, structure, and adherence to the very specific language of resumes are all vital elements that will determine whether your resume will move onto the "call list" or whether you'll receive a rejection letter or no response at all.

Although there are many factors that will determine your resume's impact, the most important rule to remember is simply that it's not just the document an employer is reviewing—it's you.

A good resume should result in one thing: an interview. In the following pages we'll show you, step by step, how to get there. Our strategies have turned those precious 10 seconds into interviews for thousands of clients throughout the world.

AN INTERNET PRIMER

A lot has changed in the years since a company ran an ad in the Sunday newspaper for a few hundred dollars and received 50 to 100 responses. The advent of the Internet has shifted every stage of the job application and hiring process, from how you'll write and distribute your resume to the steps you'll take to research and apply for openings.

Competition among job seekers is at an all-time high, and this is due partly to the ease with which one can apply for a job. A simple click of the button can distribute your resume to a prospective employer (or even hundreds in some cases), and this ease of distribution often creates an overwhelming response to advertised positions.

To combat this overwhelming response, companies have started using technology to their advantage, and some even use special search software that scans and eliminates applicants before a human being has looked at a resume. Although not every company uses this type of software, technology is a primary force in the job application process, and that's a reality that every job seeker should be aware of. We'll discuss how to avoid being eliminated from consideration by scanning software in Chapter 8, but resume-filtering tools are just one of the many applications that hiring managers use to divide and eliminate applicants solely on the basis of the inadequacy of their resumes.

The resume is no longer a two-dimensional object to only be mailed or handed to an old friend. A twenty-first-century resume is your personal recruiter and perhaps the only marketing tool that you have to ensure that hirers immediately recognize your accomplishments and skills.

Twenty-first-century resumes are by no means identical: They come in many different formats and layouts. However, despite the amazing array of fonts, colors, styles, and options you have to choose from, there is a set of rules and guidelines you should always follow to create your own professional resume.

SEVEN STEPS TO BUILDING A GREAT RESUME

There are certain key elements that go into every great resume. Although we'll explore them in greater depth when we review the resume-building process in Chapter 6, let's take a brief look at **the seven rules that should never be violated in writing a resume.**

Although every resume will be different, depending on your unique employment history, level of expertise, and profession, each resume should be organized in a way that creates an optimal synergy between past accomplishments and future career goals.

Following are seven basic steps for building the solid foundation of a great resume.

1. Use the Right Point of View

The main goal of your resume is to create a direct relationship between you and the employer. The easiest way to accomplish this is by always staying in the first person. Although the first person means writing from your point of view (or using the word "I" to begin every sentence), resume writers employ a trick called using the **silent I**. This means that the "I" is always implied in every sentence; it's just never written on the page. The examples below demonstrate how to use your voice when writing a resume, using the first person but never writing "I."

Correct: Manage 10 Sales Associates responsible for generating 80% of company revenue.

Incorrect: I manage 10 Sales Associates responsible for generating 80% of company revenue.

Incorrect: Manage**s** 10 Sales Associates responsible for generating 80% of company revenue. (You never want to write "he or she manage**s**"; that's the third person.)

An easy way to remember this is to pretend that you're in an interview but can't say the word "I." If during an interview for a management position a potential employer asks you how many people you supervise, you might respond, "I supervise seven sales professionals." That's first person, and it's the correct approach in resume writing. You wouldn't answer, "He (or She) manages seven sales professionals." When writing a resume, use the silent "I" to create an instant sense of correlation and responsibility between the applicant and the accomplishment. An employer probably would reject the incorrect examples shown above. Why?

"I" is a word hirers never like to see. Remember that most businesses are teams, and there's no "I" in "team." The third example is incorrect because it shifts to the third-person point of view. When the "s" is added to "manage," the structure shifts the sentence to an action that somebody else is responsible for (*He or she manages 10 sales associates*). Remember: Never use the words "he," "she," "our," and "their" in a resume. (These are those pesky third-person pronouns we all learned and forgot about in high school.)

2. Use Action Verbs

Action verbs are an essential part of a resume and an important part of producing a resume that gets you noticed. ***They are generally effective when used as the first word in an accomplishment statement,*** as they grab an employer's attention and clearly demonstrate what you've achieved. Action verbs also are always used within ***responsibility statements;*** these are sentences highlighting your overall duties that we recommend writing in a paragraph format. Responsibility statements generally precede your accomplishment bullets but also can stand alone.

Dramatically different action verbs may be used to express the accomplishments or responsibilities of a Chief Operating Officer as opposed to a Managing Editor. The bottom line is that no two resumes are alike, and powerful action verbs should be selected carefully, depending on your industry.

Appendix C includes a comprehensive list of action verbs by category. A few examples of powerful action verbs that are great to start off a sentence include Manage or Managed, Direct or Directed, Implement or Implemented, Analyze and Analyzed, Guide and Guided, and Oversee and Oversaw.

These verbs will change tenses (from present tense to past tense), depending on whether the skill, accomplishment, or duty is from a current position or a previous one.

3. Use a Headline to Hook Hirers

A headline is your major selling point and will sum up your objective and your strongest skills in a one- or two-line statement. ***The key to the headline is telling a potential employer what you have to offer the company, not what you want from it.*** Headlines combine the advantages of professional objectives with the advantages of accomplishments. A *personal* objective can be very vague, and has no appeal to the employer. For example:

I'm looking for a position that offers growth and the chance to utilize my skills and accomplishments in a career-oriented position.

This vague statement can be strengthened by converting it to a *professional* objective, combining it with your most attractive attributes or skills, and telling the employer what you have to offer.

Headline: *Award-winning sales professional with quota-shattering background and demonstrated expertise in training, motivating, and overseeing junior employees*

This is the first sentence that will follow your contact information at the top of the resume, and it's so important that we've devoted a significant portion of Chaper 6 to creating a good headline. One note: Don't add a period after the headline; we want to keep this like a brief slogan that encourages you to read the entire advertisement.

4. Don't Use Articles

Resume writing uses a telegraphic style that avoids using very basic words such as "a," "an," and "the," which are known as articles. When telegrams were the main form of communication, every word added to a telegram was an additional cost to the sender. That's why articles usually were eliminated. The time that you have to convey your message is extremely valuable, and you should always remember to cut excess words in a resume, especially articles.

Time is also a valuable part of an employer's day, and the faster he or she is able to review your resume and understand your accomplishments, the more powerful the resume is. A watered-down sentence will use "a," "an," and "the" when it is not necessary:

Incorrect Example: *Managed a team of three employees and directed the benefits administration for a major accounting firm.*

A stronger sentence avoids these articles and is crisp and concise:

Correct Example: *Managed team of three employees and directed benefits administration for major accounting firm.*

Although the difference may seem subtle, this is a key element of a powerful resume.

5. Use Numbers and Symbols Effectively

The standard rule of spelling out numbers from one to nine applies to professional resumes. However, when you are citing monetary amounts of $1 million or more, use the numeral. When you use numerals, these highly attractive figures jump off the page faster than they would if they were spelled out.

Correct: Directed seven employees and oversaw $1 million budget.

Incorrect: Directed **7** employees and oversaw **a one million dollar** budget.

6. The Header Is the Most Important Part of a Resume

Although it may sound like something that's so basic that it doesn't need to be mentioned, the most important part of your resume is the header, which includes your name, address, phone number, and e-mail. If these things aren't included or if there's a spelling mistake or typo in this part of the resume, the employer will not be able to contact you. You can have the most beautiful, well-written resume in the world, and it will be completely irrelevant. An employer will not try to track you down.

Chapter 6 discusses how to format great headers, but for now remember that a phone number and an e-mail address are vital to your success. If you don't have an e-mail account, sign up for one before you send out your first resume. They're free, and you can go to www.yahoo.com or www.hotmail.com and sign up for one in a few minutes.

7. Avoid Topics That Can Screen You Out

Whether you were a member of your church's choir or the leader of a group dedicated to advancing sexual equality, avoid including information on your resume that does not support your professional objective.

Let your accomplishments and skills speak for you. Don't give a hirer any reason to reject your application outside of the qualifications. You should omit from your resume height, weight, sexual orientation, religion, race, ethnicity, national origin, and physical disabilities unless they are job-related or you are applying to organizations that you know will see them as pluses.

Age and photographs are other areas to avoid including in a resume.

After you've completed your resume, a quick review of these areas will ensure that you won't be eliminated from consideration because of simple mistakes. Next, we'll discuss the steps to building a powerful resume. The first step is deciding which format is right for you.

CHOOSING THE RIGHT FORMAT FOR YOU

Choosing the right format is essential to your job search, as your work history and accomplishments need to be reflected clearly to impress employers. The good news is that it's a relatively easy choice. By answering a few questions, you'll be able to determine the right format and begin creating a power resume. Resumes are divided into three major categories:

1. **The chronological resume** is a step-by-step breakdown of your career by dates. **Job seekers with a steady work history primarily use this format**, as it highlights the applicant's most recent position and moves backward in a linear time frame. Over 90% of all resumes use the chronological format, and if you've ever created a resume by using a template from a word-processing program, the odds are that it follows this format.

2. **The functional resume** emphasizes two to four major skills you would want to showcase to an employer, such as sales, administration, and management. As opposed to highlighting a steady track record of employment in a direct timeline, **individuals who prefer the functional format are usually reentering the workforce after a hiatus or are changing careers.**

3. **The combination resume** is a hybrid of the two and is used primarily by applicants who have a steady work history but wish to emphasize their functional skill sets. **Self-employed professionals and consultants frequently use a combination resume.**

Students can use both the chronological and functional formats.

In the next few chapters we'll focus on the unique attributes, advantages, and weaknesses of these major resume formats.

2

The Chronological Resume Format

The overwhelming majority of resumes follow the chronological format as it's the easiest type of document both to create and to read. The chronological resume lists your responsibilities, skills, accomplishments, and work history by highlighting your most recent position and working backward to include all relevant employment.

The chronological format is ideal if you fit into one of the following categories:

- You have a steady work history.
- You are able to demonstrate upward mobility or promotions with one or more companies following a single career path.
- You are applying for a job similar to your present or last position.
- You have worked at Fortune 1000 companies with impressive name recognition.
- You are working with a recruiter or staffing agency.

A chronological resume sorts your employment history by date, and the purpose of this format is to demonstrate a job seeker's professional advancement and highlight his or her strengths as a career-oriented professional.

By listing data in "reverse chronological order"—or moving backward from today to over 20 years ago, for example—you emphasize the most recent and most relevant information in your career. Your educational degrees, memberships, certificates, and awards (if applicable) follow your employment history. We'll break this down for you step by step in Chapter 6.

STRENGTHS OF THE CHRONOLOGICAL FORMAT

- It calls attention to a stable work history or employers with strong name recognition.
- It demonstrates upward mobility and promotions (with one or more companies) in the course of a single career path.
- It is favored by employers for purposes of making comparisons.

WEAKNESSES OF THE CHRONOLOGICAL FORMAT

- The strong emphasis on work history is less than ideal for many people.
    Solution: Use the functional format.
- Your most recent experience has to be relevant to the job for which you're applying.
    Solution: Use the functional or combination format.

If you have a strong work history, however, and think that this is the right resume for you, don't hesitate to use it. There are ways to deemphasize gaps in employment, including listing positions by year instead of by month/year and including your activity and purpose during your period of unemployment. In the example below there's an 11-month gap in employment that is downplayed simply by listing the year:

Correctly Covering Gaps in a Chronological Resume

Company Name, City, State   **2000 – 2002**
Job Title

Company Name, City, State   **1998 – 2000**
Job Title

Incorrectly Exposing Gaps in a Chronological Resume

Company Name, City, State   **12/00 – 05/02**
Job Title

Company Name, City, State   **11/98 – 02/00**
Job Title

The next few pages contain a chronological resume template and examples of resumes that follow this format. An introduction to the advantages and disadvantages of the functional resume appears in the next chapter, and if you're not sure which resume format best suits your needs take the quick quiz in Appendix A to help you decide.

CONTACT INFORMATION NAME

Street Address • City, State ZIP • Phone Number • E-mail Address

Your Headline should directly follow your contact information

SUMMARY OF QUALIFICATIONS

➢ 1
➢ 2
➢ 3
➢ 4
➢ 5

PROFESSIONAL EXPERIENCE

Company Name, City, State   08/00 – 12/02
Job Title
Responsibility statement describing your overall job duties.
- Accomplishments statements describing your actions and their results.
- 2
- 3
- 4
- 5

Company Name, City, State   03/97 – 07/00
Job Title
Responsibility statement describing y
- Accomplishments statements d
- 2

> The key to the chronological resume is listing dates of employment in reverse order. Start with the date of your most relevant position (or when you graduated college or high school) and work up to your most recent position.

Company Name, City, State   05/96 – 02/97
Job Title
Responsibility statement describing your overall job duties.
- Accomplishments statements describing your actions and their results.
- 2

Company Name, City, State   07/94 – 04/96
Job Title
Responsibility statement describing your overall job duties.
- Accomplishments statements describing your actions and their results.
- 2

EDUCATION

College or University, City, State
Degree, Graduation Date

KEYWORDS

A set of words that will help ensure that you're not eliminated because of a missing word or phrase in your resume. For example, for Accounts Payable, the keyword would be A/P.

MARINA APPESSOS

35 Conch Shell Road • Tallahassee, FL 32399 • (800) 737-8637 • mappessos@resume.com

Award-winning sales professional with quota-shattering background and demonstrated expertise training, motivating, and overseeing sales professionals

SUMMARY OF QUALIFICATIONS

- Over six years of sales and merchandising experience, with track record of consistently exceeding sales quotas.
- Strong background in managing both teams and individuals, including 22 in-house sales representatives.
- Forge and maintain excellent relationships with wholesale representatives, including buyers from major retailers, merchandising assistants, and store managers.
- Self-starter with ability to multitask. Exceptional organization and administration skills.
- Achieved 95% customer satisfaction rating, earning consistent repeat business for company.
- Superior communication abilities with fluency in Spanish.
- Proficient in MS Office, Windows, Mac OS, AS/400, MovJ wholesale software, Quark, and Lotus Notes.

PROFESSIONAL EXPERIENCE

Lebron Accessories Company, Tallahassee, FL   08/00 – 12/02
Promotions Coordinator (10/01 – 12/02)
Monitored group line merchandise throughout retail establishments, and directed sales representatives in determining and tracking cut-off dates for all show merchandise. Supervised new line deliveries, past merchandise allocation and sample inventory management. Assured correct shipment of merchandise from production facilities throughout the United States. Ensured on-time and appropriate delivery of merchandise, color cards, and theft tags to large retail.
- Reengineered inventory processes and procedures, increasing efficiency 190% within six months.
- Administered and tracked sample stock, consisting of more than 5,000 items.

Sales and Promotions Coordinator (08/00 – 10/01)
Designed allocation, scheduling and distribution initiatives for promotional items. Scheduled, monitored and bought sales materials at key industry events.
- Successfully delivered promotional items for over 1000 retail establishments throughout United States.
- Created and executed all initiatives for promotional purchase program.
- Interfaced extensively with 18 sales representatives and buyers.

Orange Products, Tallahassee, FL   03/97 – 07/00
National Sales Assistant
Managed day-to-day merchandising operations, ensuring precise delivery of goods to retail establishments throughout West Coast. Collaborated with regional manager to establish corporatewide merchandising processes and procedures. Analyzed, tracked and confirmed all shipments and deliveries. Produced weekly sales reports for management. Reviewed and resolved all customer service issues. Oversaw and administered showroom, including inventory control and quality adherence.
- Interfaced with buyers and assistants from Saks Fifth Avenue, Neiman Marcus, Macy's and Liberty House.
- Provided administrative and sales support to regional manager and three sales representatives.

Sunshine Marine Ltd., Miami, FL   05/96 – 02/97
Sales Associate
Supported sales reps in Junior and Fashion Jewelry departments. Assessed daily sales statistics; focused on identifying consumer trends and purchases. Trained and mentored new employees on customer service and corporate processes and procedures.
- Awarded "Customer Service Associate of the Year."
- Designed and executed sales/marketing strategies, successfully exceeding all sales goals.

EDUCATION
University of Miami, Miami, FL
Bachelor of Arts Degree in Fashion Merchandising, 1996

Keywords: Merchandiser, Promotions Manager, Public Relations, Purchaser

MARINA APPESSOS

A strong **headline** introduces multiple skills and/or accomplishments.

35 Conch Shell Road • Tallahassee, FL 32399 • (800) 737-8637 • mappessos@resume.com

Award-winning sales professional with quota-shattering background and demonstrated expertise training, motivating, and overseeing sales professionals

SUMMARY OF QUALIFICATIONS

- Over six years of sales and merchandising experience, with track record of consistently exceeding sales quotas.
- Strong background in managing both teams and individuals, including 22 in-house sales representatives.
- Forge and maintain excellent relationships with wholesale representatives, including buyers from major retailers, merchandising assistants, and store managers.
- Self-starter with ability to multitask. Exceptional organization
- Achieved 95% customer satisfaction rating, earning consistent
- Superior communication abilities with fluency in Spanish.
- Proficient in MS Office, Windows, Mac OS, AS/400, MovJ wholesale software, Quark, and Lotus Notes.

A good resume will include four to eight bullets in the **Summary of Qualifications** section to keep employers focused on your strongest assets.

PROFESSIONAL EXPERIENCE

Lebron Accessories Company, Tallahass...

Promotions Coordinator (10/01 – 12/02)

Include your **professional experience** and responsibilities in paragraph form and bullet your accomplishments, showing actions taken and achieved results.

08/00 – 12/02

Monitored group line merchandise througho... ...representatives in determining and tracking cut-off dates for all show merch... ...ast merchandise allocation and sample inventory management. Assured correct shipment of merchandise from production facilities throughout the United States. Ensured on-time and appropriate delivery of merchandise, color cards, and theft tags to large retail.

- Reengineered inventory processes and procedures, increasing efficiency 190% within six months.
- Administered and tracked sample stock, consisting of more than 5,000 items.

Sales and Promotions Coordinator (08/00 – 10/01)

Designed allocation, scheduling and distribution initiatives for promotional items. Scheduled, monitored and bought sales materials at key industry events.

- Successfully delivered promotional items for over 1000 retail establishments throughout United States.
- Created and executed all initiatives for promotional purchase program.
- Interfaced extensively with 18 sales representatives and buyers.

A steady track record of employment **dates** is a key to the chronological resume's appeal.

Orange Products, Tallahassee, FL

National Sales Assistant

03/97 – 07/00

Managed day-to-day merchandising operations, ensuring precise delivery of goods to retail establishments throughout West Coast. Collaborated with regional manager to establish corporatewide merchandising processes and procedures. Analyzed, tracked and confirmed all shipments and deliveries. Produced weekly sales reports for management. Reviewed and resolved all customer service issues. Oversaw and administered showroom, including inventory control and quality adherence.

- Interfaced with buyers and assistants from Saks Fifth Avenue, Neiman Marcus, Macy's and Liberty House.
- Provided administrative and sales support to regional manager and three sales representatives.

Sunshine Marine Ltd., Miami, FL

Sales Associate

05/96 – 02/97

Supported sales reps in Junior and Fashion Jewelry departments. Assessed daily sales statistics; focused on identifying consumer trends and purchases. Trained and mentored new employees on customer service and corporate processes and procedures.

- Awarded "Customer Service Associate of the Year."
- Designed and executed sales/marketing strategies, successfully...

In the **Education** section include the college date if you're a recent graduate or have less than five years of professional experience.

EDUCATION

University of Miami, Miami, FL

Bachelor of Arts Degree in Fashion Merchandising, 1996

Keywords: Merchandiser, Promotions Manager, Public Relations, Purchaser

Florence Sullivan

77 Market Street • Newark, NJ 08625 • 800-737-8637 • fsullivan@resume.com

Talented Executive Assistant with strong management and administration background

SUMMARY OF QUALIFICATIONS

➢ Proven success planning and directing executive-level administrative affairs and providing support to senior management.

➢ Organized and meticulous, with exceptional communication skills. Adept at building strong business relationships with diverse range of customers, coworkers, and management.

➢ Demonstrated expertise in data entry, telephone support, scheduling, bookkeeping, and reporting.

➢ Able to coordinate and complete multiple projects in deadline-oriented environment.

➢ Quick learner, adapting easily to new protocols and changing environments.

➢ Proficient in MS Office; type 78 wpm.

PROFESSIONAL EXPERIENCE

ANDERSON AND SONS, New York, NY   1999 – Present

Executive Assistant (2001 – Present) promoted within four months of hire to provide executive support to Vice President of Marketing. Interface extensively with corporate clientele. Plan, schedule, and administer office operations, overseeing data entry, telephone support, mail distribution, scheduling, filing, and reporting.

❑ Arrange and coordinate travel itineraries, including airfare, accommodations, and dining.
❑ Manage confidential correspondence, appointments, and meetings for staff.
❑ Monitor and secure approval of all expenses.
❑ Assist Vice President with recruiting and hiring sales associates and analysts for company.

Office Coordinator (1999 – 2001) responsible for assisting with administration of day-to-day office operations for advertising department.

❑ Supervised and coordinated special events and corporate retreats.
❑ Provided administrative support to office manager and sales staff.
❑ Maintained and updated all vendor accounts and files.
❑ Supported business manager in analyzing financial investments and producing reports.

HEVLO REGIONAL OPERATIONS, Plainview, NY   1995 – 1999

Office Manager accountable for managing operations for $5 million carpet import/export company.

❑ Responsible for overseeing all facets of client contact, arranging inventory shipment, accounts payable and receivable, billing, employee supervision, correspondence, and sales.
❑ **Instrumental in increasing revenue from $2.2 million to $4.7 million within one year.**
❑ Planned and executed customer service initiatives, increased customer satisfaction 73%.
❑ Collaborated with sales and marketing teams to design business plans.
❑ Analyzed and automated bookkeeping processes, enhancing both efficiency and quality.
❑ Represented company at Hevlo's annual trade seminar.

COMPUTER SKILLS

Microsoft Office, PeopleSoft, QuickBooks, FreeTree Accounting, Internet-savvy

EDUCATION

University of Phoenix, San Francisco, CA
Bachelor of Business Administration; Concentration in Management

KEYWORDS: A/R, A/P, assistant, executive support, executive office support, management, administration, payroll

References available upon request

Florence Sullivan

77 Market Street • Newark, NJ 08625 • 800-737-8637 • fsullivan@resume.com

Talented Executive Assistant with strong management and administration background

SUMMARY OF QUALIFICATIONS

➢ Proven success planning and directing executive-level administrative affairs and providing support to senior management.

➢ Organized and meticulous, with exceptional communication skills. Adept at building strong business relationships with diverse range of customers, coworkers, and management.

➢ Demonstrated expertise in data entry, telephone support, scheduling, bookkeeping, and reporting.

➢ Able to coordinate and complete multiple projects in deadline-oriented environment.

➢ Quick learner, adapting easily to new protocols and changing environments.

➢ Proficient in MS Office; type 78 wpm.

PROFESSIONAL EXPERIENCE

ANDERSON AND SONS, New York, NY   1999 – Present

Executive Assistant (2001 – Present) promoted within four months of hire to provide executive support to Vice President of Marketing. Interface extensively with corporate clientele. Plan, schedule, and administer office operations, overseeing data entry, telephone support, mail distribution, scheduling, filing, and reporting.

❑ Arrange and coordinate travel itine... ...ommodations, and dining.

❑ Manage confidential correspond... ...ngs for staff.

❑ Monitor and secure approval of a...

❑ Assist Vice President with recruiti... ...s and analysts for company.

> Demonstrating promotions with one company is an effective way to convince employers that you're a responsible candidate.

Office Coordinator (1999 – 2001) responsible for assisting with administration of day-to-day office operations for advertising department.

❑ Supervised and coordinated special events and corporate retreats.

❑ Provided administrative support to office manager and sales staff.

❑ Maintained and updated all vendor accounts and files.

❑ Supported business manager in analyzing financial investments and producing reports.

HEVLO REGIONAL OPERATIONS, Plainview, NY   1995 – 1999

Office Manager accountable for managing operations for $5 million carpet import/export company.

❑ Responsible for overseeing all facets of client contact, arranging inventory shipment, accounts payable and receivable, billing, employee supervision, correspondence, and sales.

❑ **Instrumental in increasing revenue from $2.2 million to $4.7 million within one year.**

❑ Planned and executed customer service initiatives, increased customer satisfaction 73%.

❑ Collaborated with sales and marketing teams to design business plans.

❑ Analyzed and automated bookkeeping processes, enhancing both efficiency and quality.

❑ Represented company at Hevlo's annual trade seminar.

COMPUTER SKILLS

Microsoft Office, PeopleSoft, QuickBooks, FreeTree Accounting, Internet-savvy

EDUCATION

University of Phoenix, San Francisco, CA
Bachelor of Business Administration; Concentration in Management

KEYWORDS: A/R, A/P, assistant, executive support, executive office support, management, administration, payroll

References available upon request

3

The Functional Resume Format

The functional format allows a job applicant to highlight specific skills, responsibilities, and accomplishments, **shifting the emphasis of the resume away from recent employment**.

The functional format is ideal if you fit into one of the following categories:

- You are changing careers.
- You are returning to the workforce after a long hiatus.

The functional format showcases your most desirable traits, organizing information into two to four subsections that offer employers a wide range of attractive skills. The primary advantage of the functional format is that it allows you to highlight experiences that have no direct relationship with your recent professional history. This allows your diverse skills to speak to your professional goal, bringing your background to the foreground.

For example, if you are applying for positions in the journalism field after working for many years in information technology, you can create writing, editing, and communication skill sets that will allow you to apply for a vast array of positions not limited to your last job. Bolstering your skill sets with a powerful Summary of Qualifications and Headline will emphasize your transferable skills in an employer's eyes.

> Whereas the *chronological format* defines your background by work history, the *functional format* concentrates on skill sets that let you broaden your objective.

The functional format is ideal for individuals who are looking to change careers. It allows for shifts in professional goals by moving the focus of the resume away from a linear timetable and creating a solid foundation of transferable skills taken from many sources. It also allows students to highlight experiences that are not limited to previous paid employment. These flexible sections allow you to prioritize subheadings to tailor a resume effectively according to your needs.

The functional resume, however, is *not* the ideal format for professionals with continuous work histories who are looking for employment or advancement in the same field or a similar field. As only a small percentage of resumes use the functional format, an employer also might perceive an unorthodox format as an attempt to hide something. This format has been highly successful for many of our clients and can be a great asset to many job seekers, but verify that this format suits your background by answering some of the questions in Appendix A.

ADVANTAGES OF FUNCTIONAL RESUMES

- **They are future-oriented**. They emphasize the potential an applicant can bring to a new employer, as opposed to what he or she has accomplished in the past.
- **They highlight responsibilities and accomplishments that are not associated with recent positions or were derived from unpaid work.**
- **They are ideal for career changers.**

DISADVANTAGES OF FUNCTIONAL RESUMES

- **They can be rejected when prospective employers expect to see chronological lists of responsibilities and accomplishments linked to specific positions.**
- **They emphasize a specific skill set rather than your career path.** They should not be used if you are applying for a position in the same field as your current position.

CONTACT INFORMATION

Street Address • City, State ZIP • Phone Number • E-mail address

Your Headline should directly follow your contact information

SUMMARY OF QUALIFICATIONS

➢ 1
➢ 2
➢ 3
➢ 4
➢ 5

SKILLS AND ACHIEVEMENTS

Skill or Profession Category (Example: Accounting, Writing, or Data Processing)
- Bulleted accomplishments pertaining to this skill set.
- 2
- 3
- 4
- 5

Skill or Profession Category
- Bulleted accomplishments pertaining to this skill set
- 2
- 3
- 4
- 5

> The key to the functional resume is breaking down your work history and background into skill sets. Because you have moved the dates to the bottom of the resume, an employer's attention will be drawn to your skills.

Skill or Profession Category (Example: Project Management or Business Analysis)
- Bulleted accomplishments pertaining to this skill set.
- 2
- 3
- 4
- 5

EXPERIENCE HISTORY

XYZ COMPANY, New York, NY   2000 – Present
Senior Market Analyst

XYZ COMPANY, New York, NY   1997 – 2000
Market Analyst/Segment Manager, Financial Services

XYZ COMPANY, New York, NY   1996
Manager, Market Analysis

EDUCATION

College or University, City, State
Degree, Graduation Date

COMPUTER SKILLS

List all your computer skills, even if it's a common program.

KEYWORDS

A set of words that will help ensure that you're not eliminated because of a missing word or phrase in your resume. For example, for Accounts Payable, the keyword would be A/P.

MICHAEL WU

50 Elm Street ♦ Lansing, MI 48909 ♦ 800-737-8637 ♦ mwu@resume.com

Successful Market Analyst with expertise in research, business analysis, and project management

SUMMARY OF QUALIFICATIONS

➢ Over 10 years of experience in marketing and market analysis for diverse areas, including finance, health care, new media, and retail.

➢ Utilize exemplary research and analysis skills to develop financial strategies and business plans.

➢ Develop investment reports and competitive analyses to determine opportunities within marketplace.

➢ Superior communication and interpersonal abilities; work well with all levels of staff and management.

➢ In-depth knowledge of numerous research tools and computer programs.

SKILLS AND ACCOMPLISHMENTS

Market Research

- Developed innovative online investing report used in new electronic active trader initiative.
- Explored financial market to develop strategic product plans; expanded line to include four credit cards, three online banking packages, and student loan products from Citibank, Wells Fargo, and FleetBoston.
- Provided key senior management with daily updates on competitor offerings, fee structures, and fund and equity flows, as well as advertising strategies of electronic, discount brokerage, and mutual fund firms.
- Created industry overview reports documenting market growth, trading activity, and consumer behavior.
- Prepared comprehensive prospect reports to support sales team presentations; performed SWOT analysis of Fortune 1000 financial and health-care companies.
- Researched target firms to determine corporate structure, business needs, and strategic objectives.
- Established and enhanced research vendor relations with Dow Jones.

Project Management and Business Analysis

- Built and managed services segment of Jameson and Partners, achieving highest performance rating from company partner for specialized medical equipment.
- Increased in-house physician referrals 125% and enabled continued existence of two outpatient rehabilitation offices by administering mail surveys, telephone interviews, and targeted marketing campaigns.
- Organized grant proposal and fund-raising team efforts, raising $6 million in donations within one year.
- Managed cross-functional project teams for development and rollout of new site content and functionalities.
- Proactively conducted company break-even analysis to determine segment viability and profit margin.
- Directed new partnership integrations and ongoing product development for multiple lines simultaneously.
- Maximized internal communications and operational efficiency by streamlining regular project administration and resource management meetings.

EXPERIENCE HISTORY

JAMESON AND PARTNERS, East Lansing, MI   2000 – Present
Senior Market Analyst

BANK OF MICHIGAN, Lansing, MI   1997 – 2000
Market Analyst/Segment Manager, Financial Services

WORLDWIDE FINANCIAL SOLUTIONS, INC., Lansing, MI   1995 – 1997
Manager, Market Analysis

ELLA DIRECT, Troy, MI   1993 – 1995
Market Analyst

COMPUTER SKILLS

Lexis/Nexis, Bloomberg, SPSS, Dreamweaver 4.0, MS FrontPage, MS Office Suite, Visio, ACT!

EDUCATION

MBA DEGREE IN MARKETING, California State University, 1992
BS Degree in Business Administration; Minor in Office Management, Atlantic College, 1990

Keywords: market analyst, senior market analyst, manager, director, research analysis

MICHAEL WU

50 Elm Street ♦ Lansing, MI 48909 ♦ 800-737-8637 ♦ mwu@resume.com

Successful Market Analyst with expertise in research, business analysis, and project management

SUMMARY OF QUALIFICATIONS

➢ Over 10 years of experience in marketing and market analysis for diverse areas, including finance, health care, new media, and retail.

> Both functional and chronological resumes use **Headers**, **Headlines**, and **Summary** sections.

- arch and analysis skills to develop financial strategies and business plans.
- orts and competitive analyses to determine opportunities within marketplace.
- n and interpersonal abilities; work well with all levels of staff and management.
- numerous research tools and computer programs.

SKILLS AND ACCOMPLISHMENTS

Market Research

- Developed innovative online investing report used in new electronic active trader initiative.
- Explored financial market to develop strategic product plans; expanded line to include four credit cards, three online banking packages, and student loan products from Citibank,

> Functional resumes organize backgrounds into **Skill Sets**, unlike chronological resumes, which list responsibilities and accomplishments by date.

- Provided key senior management with daily updates on competitor nd equity flows, as well as advertising strategies of electronic, disco
- Created industry overview reports documenting market growth, trad r.
- Prepared comprehensive prospect reports to support sales team pres is of Fortune 1000 financial and health-care companies.
- Researched target firms to determine corporate structure, business needs, and strategic objectives.
- Established and enhanced research vendor relations with Dow Jones.

Project Management and Business Analysis

- Built and managed services segment of Jameson and Partners, achieving highest performance rating from company partner for specialized medical equipment.
- Increased in-house physician referrals 125% and enabled continued existence of two outpatient rehabilitation offices by administering mail surveys, telephone interviews, and targeted marketing campaigns.
- Organized grant proposal and fund-raising team efforts, raising $6 million in donations within one year.
- Managed cross-functional project teams for development and rollout of new site content and functionalities.
- Proactively conducted company break-even analysis to determine segment viability and profit margin.
- Directed new partnership integrations and ongoing product development for multiple lines simultaneously.
- Maximized internal communications and operational efficiency by streamlining regular project administration and resource management meetings.

EXPERIENCE HISTORY

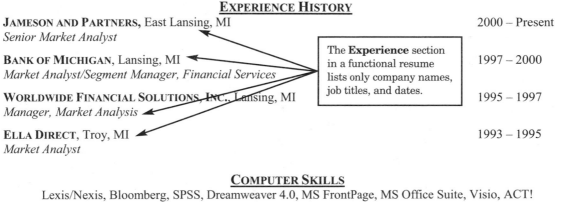

JAMESON AND PARTNERS, East Lansing, MI *Senior Market Analyst*	2000 – Present
BANK OF MICHIGAN, Lansing, MI *Market Analyst/Segment Manager, Financial Services*	1997 – 2000
WORLDWIDE FINANCIAL SOLUTIONS, INC., Lansing, MI *Manager, Market Analysis*	1995 – 1997
ELLA DIRECT, Troy, MI *Market Analyst*	1993 – 1995

> The **Experience** section in a functional resume lists only company names, job titles, and dates.

COMPUTER SKILLS

Lexis/Nexis, Bloomberg, SPSS, Dreamweaver 4.0, MS FrontPage, MS Office Suite, Visio, ACT!

EDUCATION

MBA DEGREE IN MARKETING, California State University, 1992
BS Degree in Business Administration; Minor in Office Management, Atlantic College, 1990

Keywords: market analyst, senior market analyst, manager, director, research analysis

> **Keywords** are an integral part of all successful resumes.

Sonia Flores

41 Meade Avenue ♦ Annapolis, MD 21401 ♦ 800-737-8637 ♦ sflores@resume.com

Award-winning Pharmaceutical Sales professional with proven success prospecting contacts, establishing clientele, and increasing revenue

SUMMARY OF QUALIFICATIONS

➢ Extensive experience within medical field, including over 10 years in pharmaceutical sales.
➢ Consistently meet or exceed sales quotas and goals. Received award for telemarketing sales.
➢ Established and sustain wide-ranging contact list of nationwide medical professionals.
➢ Excellent communication, interpersonal, and negotiation skills facilitate successful interaction with clients from diverse ages, cultures, professions, and socioeconomic levels.
➢ Consistently provide superior customer service; focused on establishing trust with clientele and promoting repeat business.
➢ Track record of converting patient requests, resulting in significant company savings.

SKILLS AND ACCOMPLISHMENTS

Sales

• Successfully directed all aspects of Acme Pharmaceutical's patient assistance program, including contact with numerous physicians, nurses, medical staff, and patients.
• Performed extensive research on prescription drug reimbursement programs and converted over 300 patient requests, resulting in savings of $165,000 annually.
• Drove sales of medications and products to physicians and medical staff, as well as to consumers.
• Examined operational procedures and developed initiatives that reduced costs and streamlined processes, including creation and implementation of online patient applications.
• Assisted employee management and mentoring for Acme, improving company morale.

Business Development

• Networked with various medical professionals and established contacts by regularly attending INCOR meetings to discuss new federal and state prescription drug programs.
• Worked closely with product development managers on forecasting of future drug usage.
• Oversaw inventory management, vendor mailing program coordination, and product tracking system maintenance for Acme Pharmaceutical.

EMPLOYMENT HISTORY

X-AON COMPANY, Baltimore, MD   2000 – Present
Sales Associate

ACME PHARMACEUTICAL COMPANY, Annapolis, MD   1988 – 2000
Administrator, Sales/Patient Assistance Program

FEDERAL EYE COMPANY, Washington, DC   1985 – 1987
Telemarketing Sales Assistant

EDUCATION

Bachelor of Arts, Political Science, George Washington University, Washington, DC

KEYWORDS: Pharmaceutical Sales Representative, Pharmaceutical Marketing Associate, Marketing Executive, Account Manager, business-to-business sales, clinical, laboratory, inside sales

Sonia Flores

41 Meade Avenue ♦ Annapolis, MD 21401 ♦ 800-737-8637 ♦ sflores@resume.com

Award-winning Pharmaceutical Sales professional with proven success prospecting contacts, establishing clientele, and increasing revenue

SUMMARY OF QUALIFICATIONS

➤ Extensive experience within medical field, including over 10 years in pharmaceutical sales.
➤ Consistently meet or exceed sales quotas and goals. Received award for telemarketing sales.
➤ Established and sustain wide-ranging contact list of nationwide medical professionals.
➤ Excellent communication, interpersonal, and negotiation skills facilitate successful interaction with clients from diverse ages, cultures, professions, and socioeconomic levels.
➤ Consistently provide superior customer service; focused on establishing trust with clientele and promoting repeat business.
➤ Track record of converting patient requests, resulting in significant company savings.

SKILLS AND ACCOMPLISHMENTS

Sales

- Successfully directed all aspects of Acme Pharmaceutical's patient assistance program, including contact with numerous physicians, nurses, medical staff, and patients.
- Performed extensive research on prescription drug reimbursement programs and converted over 300 patient requests, resulting in savings of $165,000 annually.
- Drove sales of medications and products to physicians and medical staff.
- Examined operational procedures and developed initiatives that reduced processes, including creation and implementation of online patient applications.
- Assisted employee management and mentoring for Acme, improving company morale.

> Two **Skill Sets** allow a candidate to target numerous positions in a job search.

Business Development

- Networked with various medical professionals and established contacts by regularly attending INCOR meetings to discuss new federal and state prescription drug programs.
- Worked closely with product development managers on forecasting of future drug usage.
- Oversaw inventory management, vendor mailing program coordination, and product tracking system maintenance for Acme Pharmaceutical.

EMPLOYMENT HISTORY

X-AON COMPANY, Baltimore, MD *Sales Associate*	2000 – Present
ACME PHARMACEUTICAL COMPANY, Annapolis, MD *Administrator, Sales/Patient Assistance Program*	1988 – 2000
FEDERAL EYE COMPANY, Washington, DC *Telemarketing Sales Assistant*	1985 – 1987

EDUCATION

Bachelor of Arts, Political Science, George Washington University, Washington, DC

KEYWORDS: Pharmaceutical Sales Representative, Pharmaceutical Marketing Associate, Marketing Executive, Account Manager, business-to-business sales, clinical, laboratory, inside sales

KENNETH VAN ENTWISTLE

4826 James Drive • Harrisburg, PA 17120 • (800) 737-8637 • kvanentwistle@resume.com

SUMMARY

Multifaceted business, finance, and IT professional with exceptional background building and implementing processes that increase revenue, reduce downtime, and allow for peak operations across multiple divisions. Exceptional research and analysis background, with a demonstrated ability to clearly assess fragmented information and create successful solutions. Extensive background leading and overseeing professional teams, including mentoring employees. Premier IT experience, including managing computing platforms, data and voice networks, applications systems, databases, accounting systems, and remarkably effective development tools. Strong emphasis on process reengineering and Total Quality Management. Adept manager, experienced in overseeing budgets exceeding $10 million annually. Able to explain complex technical and financial concepts to diverse audiences.

SKILLS AND ACCOMPLISHMENTS

BUSINESS ANALYSIS AND ACCOUNTING

➤ Expertise creating and implementing processes that provide detailed financial analysis, including applications in Excel.
➤ Develop and oversee business tools analyzing multiple aspects of company operations, including day-to-day and long-term analysis on both a global and a customer-specific basis.
➤ Strong background designing and programming the integration of transaction details with MAS90 and AccountMate accounting systems, achieving seamless feed for billing.
➤ Taught first commercially available, publisher-sanctioned Peachtree Accounting Software class.
➤ Created automated reporting and alarming tools that alerted company to deviations in performance; application monitored financial health and provided staff with alerts regarding system-processing anomalies.
➤ Performed initial setup and oversaw consulting of QuickBooks accounting system, creating full charts.
➤ Created applications in Excel for use in the daily operations of medical practice, with complete partner profit division program used to distribute practice profits among the physician-partners.
➤ Demonstrated background dramatically reducing client billing, including serving as expert witness for several law firms, in one case cutting client liability from $2.4 million to $200,000.

IT/MIS TECHNICAL

➤ Exceptional background in diverse facets of IT and MIS areas, including Web development, software development, databases, processes and applications using MS Excel/Word/Visio/Project.
➤ Fluent understanding of FoxPro, SQL Server, Visual Basic, and CRM Design; taught database development, administration, and management classes for Southern Polytechnic State University.
➤ Reengineered and developed over 200 discrete back-office applications.
➤ Taught corporate clientele in dBase, FoxPro, and Visual FoxPro and provided ad hoc sales engineering to Microsoft during and after acquisition of FoxPro.
➤ Created and implemented applications for property and evidence management for Atlanta Police Department, virtually eliminating lost and stolen items.
➤ Extensive work designing and programming the integration of transaction details (call detail records).
➤ Architect of POS system allowing point-of-sale transactions to interact with database system through dialup, TCP/IP, and/or nailed-up connection instigated from POS terminals, computers systems, or the Web.
➤ Developed migration plan to move databases (100+) from FoxPro to SQL Server 6.5. SQL architecture improved capacity, increasing available current records from one month to three years.
➤ Developed automated pricing tools for sales force, creating system of immediate pricing for prospects with no downtime from home office. Supported senior management with advanced revenue/profit evaluations.
➤ Provided sales engineering support in closing sales in excess of $12 million annually.

MANAGEMENT

➤ Brought industry standardization, quality assurance, professional structure, and development standards to the extensive database system that managed information for calling card company's product line.
➤ Reviewed entire operations, eliminating redundancy, adjusting personnel, and ensuring standards were met.
➤ Using a combination of Excel, SQL Server, Visual FoxPro, and Visual Basic, defined and implemented processes, including software and development.
➤ Successfully performed vendor negotiations, reducing company debt by $3 million.

(Management Continued …)

The Functional Resume Format

➢ Built issues management system for Industry Systems, providing management-decision support adopted by three nuclear sites.

➢ Directed relocation of engineering department from Arizona to New York, including permanent and temporary relocation of engineers, their families, and equipment.

➢ Established relationships with vendors to provide best of breed products and services.

➢ Defined and implemented efforts to understand and document existing manual processes.

➢ Interfaced with various last-mile and long-distance carriers to document facilities, determining usage and requirements that had no prior documentation or day-to-day strategic management.

➢ Developed budget that allowed for proposed company growth and necessary structural changes.

➢ Project manager for revision of all internal applications to current industry standards and architecture.

➢ Reduced senior management expense by over $140,000 annually. Restructured technical departments, allowing for 5 to 15% staff expense reduction, and consolidated server farm, reducing server number by over 35%.

WORK EXPERIENCE

GENERAL BUSINESS SOLUTIONS, Philadelphia, PA　　　　　　　　　　2002 – Present
Sales Manager

DONNERSON TELECOMMUNICATIONS, Philadelphia, PA　　　　　　　　1999 – 2002
Regional Sales Manager

BREVERMAN'S PHONE SERVICES, Atlanta, GA　　　　　　　　　　　1998 – 1999
Sales Manager

CLARK INDUSTRIES, Canton, GA　　　　　　　　　　　　　　　　1993 – 1997
Program Manager/Engineer

SOUTHERN GRAND CORPORATION, Marietta, GA　　　　　　　　　　1987 – 1993
Sales Manager

SPECIALIZED TRAINING

- Systems Administration for MS-SQL Server
- Supporting MS Windows NT 4.0 – Core Technologies
- Visual Basic for Applications
- Java SL-210
- IBM OS/2 LAN Server 4.0 Administration
- Sybase – Fast Track to Sybase
- Heverman & Associates Software Requirements
- Extensive training includes but not limited to:
  LAN/WAN Technology • Server Administration • Database Development

COMPUTER SKILLS

MS Word/Excel/Access/PowerPoint/Visio/Project, Visual FoxPro, Visual Basic, FrontPage

KEYWORDS: Billing, profit & loss, P&L, A/R, accounting, analysis, organization, quantification, database, design, process, management, back office, development, analysis, tools, bookkeeping, operations, data

KENNETH VAN ENTWISTLE

4826 James Drive • Harrisburg, PA 17120 • (800) 737-8637 • kvanentwistle@resume.com

SUMMARY

Multifaceted business, finance, and IT professional with exceptional background building and implementing processes that increase revenue, reduce downtime, and allow for peak operations across multiple divisions. Exceptional research and analysis background, with a demonstrated ability to clearly and create successful solutions. Extensive background leading and overseeing mentoring employees. Premier IT experience, including managing computing platf applications systems, databases, accounting systems, and remarkably effective devel on process reengineering and Total Quality Management. Adept manager, expe exceeding $10 million annually. Able to explain complex technical and financial con

> The executive functional resume begins with **Contact Information** and a profile of career highlights. A headline is incorporated into this **Summary** section for the executive resume.

SKILLS AND ACCOMPLISHMENTS

BUSINESS ANALYSIS AND ACCOUNTING

➤ Expertise creating and implementing processes that provide detailed financial analysis, including applications in Excel.
➤ Develop and oversee business tools analyzing multiple aspects of company operations, including day-to-day and long-term analysis on both a global and a customer-specific basis.
➤ Strong background designing and programming the integration of transaction details with MAS90 and AccountMate accounting systems, achieving seamless feed for billing.
➤ Taught first commercially available, publisher-sanctioned Peachtree Accounting Software class.
➤ Created automated reporting and alarming tools that alerted company to deviations in performance; application monitored financial health and provided staff with alerts regarding system-processing anomalies.
➤ Performed initial setup and oversaw consulting of QuickBooks accounting system, creating full charts.
➤ Created applications in Excel for use in the daily operations of medical practice, with complete partner profit division program used to distribute practice profits among the physician-partners.
➤ Demonstrated background dramatically reducing client billing, including serving as expert witness for several law firms, in one case cutting client liability from $2.4 million to $200,000.

> Three **Skill Sets** should be used for the executive functional resume. You can apply for numerous jobs with this format.

IT/MIS TECHNICAL

➤ Exceptional background in diverse facets of IT and MIS areas, including Web dev development, databases, processes and applications using MS Excel/Word/Visio/F
➤ Fluent understanding of FoxPro, SQL Server, Visual Basic, and CRM Design; taught database development, administration, and management classes for Southern Polytechnic State University.
➤ Reengineered and developed over 200 discrete back-office applications.
➤ Taught corporate clientele in dBase, FoxPro, and Visual FoxPro and provided ad hoc sales engineering to Microsoft during and after acquisition of FoxPro.
➤ Created and implemented applications for property and evidence management for Atlanta Police Department, virtually eliminating lost and stolen items.
➤ Extensive work designing and programming the integration of transaction details (call detail records).
➤ Architect of POS system allowing point-of-sale transactions to interact with database system through dialup, TCP/IP, and/or nailed-up connection instigated from POS terminals, computers systems, or the Web.
➤ Developed migration plan to move databases (100+) from FoxPro to SQL Server 6.5. SQL architecture improved capacity, increasing available current records from one month to three years.
➤ Developed automated pricing tools for sales force, creating system of immediate pricing for prospects with no downtime from home office. Supported senior management with advanced revenue/profit evaluations.
➤ Provided sales engineering support in closing sales in excess of $12 million annually.

MANAGEMENT

➤ Brought industry standardization, quality assurance, professional structure, and development standards to the extensive database system that managed information for calling card company's product line.
➤ Reviewed entire operations, eliminating redundancy, adjusting personnel, and ensuring standards were met.
➤ Using a combination of Excel, SQL Server, Visual FoxPro, and Visual Basic, defined and implemented processes, including software and development.
➤ Successfully performed vendor negotiations, reducing company debt by $3 million.

(Management Continued …)

➢ Built issues management system for Industry Systems, providing management-decision support adopted by three nuclear sites.

➢ Directed relocation of engineering department from Arizona to New York, including permanent and temporary relocation of engineers, their families, and equipment.

➢ Established relationships with vendors to provide best of breed products and services.

➢ Defined and implemented efforts to understand and document existing manual processes.

➢ Interfaced with various last-mile and long-distance carriers to document facilities, determining usage and requirements that had no prior documentation or day-to-day strategic management.

➢ Developed budget that allowed for proposed company growth and necessary structural changes.

➢ Project manager for revision of all internal applications to current industry standards and architecture.

➢ Reduced senior management expense by over $140,000 annually. Restructured technical departments, allowing for 5 to 15% staff expense reduction, and consolidated server farm, reducing server number by over 35%.

WORK EXPERIENCE

GENERAL BUSINESS SOLUTIONS, Philadelphia, PA *Sales Manager*	2002 – Present
DONNERSON TELECOMMUNICATIONS, Philadelphia, PA *Regional Sales Manager*	1999 – 2002
BREVERMAN'S PHONE SERVICES, Atlanta, GA *Sales Manager*	1998 – 1999
CLARK INDUSTRIES, Canton, GA *Program Manager/Engineer*	1993 – 1997
SOUTHERN GRAND CORPORATION, Marietta, GA *Sales Manager*	1987 – 1993

SPECIALIZED TRAINING

- Systems Administration for MS-SQL Server
- Supporting MS Windows NT 4.0 – Core Technologies
- Visual Basic for Applications
- Java SL-210
- IBM OS/2 LAN Server 4.0 Administration
- Sybase – Fast Track to Sybase
- Heverman & Associates Software Requirements
- Extensive training includes but not limited to:
 LAN/WAN Technology • Server Administration • Database Development

> A **Specialized Training** section is common for professionals with extensive work histories. See Chapter 17 for the fundamentals of the executive resume.

COMPUTER SKILLS

MS Word/Excel/Access/PowerPoint/Visio/Project, Visual FoxPro, Visual Basic, FrontPage

KEYWORDS: Billing, profit & loss, P&L, A/R, accounting, analysis, organization, quantification, database, design, process, management, back office, development, analysis, tools, bookkeeping, operations, data

4
The Combination Resume Format

The combination resume highlights the key strengths of both the chronological format and the functional format, allowing a job seeker to emphasize *both* a steady work history *and* diverse skill sets. Although all good resumes meet these qualifications to a certain extent, the goal of the combination format is to showcase both a consistent employment record and a specific list of skill sets, incorporating a sound time frame to serve as the backbone of the resume.

Demonstrating to an employer **how your skills directly resulted in accomplishments for the company** in both **the skill sets section and the work history section** is the defining characteristic of the combination resume, as opposed to the functional resume, which keeps skills and work history separate.

The combination format also allows professionals to apply for a broader range of jobs than does the strict chronological format. The combination resume has been a successful choice for consultants, as a strong work history is backed by individual success at specific companies or while overseeing key projects. It is also a good choice if you have both strong skills and a steady employment record but need a resume that will overcome the objections some employers may have to the functional format. The emphasis of this resume, remember, is on the specific skills you can bring to a future employer.

ADVANTAGES OF THE COMBINATION RESUME

- Combines the defining strengths of chronological and functional resumes: a steady work history and diverse skill sets.
- Allows a broader range of professional objectives than does the strict chronological resume.
- Is great for consultants because it specifies how they influenced a business's success.

DISADVANTAGES OF THE COMBINATION RESUME

- If you are applying for positions in multiple industries, skill sections and accomplishment bullets may have to be reorganized and tweaked accordingly.
- Conservative employers may desire the chronological resume, especially for executives.

The next few pages contain samples of combination resumes, followed by insider tips, tricks, and writing guidelines that show how our professional resume writers and editors create attractive resumes that grab a hirer's attention and leave a powerful, lasting impression.

Contact Information

Street Address ◆ City, State ZIP ◆ Phone Number ◆ E-mail Address

Your headline should directly follow your contact information

SUMMARY OF QUALIFICATIONS

➤ 1
➤ 2
➤ 3
➤ 4
➤ 5

CAREER HIGHLIGHTS

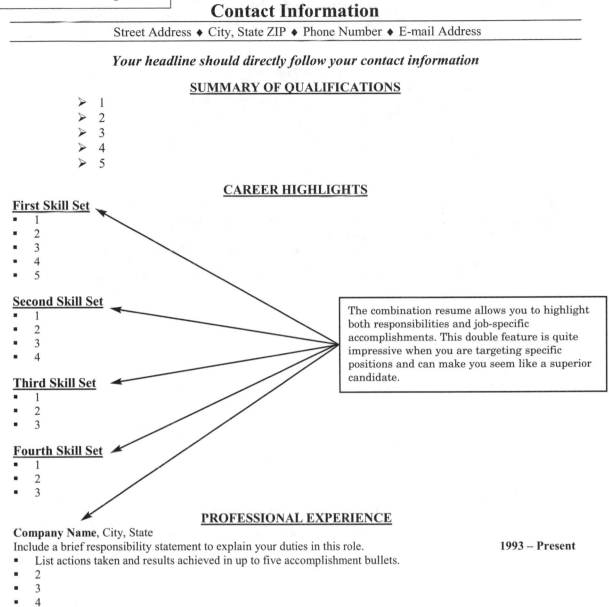

First Skill Set
- 1
- 2
- 3
- 4
- 5

Second Skill Set
- 1
- 2
- 3
- 4

Third Skill Set
- 1
- 2
- 3

Fourth Skill Set
- 1
- 2
- 3

> The combination resume allows you to highlight both responsibilities and job-specific accomplishments. This double feature is quite impressive when you are targeting specific positions and can make you seem like a superior candidate.

PROFESSIONAL EXPERIENCE

Company Name, City, State   **1993 – Present**
Include a brief responsibility statement to explain your duties in this role.
- List actions taken and results achieved in up to five accomplishment bullets.
- 2
- 3
- 4

Company Name, City, State   **1990 – 1993**
Include a brief responsibility statement to explain your duties in this role.
- List actions taken and results achieved in up to five accomplishment bullets.
- 2
- 3

EDUCATION
Degree, University, City and State, GPA (if 3.0 or better)

TRAINING AND CERTIFICATION
Professional development, seminars, and special training are listed here

COMPUTER SKILLS
List all your computer skills, even if it's a common program

Keywords: A set of words that will help ensure that you're not eliminated because of a missing word or phrase in your resume. For example, for Accounts Payable, the keyword would be A/P.

Deborah Goldberg

7 Vineyard Lane ♦ Sacramento, CA 95814 ♦ (800) 737-8637 ♦ dgoldberg@resume.com

Successful manager with over 10 years of expertise in operations, team development, sales, and production

SUMMARY OF QUALIFICATIONS

➢ Demonstrated expertise in dramatically reducing cost expenditures while increasing productivity.
➢ Diverse knowledge of federal and state regulations governing workplace safety.
➢ Proactive, hands-on style; extensive team leadership and personnel development skills.
➢ Adept at training and managing employees across numerous divisions in several key areas.
➢ Superior communication, interpersonal, and negotiation skills.

CAREER HIGHLIGHTS

Business and Operations
- Direct and monitor warehousing and retail facility activities in world-class enterprise.
- Maintain responsibility for developing, administering, and monitoring multi-million-dollar budgets.
- Build and foster proactive workplace environment conducive to highest levels of employee participation.
- Maintain inventory, logistics, purchasing, and procurement of products and supplies with TQM/JIT techniques.
- Effect significant expense reduction through manpower and raw material cost control processes.

Warehousing
- Lead up to 100 team members in storage, transportation, and production of products and supplies.
- Assure personnel comply with all applicable health and safety guidelines and regulations, including OSHA, HAZMAT, and local/organizational mandates.
- Understand and maintain compliance with all specifications of OSHA, EPA, and UL.
- Manage all aspects of manufacturing projects from planning through shipment, including tariff compliance, transportation contracting, and process reviews.

Retail Store Management
- Possess experience in budget management, forecasting, project planning and execution, and program direction.
- Utilize customer service and public relations skills to develop successful business and community relations.
- Monitor and mentor sales associates and team leaders, providing all employees with necessary training and development to achieve personal and organizational goals.

Human Resources
- Foster workplace diversity and ensure all team members remain in compliance with EEOC regulations.
- Motivate, train, and mentor individuals, providing necessary tools to meet or exceed company expectations.
- Streamline work processes to decrease wage and salary expenses through well-managed scheduling.

PROFESSIONAL EXPERIENCE

Operations, Logistics, Materials Manager, Laser Precision Equipment, Davis, CA   **1993 – Present**
Oversee all facets of operation for 260,000-sq. ft warehouse; direct and schedule 100 personnel.
- Administer combined budgets of more than $3.5 million, including production, warehousing, and shipping.
- Successfully manage costs though application of numerous software applications and other techniques.
- Spearheaded and assisted with changes resulting in $10.5 million savings over 10-year time frame.

Merchandise Manager, South Park Solutions, San Francisco, CA   **1990 – 1993**
Managed more than 50 personnel and supervisors in Receiving Department, Business Office, and Sales.
- Led preopening activities for three geographical facilities, including professional development and planning.
- Designed and implemented 30-60-90-day planner, floor plans, and seasonal merchandising projects.

EDUCATION
Bachelor of Business Administration in Management (Minor in Marketing), SFSU, 3.47 GPA

TRAINING AND CERTIFICATION

Certified Production Inventory Manager – American Production and Inventory Control Association (28 Credits)

COMPUTER SKILLS
Proficient in Microsoft/IBM-based PCs, Software, Hardware, Networking, Windows XP/2000/NT/9x/3.1/DOS

Keywords: Retail Store Manager, Warehouse Manager, Production Manager, Merchandise Manager, Team Leader, Assistant Manager, Warehouse Supervisor

Deborah Goldberg

7 Vineyard Lane ♦ Sacramento, CA 95814 ♦ (800) 737-8637 ♦ dgoldberg@resume.com

Successful manager with over 10 years of expertise in operations, team development, sales, and production

> The combination resume begins with your **Contact Information** and a **Headline**.

SUMMARY OF QUALIFICATIONS

➤ Demonstrated expertise in dramatically reducing cost expenditures while incre[...]
➤ Diverse knowledge of federal and state regulations governing workplace safety.
➤ Proactive, hands-on style; extensive team leadership and personnel development skills.
➤ Adept at training and managing employees across numerous divisions in several key areas.
➤ Superior communication, interpersonal, and negotiation skills.

CAREER HIGHLIGHTS

Business and Operations
- Direct and monitor warehousing and retail facility activities in world-class enterprise.
- Maintain responsibility for developing, administering, and monitoring multi-million-dollar budgets.
- Build and foster proactive workplace environment conducive to highest levels of employee participation.
- Maintain inventory, logistics, purchasing, and procurement of products and supplies with TQM/JIT techniques.
- Effect significant expense reduction through manpower and raw material cost control processes.

Warehousing
- Lead up to 100 team members in storage, transportation, and production of products and supplies.
- Assure personnel comply with all app[...]delines and regulations, including OSHA, HAZMAT, and local/organizational r[...]
- Understand and maintain compliance [...]SHA, EPA, and UL.
- Manage all aspects of manufacturing [...]gh shipment, including tariff compliance, transportation contracting, and proces[...]

> Two to four **Skill Sets** are a great way to build your appeal to a potential employer and qualify for numerous openings.

Retail Store Management
- Possess experience in budget management, forecasting, project planning and execution, and program direction.
- Utilize customer service and public relations skills to develop successful business and community relations.
- Monitor and mentor sales associates and team leaders, providing all employees with necessary training and development to achieve personal and organizational goals.

Human Resources
- Foster workplace diversity and ensure all team members remain in compliance with EEOC regulations.
- Motivate, train, and mentor individuals, providing necessary tools to meet or exceed company expectations.
- Streamline work processes to decrease wage and salary expenses through well-managed scheduling.

PROFESSIONAL EXPERIENCE

Operations, Logistics, Materials Manager, Laser Precision Equipment, Davis, CA   **1993 – Present**
Oversee all facets of operation for 260,000-sq. ft warehouse; direct [...]el.
- Administer combined budgets of more than $3.5 million, inclu[...]sing, and shipping.
- Successfully manage costs though application of numerous soft[...]er techniques.
- Spearheaded and assisted with changes resulting in $10.5 milli[...]me frame.

> The combination resume includes **Bullets** highlighting your responsibilities or accomplishments for each employer.

Merchandise Manager, South Park Solutions, San Francisco, CA   **1990 – 1993**
Managed more than 50 personnel and supervisors in Receiving Dep[...] and Sales.
- Led preopening activities for three geographical facilities, including professional development and planning.
- Designed and implemented 30-60-90-day planner, floor plans, and seasonal merchandising projects.

EDUCATION
Bachelor of Business Administration in Management (Minor in Marketing), SFSU, 3.47 GPA

TRAINING AND CERTIFICATION
Certified Production Inventory Manager – American Production and Inventory Control Association (28 Credits)

COMPUTER SKILLS
Proficient in Microsoft/IBM-based PCs, Software, Hardware, Networking, Windows XP/2000/NT/9x/3.1/DOS

Keywords: Retail Store Manager, Warehouse Manager, Production Manager, Merchandise Manager, Team Leader, Assistant Manager, Warehouse Supervisor

Leroy Brown

11 Golden Road, Apt. 4G • Little Rock, AR 72201 • (800) 737-8637 • LBROWN@RESUME.COM

A highly skilled Java and C++ Software Engineer with strengths in quality assurance and testing

Summary of Qualifications

➢ Three years of object-oriented software development and quality assurance experience.
➢ Java and C++ application-development expertise in Windows NT environment.
➢ Adept at troubleshooting by identifying problems and implementing comprehensive solutions.
➢ Skilled communicator. Able to interface with all levels of management, clients, and specialists.
➢ In-depth technical skills complemented by BS degree in Computer Engineering.

Technical Skills

Languages:	Java, C, C++, HTML, JavaScript, OpenGL
Java Skills:	Swing, AWT, RMI, JDBC, Java Server Pages
Tools:	Microsoft Visual C++, Microsoft SQL, Apache Tomcat Server
Platforms:	Windows NT / 2000 / 98, UNIX, Linux, CGI

Professional Experience

GreatSolutions Company, Little Rock, AR   1998 – Present
Software Engineer creating and implementing comprehensive applications and databases for diverse range of clientele, including:

Wayne Software Application
- Led four junior engineers in development and delivery of multitiered application for France Telecom.
- Designed server application using Java RMI (Remote Method Invocation), linking multiple merchants to one Web portal.
- Created enterprise information system application connecting to SQL database via JDBC.
- Oversaw development of Java Server Pages (JSP) for Web client application.
- Installed, demonstrated, and provided support for completed software.
- Represented WebXchange, Inc., on location in France.

P.C. Titleman Company Project
- Designed database management system.

Sales/Inventory Applications
- Supervised five junior engineers; utilized Java RMI to design and implement client/server applications for sales offices and warehouses.
- Enabled real-time sales, shipping, and ordering information.

Beta Alpha Command Computers, Texarkana, AR   1997 – 1998
Quality Assurance Engineer/Black-Box Testing
- Performed functionality and performance testing; launched *StrikerNow* video game program.
- Wrote extensive batch files to automate testing process.
- Identified memory leaks and reduced software's minimum system requirements.

Education

Bachelor of Science in Computer Engineering, 1996
Technical Institute of Iowa, Des Moines, IA

Keywords: QA Engineer, Technical Support, Tester, Programmer, Manager, Team Lead

Leroy Brown

11 GOLDEN ROAD, APT. 4G • LITTLE ROCK, AR 72201 • (800) 737-8637 • LBROWN@RESUME.COM

A highly skilled Java and C++ Software Engineer with strengths in quality assurance and testing

SUMMARY OF QUALIFICATIONS

➢ Three years of object-oriented software development and quality assura
➢ Java and C++ application-development expertise in Windows NT envir
➢ Adept at troubleshooting by identifying problems and implementing con
➢ Skilled communicator. Able to interface with all levels of management,
➢ In-depth technical skills complemented by BS degree in Computer Engineering.

> This combination resume begins with **Contact Information** and a **Headline** and is followed by a **Summary of Qualifications**.

TECHNICAL SKILLS

Languages:	Java, C, C++, HTML, JavaScript, OpenGL
Java Skills:	Swing, AWT, RMI, JDBC, Java Server Pages
Tools:	Microsoft Visual C++, Microsoft SQL, Apache Tomca
Platforms:	Windows NT / 2000 / 98, UNIX, Linux, CGI

> We'll discuss information technology resumes and computer skills in Chapter 12. A great option for computer pros is to list **Technical Skills** high in the resume.

PROFESSIONAL EXPERIENCE

GREATSOLUTIONS COMPANY, Little Rock, AR   1998 – Present
Software Engineer creating and implementing comprehensive applications and databases for diverse range of clientele, including:

Wayne Software Application
• Led four junior engineers in development and delivery of multitiered application for France Telecom.
• Designed server application using Java RMI (Remote Method Invocation), merchants to one Web portal.
• Created enterprise information system application connecting to SQL datab
• Oversaw development of Java Server Pages (JSP) for Web client applicati
• Installed, demonstrated, and provided support for completed software.
• Represented WebXchange, Inc., on location in France.

> Demonstrating **numerous projects under one date** is a great way to impress employers and the key to showing a steady work history as a consultant.

P.C. Titleman Company Project
• Designed database management system

Sales/Inventory Applications
• Supervised five junior engineers; utilized Java RMI to design and implement client/server applications for sales offices and warehouses.
• Enabled real-time sales, shipping, and ordering information.

BETA ALPHA COMMAND COMPUTERS, Texarkana, AR   1997 – 1998
Quality Assurance Engineer/Black-Box Testing
• Performed functionality and performance testing; launched *StrikerNow* video game program.
• Wrote extensive batch files to automate testing process.
• Identified memory leaks and reduced software's minimum system requirements.

EDUCATION

BACHELOR OF SCIENCE IN COMPUTER ENGINEERING, 1996
Technical Institute of Iowa, Des Moines, IA

Keywords: QA Engineer, Technical Support, Tester, Programmer, Manager, Team Lead

5

Step-by-Step Guide to Resume Formatting

Your professional resume serves as a billboard to hirers, making them stop in their tracks and take notice of what you are selling: your talents, skills, and accomplishments. Every effective billboard utilizes advertising techniques that years of research have validated. People will be more receptive to messages depending on the way a page is set up and organized, and the hirers who read your resume are no different: The same rules apply. By taking advantage of proven advertising techniques, Resume.com's resumes attract hirers and keep their interest.

In this chapter, we will guide you through the different tools and selections you will use to create a resume on your computer.

Rule 1 is not to be intimidated by a word-processing program. Most word-processing programs are packed with valuable styling and editing tools, and we will explain how to use them even if you have very little experience with computers. We'll start with the general areas of formatting your resume. As we proceed throughout the overall construction of your resume, we'll be guiding you through the easiest way to build a professional document. We've decided to use Microsoft Word to demonstrate numerous formatting and writing tools that you can use to create your own unbeatable resume.

THE TOOLBAR

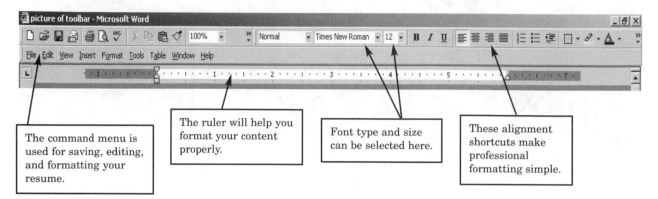

The command menu is used for saving, editing, and formatting your resume.

The ruler will help you format your content properly.

Font type and size can be selected here.

These alignment shortcuts make professional formatting simple.

Step 1: Opening and Saving a Word File

To begin, open a new Word document by Selecting File, New, and Save As.

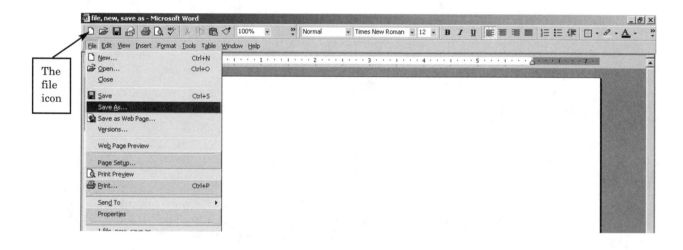

The file icon

Save this document as your "last name, first name" (Doe, Jane) to make the title easily identifiable to a potential hirer. Whether you are a novice or an experienced user of Microsoft Word, this should be the first step you follow whenever you create a resume. Remember to save the document regularly.

Step 2: Setting the Page Margins

The Microsoft Word Ruler: Setting Up Margins and Tabs

The importance of using adequate white space and correct margins on a resume cannot be overstated. Your resume is half content and half presentation. Too little white space makes your document appear cramped and difficult to read; too much leaves your resume looking empty and inadequate. If the document is hard to read, a prospective employer will bypass the information, and an ugly format almost certainly will eliminate you from consideration.

To manipulate your margins, Select File, Page Setup, and then Margins.

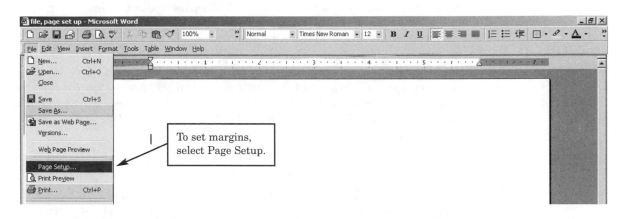

The left and right margins should always be set at 1 inch. This is the standard for all Resume.com resumes, as it has proved to be the most successful. The top and bottom margins can vary from a minimum 0.5 inch to a maximum of 1 inch, depending on how much content will appear in your resume. After you have selected these margins, hit OK.

Try adjusting the top and bottom margins to fashion the length and overall appearance of the resume. Remember, this is a key element of your resume's appeal and success.

Step 3: The Right Fonts and Font Sizes to Use

There are a few rules governing the practicality of **font types** and **font sizes**. Some examples of **font type** include Times New Roman, Garamond, Arial, and *Script.* Font size determines the size of each letter, for example:

16, 14,12, 10, 8.

Extensive research has shown that people are much more likely to read and understand content when it is written in a font with serifs; an example would be this book, which is written in Times New Roman, a font with serifs.

Font size also plays a key role in the appearance of a resume. If the font size is too small or the typeface is difficult to read, chances are that a person will pass right over the content or have a difficult time retaining the information.

As a rule of thumb, your document should use at least a 10-point font, and a 12-point font is ideal. Although the contents of a resume are always vital to its success, it is essential to ensure that your document is as aesthetically pleasing as it is strongly worded. You can tell a font with serifs by the curves and accents on certain letters, such as t's and p's. An easy comparison of two fonts is that between Times New Roman and Arial. Times New Roman is easy to read and pleasing to the eye. Arial is a font that has no design variation or distinction between strokes.

Some Examples of Font Sizes and Type Sizes

With Serifs	Without Serifs
Times New Roman, 10-pt	Arial, 10-pt
Times New Roman, 12-pt	Arial, 12-pt
Garamond, 10-pt	Helvetica, 10-pt
Garamond, 12-pt	Helvetica, 12-pt
Book Antiqua, 10-pt	**Hobo, 10-pt**
Book Antiqua, 12pt	**Hobo, 12-pt**
Courier, 10-pt	Kabel™, 10-pt
Courier, 12-pt	Kabel™, 12-pt

To select a font type for your resume, you can use two options:

You can use the drop-down menus on the **Font** and **Font Size** slots on the toolbar.

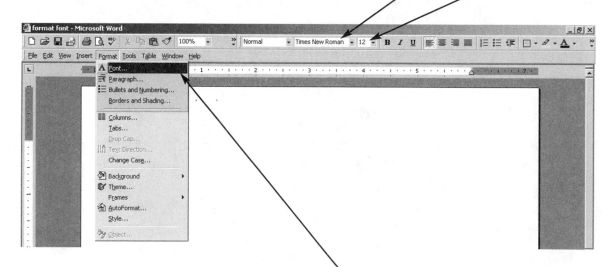

A second option is to select **Format** and **Font** from the command menu.

After selecting Format and Font, you will have a multitude of choices for font types and sizes.

Although research indicates that fonts with serifs lead to better results, fonts without serifs are gaining popularity because of the increasing use of computers in the job application process. Fonts without serifs often are preferred, as computers frequently have a difficult time translating e-mailed documents sent from one computer to another when the documents are written in serifs. This often happens when one person is using a personal computer (PC) and another is using a Macintosh (Mac). Although both documents may appear perfect on the screen when they are being written, they can appear jumbled or incoherent when viewed after being e-mailed.

Fonts without serifs increase the chances that another computer will be able to read your information without any formatting inconsistencies. Not only do fonts without serifs improve the odds that a person will be able to read your document, but as we will discuss in Chapter 8, many employers have implemented computer scanning software to eliminate candidates whose resumes do not contain certain key words.

Computer scanning software reads your resume by using a technique called optical character recognition, and complicated fonts such as *Script* can prove unreadable to these programs, immediately eliminating a candidate from consideration.

Use a font with serifs when sending your resume by mail or fax or for job fairs. For e-mail applications, you can easily create a resume without serifs, as we'll discuss in Chapter 8.

6

Step-by-Step Guide to Writing Your Resume

In Chapter 5 we reviewed the basic formatting tools of your Microsoft Word word-processing program, including saving your document, the best fonts to use, and the maximum margins you should set to create a highly readable resume. In this chapter we will discuss the essential elements of the resume, beginning with a discussion of catching and eliminating common resume errors.

Every section of your resume should be written from the **first-person point of view**, or what we call the silent "I," as was discussed in Chapter 1. You should never use the third-person point of view, which only deemphasizes your accomplishments. The following example demonstrates the difference between writing with the silent "I" and using the third person:

Correct: **First person:** "Drive over 300 tons of widgets each quarter."

Incorrect: **Third person:** "Drives over 300 tons of widgets each quarter."

Using the first person, or silent "I," you are essentially saying, "I drive over 300 tons of widgets each quarter." Conversely, when you use the third-person point of view, you're subconsciously attributing the accomplishment to someone else: "He drives over 300 tons of widgets each quarter."

Would you ever give someone else credit for your work? No. That's why using the silent "I" is an integral component of all successful professional resumes.

A **thesaurus** is another tool that is very helpful when you create a resume. One of the most common mistakes in amateur resumes is to begin multiple sentences with the same word. **Avoid repeating the same word over and over in your bullets.**

Bob's Building Company, Millburn, NJ   **1993 – Present**
Communications Director
- Experience in marketing, public relations, and promotions.
- Experience producing and promoting events that dramatically increase sales.
- Skilled in developing promotional materials and writing copy for print advertising, television, and radio.
- Excellent relationship-building skills.
- Skilled media spokesperson. Effective at generating positive publicity.

Although you don't have to be a word guru to use appropriate synonyms, it pays to invest in a good thesaurus or at least use the thesaurus that is built into most MS Word programs. There are additional sites online that can be accessed by simply typing the word "thesaurus" into any search engine.

To access your thesaurus, highlight a word you would like to replace and then go on to Tools, Language, Thesaurus.

Your computer's thesaurus will list words that are close in meaning to the word you have highlighted. Although synonyms by definition have similar meanings, the shades of difference in each word can change your intended message. For example, although a common synonym for "manage" is "supervise," these words have different meanings:

Manage:
v. man·aged, man·ag·ing, man·ag·es
v., v.t. 1. To direct or control the use of; handle: *manage a complex machine tool.*

Supervise:
v.t. su·per·vised, su·per·vis·ing, su·per·vis·es

1. To have the charge and direction of; superintend.

As this example shows, although using the thesaurus is a good way to find alternative words, consult a dictionary to ensure that the word you're using is indeed what you mean to say.

Spell check is also an integral part of writing a resume. **Typos are a terrible mistake that hirers won't overlook.** There's no better way to make you seem unprofessional. Spell check is an instantaneous and easy part of your writing. To spell check your document, go to Tools and select Spelling and Grammar.

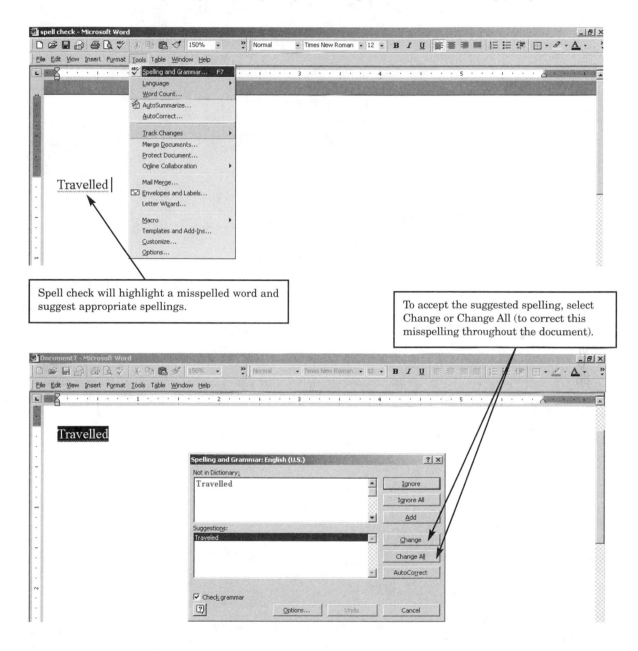

Spell check will highlight a misspelled word and suggest appropriate spellings.

To accept the suggested spelling, select Change or Change All (to correct this misspelling throughout the document).

Not only will your computer alert you to potential spelling mistakes, it also will make grammar and punctuation suggestions. You should spell check all materials before sending them to an employer. Your correspondence is a reflection of yourself, and you want to demonstrate the best of your abilities.

One caveat about spell check: Although it is an excellent tool, spell check doesn't pick up all errors. Homonyms (two words that sound the same but are spelled differently, such as "sea" and "see"), proper nouns, and abbreviations may pass unsuspected through spell check. Additionally, spell check may highlight a correct spelling (such as a company name) as incorrect.

A good example of something that would not be picked up by the spell-check radar would be "boosted moral" when you meant to say "boosted morale." Another common mistake is "Database Manger" when the correct term is "Database Manager." This is why it is always important to read and reread documents before submitting them even if you've spell checked the document. Try having a close friend, relative, or associate read your documents for clarity and correct spelling. The same rule applies for writing and editing: No matter how many times you've read what you've written, another set of eyes can help pick up small errors.

Follow these simple tips to avoid fatal errors in your resume. Now let's begin building your brand-new resume with Step 1: Your Contact Information, also known as the header.

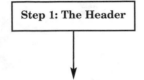

Step 1: The Header

John Doe

248 W. 35th Street • New York, NY 10001 • (800) 737-8637 • info@resume.com

STEP 1: WRITING AND CREATING POWERFUL HEADERS

The header provides the first visual impression of a resume. You need to pack a strong punch in this section, as it is your first chance to make a lasting impression.

Follow These Simple Steps to Format Your Resume Header

1. Type your name on the first line, and right below this information enter your street address, city, state, Zip Code, home phone number, and e-mail address. **Example:**

John Doe

248 W. 35th Street, 12A New York, NY 10001 (800) 737-8637, info@resume.com

2. Then separate each item on the second line by inserting a symbol that clearly differentiates the components of your contact information, including street address (and apartment), city/state/Zip Code, phone number, and e-mail adress. You can insert a symbol by going to Insert and then Symbol.

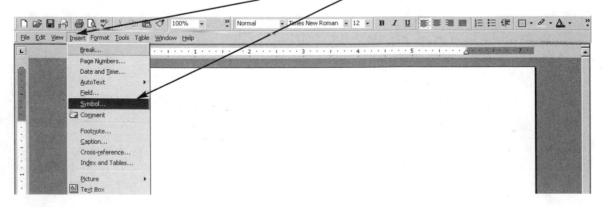

Always choose a conservative symbol, such as blocks or circles.

After you've selected a symbol, place the cursor after each item on your contact information (e.g., after the street address and before the city) and click Insert. **Example:**

John Doe

248 W. 35th Street, 12A • New York, NY 10001 • (800) 737-8637 • info@resume.com

3. Next, center your name on the page or left justify it to grab an employer's attention. To align your name, simply highlight it and choose the left alignment or centering option on the toolbar. Here the alignment is to the left.

Here the name is centered.

4. Your name should stand out clearly. Make sure the font size here is a maximum of 22 points and a minimum of 14 points. Your name should always be the largest piece of information on the resume, and it should be in **bold**.

Example:

John Doe

248 W. 35th Street, 12A ● New York, NY 10001 ● (800) 737-8637 ● info@resume.com

5. Now create a line (or border) underneath your name or your name and contact information.

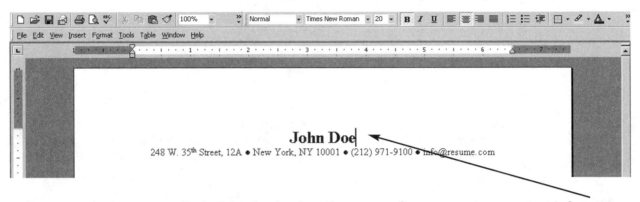

To do this, simply place the cursor after your name or contact information. Then click the Border Box on the toolbar.

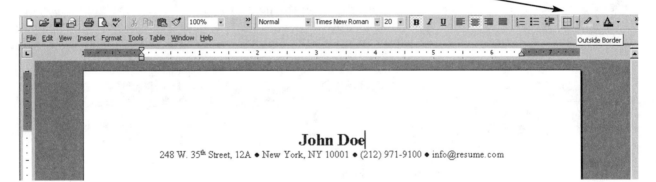

Then choose the border you would like to use from the drop-down menu. We recommend a single line between your name and your contact information.

Finally, click on the bottom border button. If the cursor is lined up after your name, an aesthetically pleasing line will appear directly below it.

John Doe
248 W. 35ᵗʰ Street, 12A ● New York, NY 10001 ● (800) 737-8637 ● info@resume.com

You also can add a line directly underneath your contact information by placing the cursor at the end of your contact information and repeating these steps.

John Doe
248 W. 35ᵗʰ Street, 12A ● New York, NY 10001 ● (800) 737-8637 ● info@resume.com

Examples of Attractive Professional Headers

(1)
Patty O'Henry
6 Northern Creek Rd. ■ Augusta, ME 04330 ■ (800) 737-8637 ■ pohenry@resume.com

(2)
Takeshi Murikawa
534 Red Clay Drive ♦ Honolulu, HI 96813 ♦ (800) 737-8637 ♦ tmurikawa@resume.com

(3)
Gertrude Cartier
87 Maize Lane, #3 ● Des Moines, IA 50319 ● 800-737-8637 ● gcartier@resume.com

Another formatting tip is to left justify your name and leave your contact information centered to create a nice offset effect that gives a professional look to your header:

(4)
IVAN KRISTOV
67 WEST ODYSSEY DRIVE ♦ PHOENIX, AZ 85007 ♦ (800) 737-8637 ♦ ikristov@resume.com

By experimenting with both the **format** and **alignment** selections, you can create an attractive resume header. Additional font types, font styles, and the borders that separate your name from your contact information can be effective ways to impress employers.

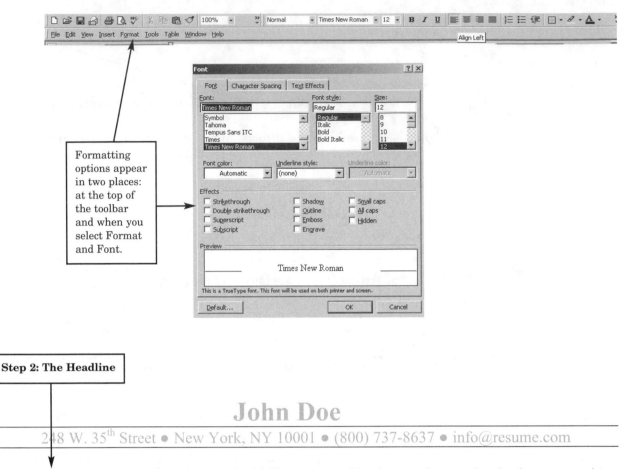

Formatting options appear in two places: at the top of the toolbar and when you select Format and Font.

Step 2: The Headline

John Doe
248 W. 35th Street ● New York, NY 10001 ● (800) 737-8637 ● info@resume.com

Award-winning retail sales professional with demonstrated background managing business operations and creating successful in-store promotions

STEP 2: THE HEADLINE VERSUS THE OBJECTIVE

The top section of your resume is the most important real estate you have to impress the reader. That's why all Resume.com resumes start out with a strong headline, incorporating a professional objective with key talents or achievements that you can offer an employer by emphasizing both what you're looking for and what you have to offer, thus creating a strong hook that catches a potential employer's attention.

All hiring situations represent an attempt by the company to solve a problem or fill a need within the organization. A headline announces what you will do to solve that problem.

You'll be much more successful if your headline is specifically tailored to the position you are applying for; this information is in essence the appetizer that entices the hirer to keep reading. Making a hirer feel that you're applying only for this job, not simply applying for *any* job, is a great way to make a positive first impression.

The headline should always be in bold, centered, and italicized with an 8- to 12-point blank space directly below your contact information:

John Doe

248 W. 35th Street, 12A • New York, NY 10001 • (800) 737-8637 • info@resume.com

Award-winning retail sales professional with demonstrated background managing business operations and creating successful in-store promotions

Many times it's easier to write the headline after completing the resume, as you'll have a stronger understanding of your key accomplishments. Here are some tips for creating a great headline:

- Never use a period at the end of a headline. Remember, you want the hirer to keep reading.
- If you've ever won an award that relates to the position you're applying for, always start off your headline with the term "Award-Winning."
- Limit the headline to two lines. Three lines are okay for professionals with extensive experience but should be avoided if possible.
- For executive resumes, incorporate the headline into the summary or profile section that begins the resume. For examples, jump ahead to Chapter 14.

It's Simple to Build Your Headline: Follow These Easy Steps

1. Start your headline with a powerful adjective that modifies your title. "Talented," "successful," "experienced," "efficient," and "dedicated" are great adjectives for starting a headline.

2. After you've picked out your adjective, add the function that defines your position. For example, "marketing," "journalism," "finance," "sales," or "public relations" would go next.

3. Then add a word that indicates level of experience, such as "manager," "associate," or "assistant." A great word that can apply to practically any applicant is "professional."

A strong way to start off your headline, building on our initial 1-2-3 approach would be:

❑ Talented marketing professional

Additional examples:

❑ Award-winning art director
❑ Accomplished financial associate
❑ Top-producing sales professional
❑ Dedicated financial analyst

You also can add additional functions to bolster your background:

❑ Accomplished sales and marketing professional

Or scale it back to keep the introduction simple:

❑ Experienced journalist

After you've completed this part of your headline, you should list the defining skills, responsibilities, or accomplishments that apply to your desired position or industry.

A great way to present these skills or accomplishments after your title is by using the words "with," "possessing," "adept at," "skilled in," or "proficient at":

❑ Accomplished sales and marketing professional **with** the power and drive to penetrate new markets, lead a sales force, and deliver quota-shattering results

❑ Top-performing financial associate **adept at** overseeing all facets of business development and financial management

❑ Top-producing sales and marketing professional **with** strong background shattering quotas and opening new markets

❑ Talented journalist **with** 18 years of experience covering city politics

---

In the last example, the resume incorporates a simple and powerful tool that hirers love to see: experience. If you list years of experience, a host of attributes—including knowledge, skills, and abilities—are conveyed immediately to the employer. However, avoid listing more than 25 years of experience in the headline to preclude age discrimination.

❑ Award-winning art director **with** proven track record working in multimedia production and publishing

❑ Efficient manager **proficient at** directing employees and overseeing sales transactions

❑ Experienced financial professional skilled in numerous business processes, including forecasting, accounting, and budgeting

To expand your headline, you can always use the word "including" after you introduce your key attribute. Breaking down our last example, notice how each word helps move the sentence to its conclusion:

Experienced financial professional
skilled in numerous business processes,
including forecasting, accounting, and budgeting

Using this type of headline allows you to include numerous duties in one sentence and will expand the openings you can apply for.

Grab an Employer's Attention: 30 Examples of Powerful Headlines

➤ Dedicated finance professional with 11 years of experience in accounts payable, shipping, and inventory management

➤ Experienced retail sales professional with strong track record of developing customer loyalty and managing retail sales operations

➤ An effective networking professional with noted success completing numerous projects on time and within budget

➤ District manager offering exemplary rapport with prospects and five years of proven experience in medical software sales

➤ Hardworking videographer and multimedia artist with solid background and education in design, photography, and film

➤ An accomplished sales professional with proven entrepreneurial success and expertise in computer programming, management, and employee training

➤ A creative management major with a positive attitude and experience in sales and customer satisfaction seeks entry-level position with telemarketing firm

> Remember, avoid using articles (words such as "a" and "an) unless they are vital to the sentence.

➤ An enthusiastic international project management professional who demonstrates resourcefulness, integrity, and **a** tireless drive to succeed

➤ Accomplished IT professional whose continued advancement in database design, system analysis, and application development predicts continued management success

➤ Talented administrative professional with over 20 years of experience providing outstanding support to entertainment-industry executives

➤ Talented administrative and operations management professional with exceptional Fortune 500 background

➤ Recent masters graduate fluent in Korean and English with strong international business acumen and outstanding background in document translation

➤ An experienced, detail-oriented systems engineer with strong sales, marketing, and project management skills

➤ IT technical support professional with over 15 years of experience seeks system engineer position

> If you want to apply for a position in only one field, you can use the word "seeks."

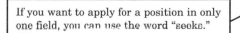

- Highly qualified and dynamic professional with expertise in payroll administration, insurance claims processing, and office management

- Top-performing sales and marketing manager with demonstrated ability to increase revenues through creative marketing techniques and exceptional negotiation skills

- An imaginative interior design major with a positive outlook and experience in office protocol and administration

- Dynamic financial professional with demonstrated expertise in product cost and inventory management

- A highly successful distribution systems manager skilled in database design, technology enhancements, and operations

- An experienced, self-motivated business management professional with outstanding customer service and corporate development skills

- A highly experienced senior financial manager with extensive financial planning, profitability analysis, and project management skills

- Talented manager with nine years of leadership experience in warehouse management, possessing dynamic teaming and interpersonal skills

- Talented and well-educated UC Berkeley graduate with successful academic background seeks entry-level opportunity within marketing or public relations field

- A strategic, visionary marketing professional with a master's degree and extensive experience in new market expansions, new product development, and B2B marketing

- Accomplished machinist with more than 20 years of experience and strong record of successfully resolving critical, time-sensitive problems

- A uniquely experienced bookkeeper and office support technician skilled in accounting software, product quality control, and Website design

- A highly qualified industrial sales and servicing professional with proven track record seeks opportunity to demonstrate technical skills

- Multi-faceted UNIX system administrator with exceptional background in software design, development, and testing; adept at creating key solutions to complex problems

- Talented finance student with strong management skills and demonstrated record of academic success seeks position in business and finance industry

- Award-winning, motivated sales manager with proven track record exceeding targets and building and developing highly profitable accounts

John Doe

248 W. 35^h Street ● New York, NY 10001 ● (800) 737-8637 ● info@resume.com

Award-winning retail sales professional with demonstrated background managing business operations and creating successful in-store promotions

SUMMARY OF QUALIFICATIONS

- Continually recognized with positions of increasing responsibility for outstanding work ethic.
- Strong communicator with dynamic training and management abilities.
- Selected by corporate headquarters to lead six-member team that trained and updated computer system for 17 stores nationwide.
- Team leader who establishes goals and motivates employees to achieve objectives.
- Excellent contributor to corporate sales and success.

STEP 3: THE SUMMARY OF QUALIFICATIONS

When you think about the 10-second rule, which states that your resume has only 10 seconds to make the cut or be rejected by a potential employer, you realize how important it is to impress an employer right from the start. The Summary of Qualifications is designed to maximize the success of your resume within these tight time constraints.

The Summary of Qualifications directly follows the headline and is a key component of building your professional worth. This section should include the highlights of your professional or academic career, including the key achievements, skills, and talents you can offer a new employer. You should include at least five bullets that discuss these characteristics, but this section should never exceed eight bullets; that would make the resume appear too text-heavy.

The Summary of Qualifications can include:

➢ Years of experience and the areas of expertise within your field

➢ Awards or recognition

➢ Industry-specific certifications or professional training

➢ "Soft skills," which are skills that are difficult to quantify, such as communication skills or office administration skills such as "multitasking"

This section is considered your "moment of truth" in an employer's eyes, so don't be modest about your greatest selling points. We guarantee that your competition won't be.

As most hirers will reject your resume if they don't like what they see in this section, the Summary of Qualifications is vital to getting noticed by hirers.

Creating Strong Bullets

Bullets play a vital role in accentuating your most valuable skills, accomplishments, and achievements. These are the one- or two-line sentences that highlight your greatest selling points, indicating why you are the best candidate for the job. Much like headlines, bullets grab the hirer's attention. Here is a sample bullet:

- Recognized with promotions of increasing responsibility for outstanding work ethic.

There are numerous ways to create effective bullets, and this will depend primarily on your personal background. For example, here are ways to impress employers based on three specific professions:

PROFESSIONAL FOCUS: SALES

If you have extensive experience in sales, your resume should be filled with accomplishment statement that use statistics and hard data to highlight your achievements. To convey to an employer that you're too valuable to pass by, show precisely how your previous sales experience affected the company's bottom line. As we discussed in Chapter 1, use quantifiable results, including:

✓ Total sales:
Generated $380,000 in sales over six-month period.

✓ Type of product sold:
Extensive background working with cybernetics and fiber optics.

✓ Number of times you've broken your quota:
Exceeded quota 125% five times during first six months of employment.

✓ Any awards based on performance:
Received "Sales Manager of the Year Award," 2003.

✓ Any accounts that you've brought to the company or taken away from the competition:
Adept at penetrating crowded territories and increasing market share.

✓ Any geographic areas that you oversee, including territories or states:
Oversaw tristate region for four years, growing sales 288% annually.

✓ Types of sales, such as inside or outside:
Strong experience in both inside and outside sales.

✓ Any training of junior employees that you've provided:
Trained and mentored 11 junior employees on sales techniques.

✓ Communication skills and developing strong relationships with clients are the mark of a good salesman. Aim to include at least one bullet that focuses on this particular area:
Adept at building powerful working relationships with diverse range of clientele.

Management professionals need to stress the intrinsic value that they bring to a company through both hard data and proof of leadership abilities. Managers occupy a special place in an employer's organization; they are trusted with making split-second judgment calls and are in essence the key to motivating staff and ensuring high levels of productivity.

Here are some areas management professionals focus on:

✓ Number of employees they oversee:

Manage 11 in-house employees and 38 freelance consultants for $225 million medical company.

✓ Area of management:

Oversee both day-to-day and long-term operations of recycling plant with 18 employees, including inventory management, forecasting, and P&L.

✓ Promotions that have earned them the title of manager:

Quickly promoted to positions of increasing responsibility due to quota-shattering sales performance and exemplary customer service record.

✓ Administrative and organizational abilities that add to the bottom line:

Developed cost-cutting initiatives that saved company $75,000 over two years.

✓ Communication and motivation skills are vital to a manager:

Mentored junior employees to maximize productivity and efficiency, ensuring stable work environment and low turnover rates.

✓ As you can see, managers perform a diverse range of duties, depending on their field. Touch on how you've added to a company's bottom line to impress a potential hirer:

Implemented strategic initiative to automate smelting process, maximizing productivity while decreasing overtime expenditures.

PROFESSIONAL FOCUS: ADMINISTRATION

Professional support and organization are vital elements in any company's success. Clearly defining office administration talents rests heavily on skills that are often difficult to quantify with data. Whether it's corporate administration, which can delve significantly into organization, or individual administration, which generally focuses on one-to-one support, your Summary of Qualifications should highlight your professional contributions or skill set.

Resumes for these professionals generally include:

✓ Scheduling, travel arrangements, and special events:

Coordinated lodging and transportation arrangements for two company executives during business conferences throughout Pacific Northwest.

✓ Verifying company expenses:

Used key knowledge of numerous software programs, including MS Excel and QuickBooks, to create expense reports and verify expenditures.

✓ Organizational skills are essential to this position:

Updated company's filing system, creating electronic database now used throughout the business.

✓ Communication and data entry abilities:

Responsible for all correspondence between Seattle partners and office personnel in Chicago.

✓ Experiences screening employees before information is escalated to a hiring manager:

Reviewed job applications and submissions and escalated materials to appropriate personnel within sales, marketing, and information technology departments.

Formatting Bullets

Writing strong bullets is the first step in creating a powerful Summary of Qualifications section, but as with the initial sections of your resume, formatting is an important part of impressing a hirer.

Every sentence of your Summary of Qualification should be accented with the same bullet type to differentiate this section clearly from the Work History section, which we'll discuss next. The first step is simply writing the sentence:

Manage 11 in-house employees and 38 freelance consultants for $225 million medical company.

Then place the cursor at the beginning of the sentence you would like to bullet:

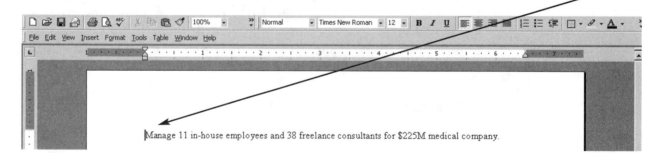

Then, go to Format, select Bullets and Numbering, and choose the bullet you would like to use.

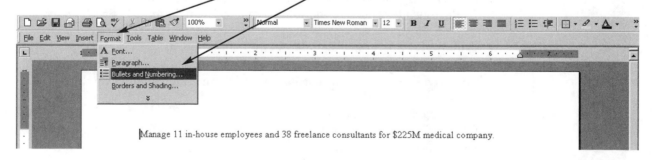

You then will be able to select a standard range of bullets to use:

By highlighting a type of bullet and selecting OK, you'll insert this bullet in front of your sentence:

• Manage 11 in-house employees and 38 freelance consultants for $225 million medical company.

To expand your choice of bullets, highlight a bullet from the previous menu and select Customize. This will bring up the following menu, allowing for greater bullet selection.

You can manipulate the size of the bullet by highlighting the bullet and choosing Font.

As with all symbols that you'll place in your resume, choose a conservative style. We recommend plain circles (•), squares (■), or arrows (➤). Don't use flowers or other creative symbols. In fact, many alternative symbols that people use in their resumes do not appear on the recipient's computer; these symbols may show up as question marks, empty circles, or empty boxes, leaving the hirer questioning your formatting—and ultimately your personality.

Here are some final tips about creating bullets:

■ List your **"selling points"** in order of importance. Quantifiable accomplishments and solid skills, such as years of experience and vital knowledge, should precede soft skills.

- Always end bullets with periods. Although you are never writing in complete sentences, periods at the ends of your bullets help contain the information you are highlighting.
- **If your spell checker indicates that your bullets are fragments, do not worry. Fragments in resumes are correct.**

Summary of Qualifications Examples

SUMMARY OF QUALIFICATIONS

➢ Over four years of experience providing short- and long-term care to patients 10 to 60 years old.

➢ Advanced educational and training background includes master's degree in social work and New York State certification.

➢ Excellent communication, leadership, and support skills with talent for responding to, and respecting, divergent opinions and interests of individuals and groups.

➢ Effective facilitator with keen analytical skills; adept at performing client/needs assessments, program efficiency, crisis intervention, and administering instructional and counseling programs.

➢ Able to thrive in deadline-oriented, high-pressure situations.

➢ Proven record of flexibility and adaptability to any assignment or position.

SUMMARY OF QUALIFICATIONS

- Progressive experience in hotel management, including serving as deputy general manager.
- Ivy League–educated at prestigious Cornell University with solid training in hospitality industry.
- Extensive hands-on experience in virtually every area of hotel operations, from staff supervision and customer service to marketing and sales.
- Adept at recognizing areas in need of improvement and applying vision to develop and execute effective action plans.
- Friendly, outgoing, charismatic; easily adapt to new environments and changing priorities.
- Able to relocate internationally; fluent in Arabic and proficient in French.

Summary of Qualifications

- Proven success in operations management, training, and administrative support.
- Develop, streamline, and implement procedures and programs that improve efficiency and reduce costs.
- Analytical and innovative; coordinate tasks and resolve problems within quality standards.
- Excellent interpersonal and communication skills; cultivate productive relationships by working effectively with students and staff at all levels.
- Advanced educational background includes master of science in College Student Personnel.

Summary of Qualifications

- Demonstrated history shattering quotas and increasing both growth and profitability in the telecommunications industry.
- Fluent understanding and extensive experience managing multiple facets of telecommunications departments, including sales, marketing, technical support, and engineering.
- Diverse equipment knowledge; in-depth understanding of optical transport, digital cross-connect systems, wave division multiplex systems, and digital loop carriers.
- Various remote and interoffice networking capabilities.
- Excellent communications skills. Effective problem solver and team player.

Summary of Qualifications

- Over 20 years of experience in business management, with expertise in business operations.
- Strong business acumen; possess master's degree in Business Administration from UCLA.
- Expert sales ability, proved by eight consecutive years of revenue growth.
- Multitalented, dedicated, and hardworking, ensuring future success.
- Diverse computer skills with proficiency in multiple software programs.

John Doe

248 W. 35th Street • New York, NY 10001 • (800) 737-8637 • info@resume.com

Award-winning retail sales professional with demonstrated background managing business operations and creating successful in-store promotions

SUMMARY OF QUALIFICATIONS

- Continually recognized with positions of increasing responsibility for outstanding work ethic.
- Strong communicator with dynamic training and management abilities.
- Selected by corporate headquarters to lead six-member team that trained and updated computer system for 17 stores nationwide.
- Team leader who establishes goals and motivates employees to achieve objectives.
- Excellent contributor to corporate sales and success.

PROFESSIONAL EXPERIENCE

McKenzie Communications, New York, NY   **1998 – Present**
Manager
Train and manage sales staff of leading national cellular company with $26 million in annual revenues. Oversee in-store promotions, including displays, point-of-sale, and general retail operations.
- ➤ Received "Manager of the Year" award in 2002.
- ➤ Oversee seven cash registers, verify receipts, handle all bank deposits, and monitor daily balances.
- ➤ Establish and maintain professional, clean, and well-stocked store.
- ➤ Continually educate staff on key products and current consumer trends.

Tralfama Digital Express, Lynbrook, NY   **1996 – 1998**
Assistant Manager
Oversaw growth of start-up store from four-employee operation to 11-employee business with $1.5 million in annual revenue.
- ➤ Established multiple sales programs, creating database of repeat customers and offering special incentives-rewards to guarantee referral business.
- ➤ Created innovative merchandise displays and promoted in-store specials and events.
- ➤ Hired and trained seven employees, monitoring performance and creating schedules.

Regional Phone Service, Manhattan, NY   **1993 – 1996**
Assistant Manager
Monitored 11 employees and handled office banking, including cash deposits and daily balances.
- ➤ Established morning and evening shift schedules for employees.
- ➤ Introduced in-store displays that increased wireless product sales 65%.

Tri-Borough Electronics, Manhattan, NY   **1992 – 1993**
Sales Associate
- ➤ Earned "Employee of the Month" award four times, working full-time while attending college.
- ➤ Sold over $4000 in products and services per month.

STEP 4: THE PROFESSIONAL EXPERIENCE SECTION

The Professional Experience section, which also can be labeled Professional Background or Professional History, is the most difficult section to create. This section is where your professional career is described, and it should give potential employers a clear idea of what you've accomplished, the industries in which you've worked, and the people with whom you've collaborated.

This section of your resume combines your **job responsibilities or duties** with targeted **accomplishment statements**. The difference between the two is that a **responsibility statement** explains the essential elements of the job and is similar to a job description. An **accomplishment statement**, in contrast, describes the particular effect you had; this can be in the form of increased efficiency, productivity, and revenues or decreased expenditures, downtime, and waste. A good tip for creating effective responsibility statements is to begin the sentence with "Responsible for" and complete the statement with a description of your general duties. Another good way to differentiate the two is to write the responsibility statement in paragraph form and the accomplishment statements as bullets, helping these significant achievements stand out on the page.

A vital component of professional resume writing is prioritizing your accomplishment statements to show a prospective employer your greatest attributes and contributions. Start with quantifiable results, such as years of experience or number of employees managed, and then move on to less significant results at the bottom of each job description.

Additionally, your resume should serve as an overview of your professional career, not take the form of an essay. Knowing what information to include and exclude is extremely important. Some areas to showcase in this section include the following:

✓ Years of experience:

Ten-year career in office management, including experience in environmental administration and government regulations.

(Avoid age discrimination by never going back farther than 25 years.)

✓ Day-to-day responsibilities and tasks:

Responsible for overseeing all data entry for northwest regional sales group.

✓ Innovations or improvements for which you were responsible:

Spearheaded use of electronic record keeping, enabling real-time data storage program.

✓ People you interacted with and supported:

Provided administrative support for telemarketing group and sales associates as well as product manufacturer representatives and third-party vendors.

✓ Any awards based on performance:

Received "Employee of the Year Award," 1995.

Writing in the correct tense is a vital part of making a clear presentation of your employment history to potential employers. Ongoing responsibilities, such as current job duties or skills that you are using currently, are written in the present tense. Promotions, accomplishments, and past results should be written in the past tense.

"Manage," "guide," "direct," and "oversee" are all present-tense verbs that might apply to current responsibility statements and skills currently being used. "Managed," "guided," "directed," and "oversaw" are all past-tense verbs and would apply to previous positions.

You might have a mix of present and past tense action verbs in your current position; that is acceptable in resume writing. However, be sure that all action verbs for previous positions are written in the past tense.

Current Position (Present Tense)

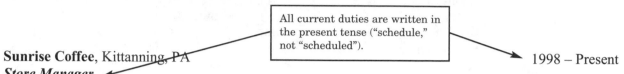

Sunrise Coffee, Kittanning, PA   1998 – Present
Store Manager
Schedule innovative and successful in-store promotions, including live music and membership beverage cards.
- Hire, train, and supervise employees; teach store procedures and provide performance reviews.
- Oversee inventory and place orders for food, equipment, and merchandise.
- Established productive incentive program, rewarding repeat customers and increasing company's bottom line.

> Accomplishment statements in current positions are in the past tense because they show the end result of your action ("established," not "establish").

Previous Position (Past Tense)

> All duties for former jobs are written in the past tense ("managed").

Sullivan Designs, Hershey, PA   1995 – 1997
Administrative Assistant
Managed all administrative operations for this $16 million interior design firm.
- Created official office correspondence and internal memoranda for Principal.
- Responsible for filing client designs and records, scheduling meetings, and dispersing mail.
- Communicated extensively with clients and vendors.

The Professional Experience Section: The Chronological Resume

If you are using the chronological format, break your professional experience section into separate job descriptions, starting with your most recent employer, job title, and dates of employment. Under that information list three to eight bullets for every position.

As we discussed above, prioritizing your strongest selling points is a key to the chronological resume. For example, if you are a sales manager applying for a sales director job, your quota-shattering results and your team's performance should be listed at the top, whereas a description of your communications skills should be listed toward the bottom. As a rule, hirers find hard statistics extremely alluring (such as sales revenue numbers), and this will maximize your resume's success.

The Professional Experience Section: The Functional Resume

If you are using the functional format, your professional experience section will be divided into two to four subheadings of skill sets labeled and prioritized to target an opening. For example, "Management," "Administration," "Communications," and "Customer Service" are all great umbrellas for a store manager. Regardless of your targeted profession, if you are using the functional format, remember that a hirer will look first for solutions to his or her needs. That's why targeting these subheadings to a specific job ad is the best approach.

Rules for Creating Effective Skill Sets for Functional Resumes

- List three to five subsections in the resume, highlighting your key skills or abilities. Under each of those subsections list your achievements, duties, and successes.

- Each subsection should be relevant to the position for which you are applying. Although this type of resume allows you to apply to numerous fields, an effective approach is to target each opening specifically.

- An excellent way to strengthen bullets is to demonstrate how you've applied your talents to leverage results. This is called a **"cause-and-effect"** relationship and is used to create effective accomplishment statements. Here is an example: "Used extensive research skills to identify and purchase less expensive equipment, saving company $2000 per quarter." By showing how your skills are applied to situations, you translate your actions into vibrant accomplishments.

Formatting Dates to Strengthen Your Work History

For many professionals one of the most common mistakes in writing a resume is to signify dates of employment by using the month-year combination (mm/yy or 12/98). Avoiding that practice can make a sporadic work history, which is common but usually detrimental to a resume, appear seamless. Omitting months therefore can camouflage potential red flags that could eliminate you from consideration.

Executives and professionals with over five years of experience usually define their periods of employment by using only years. For these professionals the need to include months becomes less important as their careers progress.

To write periods of employment, use an en dash to separate dates (1990 – 1999). An en dash is longer than a hyphen and accentuates dates clearly. To insert an en dash, write the starting employment date and then go to Insert and Symbol.

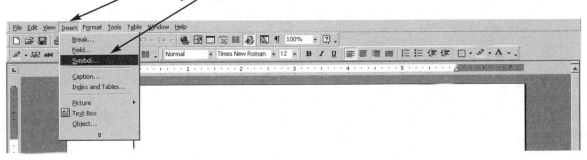

The Symbol window opens. Select Special Characters, En Dash, and Insert.

Symbol

| Symbols | Special Characters |

Character: Shortcut key:

—	Em Dash	Alt+Ctrl+Num -
–	En Dash	Ctrl+Num -
-	Nonbreaking Hyphen	Ctrl+_
¬	Optional Hyphen	Ctrl+-
	Em Space	
	En Space	
	1/4 Em Space	
°	Nonbreaking Space	Ctrl+Shift+Space
©	Copyright	Alt+Ctrl+C
®	Registered	Alt+Ctrl+R
™	Trademark	Alt+Ctrl+T
§	Section	
¶	Paragraph	

AutoCorrect...   Shortcut Key...

Insert   Cancel

Chronological Format Example

PROFESSIONAL EXPERIENCE

XYZ COMPANY, NEW YORK, NY   2001 – PRESENT
Director of Sales Engineering and Product Management (IT) for privately owned provider of Internet security applications. Manage and monitor META product development and support technologies.

- Worked with three-member management team to extensively develop and refine companywide networking functional model, including architecture and engineering.
- Created and implemented sales strategies for eight-member sales team in four-state territory; oversaw closing of up to 15 new accounts weekly.
- Instrumental in negotiating and securing high-dollar contracts, including $350,000 from state of North Carolina.
- Established and built critical alliances and partnerships.
- Conducted average of five product demonstrations/presentations weekly.
- Developed and produced curriculum and technical guides for initial and ongoing training of sales personnel, engineers, and customers.

XYZ COMPANY, NEW YORK, NY   1998 – 2001
Computer Consultant. Managed network and 30 workstations with outside contractors. Troubleshot systems and developed new computer-related solutions.

- Assisted users with technical support; optimized systems to ensure overall efficiency.
- Wrote comprehensive employee manual for newly implemented software application.

Functional Format Example

SKILLS AND ACCOMPLISHMENTS
Business and Operations

- Direct and monitor warehousing and retail facility activities in world-class enterprise.
- Maintain responsibility for developing, administering and monitoring multi-million-dollar budgets.
- Build and foster proactive workplace environment conducive to highest levels of employee participation.
- Proactive, hands-on style; extensive team leadership and personnel development skills.
- Supervise inventory, logistics, purchasing, and procurement of products and supplies with TQM/JIT techniques.
- Effect significant expense reduction through manpower and raw material cost control processes.

Warehousing

- Lead up to 100 team members in storage, transportation, and production of products and supplies.
- Assure personnel comply with all applicable health and safety guidelines and regulations, including OSHA, HAZMAT, and local/organizational mandates.
- Understand and maintain compliance with all specifications of OSHA, EPA, and UL.
- Manage all aspects of manufacturing projects from planning through shipment, including tariff compliance, transportation contracting, and process reviews.

WORK HISTORY

NAKOZOWA U.S.A., NEW YORK, NY   1994 – 2002
Regional Business Manager (2000 – 2002)
Warehouse Supervisor (1994 – 2000)

L.C.D. FINISHING, ST. LOUIS, MO   1990 – 1994
Operations Manager

BLUE OVAL SYSTEMS INC., MINNEAPOLIS, MN   1987 – 1990
Associate Operations Manager

HAYAKISA U.S.A., LOS ANGELES, CA   1985 – 1987
Sales Associate

STRUNK AMERICA CORP, BUENA PARK, CA   1982 – 1985
Sales Representative

John Doe

248 W. 35th Street • New York, NY 10001 • (800) 737-8637 • info@resume.com

Award-winning retail sales professional with demonstrated background managing business operations and creating successful in-store promotions

SUMMARY OF QUALIFICATIONS

- Continually recognized with positions of increasing responsibility for outstanding work ethic.
- Strong communicator with dynamic training and management abilities.
- Selected by corporate headquarters to lead six-member team that trained and updated computer system for 17 stores nationwide.
- Team leader who establishes goals and motivates employees to achieve objectives.
- Excellent contributor to corporate sales and success.

PROFESSIONAL EXPERIENCE

McKenzie Communications, New York, NY   1998 – Present
Manager
Train and manage sales staff of leading national cellular company with $26 million in annual revenues.
- Oversee in-store promotions, including displays, point-of-sale, and general retail operations.
- Received "Manager of the Year" award in 1999.
- Oversee cash registers, verify receipts, handle all bank deposits, and monitor daily balances.
- Establish and maintain professional, clean, and well-stocked store.
- Continually educate staff on key products and current consumer trends.

Tralfama Digital Express, Lynbrook, NY   1996 – 1998
Assistant Manager
Oversaw growth of start-up store from four-employee operation to 11-employee business with $1.5 million in annual revenue.
- Established multiple sales programs, creating database of repeat customers and offering special incentive-rewards to guarantee referral business.
- Created innovative merchandise displays and promoted in-store specials and events.
- Hired and trained seven employees, monitoring performance and creating schedules.

Regional Phone Service, Manhattan, NY   1993 – 1996
Assistant Manager
Monitored 11 employees and handled office banking, including cash deposits and daily balances.
- Established morning and evening shift schedules for employees.
- Introduced in-store displays that increased wireless product sales 65%.

Tri-Borough Electronics, Manhattan, NY   1992 – 1993
Sales Associate
- Earned "Employee of the Month" award four times, working full-time while attending college.
- Sold over $4,000 in products and services per month.

EDUCATION

Manhattan University, Manhattan, NY
Bachelor of Science, 1993. GPA: 3.5

STEP 5: EDUCATION AND PROFESSIONAL DEVELOPMENT

The education section is an important part of a resume. Employers often pay special attention to this section if the final decision comes down to two otherwise equally qualified candidates. Your education should immediately follow your Professional Experience (or Work History) section unless you are a student or have less than one year of experience.

As a rule of thumb, most employers want to know

1. Where you received your education
2. Your major or course of study
3. Any degrees you obtained

If you have a strong education, such as an Ivy League degree or additional postgraduate studies (including a master's degree or a Ph.D.), make sure to include this information *both* in your education section and as a bullet in your Summary of Qualifications. Depending on your level of education, there are a few strict guidelines to follow in this section.

1. As with the Professional History section, list your most recent degree or education first, following the reverse chronological format. Here is an example:

   Columbia University School of Journalism, New York, NY
   Master's Degree, 2002

   University of Florida, Gainesville, FL
   Bachelor's Degree, 1999, G.P.A. 3.36

2. If you have an associate's degree and a bachelor's degree (or a B.A. and additional postgraduate study), leave off your high school education.

3. If you have a bachelor's degree and an associate's degree, leave off the associate's degree; a bachelor's degree carries more weight academically.

   Cornell College, Mount Vernon, IA
   Bachelor's Degree / G.P.A. 3.42   1997

   Suffolk Community College, Suffolk, NY
   Associate's Degree   1995

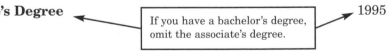
If you have a bachelor's degree, omit the associate's degree.

4. If you have college experience but did not receive a degree, include the name of the college as well as the general course of study. Here is an example:

   New York University, New York, NY
   Extensive coursework in Business Administration

5. If your education consists of a high school diploma, omit this information, as it is assumed. If the position you are applying for states that you need a high school education, include it. Here is an example:

   Everett J. Peterman High School, Austin, TX.   Graduated 1997.

6. Do not include an education section if you do not have a high school diploma.

Your value as a candidate, remember, ultimately will be based on your accomplishments; your education section becomes less important as you advance along your career path. If you're just starting out or have little experience, this section can have a tremendous impact on your job search, however. For recent graduates, the education section usually precedes Professional Experience and should include college coursework and activities relevant to a targeted job. To create a student resume step by step, see Chapter 13.

Pay special attention to the information you include in the education section; job seekers may include superfluous information, usually hurting their chances.

Grade Point Average

Grade point averages (GPAs) are important to the education section but should be listed only if they are 3.0 or higher. Although most professionals with more than 10 years of experience choose to omit their GPAs, special honors such as summa cum laude may continue to be listed.

Additional Professional Development

If you've had additional training or certifications, you can highlight this information in the education section. This can include programs an employer may have instituted or paid for, such as a management training program, or any certifications you may have earned, such as a firearms safety license. With this section, use the reverse chronological format, listing the most recent information first.

Education and Professional Development Examples

EDUCATION AND CERTIFICATIONS

Accounting and Business Administration, Los Angeles, CA
J.P. Edwards Company, 2000

J.P. Edwards Management Training Program, Los Angeles, CA
J.P. Edwards Company, 1999

University of Washington, Seattle, WA
Bachelor's Degree, 1996

EDUCATION

University of Washington, Seattle, WA
Bachelor's Degree, 1996

CERTIFICATES

Accounting and Business Administration, Los Angeles, CA
J.P. Edwards Company, 2000

J.P. Edwards Management Training Program, Los Angeles, CA
J.P. Edwards Company, 1999

Education, Seminars, and Professional Training

EASTERN CONNECTICUT STATE UNIVERSITY, Willimantic, CT
B.A. in Industrial Psychology, 2001

U.S. NAVAL SECURITY ACADEMY, San Antonio, TX
Security Specialist Course; Security Police Tactics Course, 1996

FLANDERS INTERNATIONAL SECURITY SERVICES, Greenwich, CT
Gun Supervisory Skills (Qualified Instructor), 1995

OFFICE OF ADULT PROBATION, Norwich, CT
Field work, court docket, and investigation licenses, 1993

Career-specific certifications can be listed as a separate section for highly specialized industries, such as information technology (see "IT Resumes" in Chapter 12).

Power Rules for Creating an Effective Education Section

- **The more relevant and recent the education is, the more it is emphasized.** Field of study, major, relevant coursework, honors, academic awards, and extracurricular activities may be found on a recent graduate's resume. If you have five years of experience, however, your school and your major are generally all that is relevant.
- **Your GPA should be listed if it is 3.0 or higher.**
- **Irrelevant information hurts your resume and should not be listed.** For example, if you majored in music but now have a sales career, write "Bachelor of Arts, Kent State University, Kent, OH, 1988." Omit the music major, as it is inconsequential to your career goal.
- **Do not give the graduation date for degrees earned over 15 years ago.**
- **If you went to college but did not graduate,** list relevant courses and activities that promote your professional worth. If you have over 60 credits, list the number of credits earned.
- **Avoid listing your high school education** if you have an associate's degree or higher, have more than five years of professional experience, or unless it is specifically called for in the job announcement.

Education Section Examples

EDUCATION

Accredited Asset Management Specialist   2002
College for Financial Planning, Denver, CO

Master of Business Administration Executive Program Studies   1996
University of Pennsylvania, Philadelphia, PA

Bachelor of Science, Political Science   1991
Slippery Rock University, Slippery Rock, PA

EDUCATION
MANHATTAN COLLEGE, New York, NY
BS, Business Administration, 2002

Key Courses: Management in Business, Global Business Strategies, Accounting, Macroeconomics, Statistics, Global Business

EDUCATION

LONG BEACH CITY COLLEGE, Long Beach, CA
Currently pursuing AA degree in International Business

John Doe

248 W. 35th Street • New York, NY 10001 • (800) 737-8637 • info@resume.com

Award-winning retail sales professional with demonstrated background managing business operations and creating successful in-store promotions

SUMMARY OF QUALIFICATIONS

- Continually recognized with positions of increasing responsibility for outstanding work ethic.
- Strong communicator with dynamic training and management abilities.
- Selected by corporate headquarters to lead six-member team that trained and updated computer system for 17 stores nationwide.
- Team leader who establishes goals and motivates employees to achieve objectives.
- Excellent contributor to corporate sales and success.

PROFESSIONAL EXPERIENCE

McKenzie Communications, New York, NY   1998 – Present
Manager
Train and manage sales staff of leading national cellular company with $26 million in annual revenues.
- Oversee in-store promotions, including displays, point-of-sale, and general retail operations.
- Received "Manager of the Year" award in 1999.
- Oversee seven cash registers, verify receipts, handle all bank deposits, and monitor daily balances.
- Establish and maintain professional, clean, and well-stocked store.
- Continually educate staff on key products and current consumer trends.

Tralfama Digital Express, Lynbrook, NY   1996 – 1998
Assistant Manager
Oversaw growth of start-up store from four-employee operation to 11-employee business with $1.5 million in annual revenue.
- Established multiple sales programs, creating database of repeat customers, and offering special incentives-rewards to guarantee referral business.
- Created innovative merchandise displays and promoted in-store specials and events.
- Hired and trained seven employees, monitoring performance and creating schedules.

Regional Phone Service, Manhattan, NY   1993 – 1996
Assistant Manager
Monitored 11 employees and handled office banking, including cash deposits and daily balances.
- Established morning and evening shift schedules for employees.
- Introduced in-store displays that increased wireless product sales 65%.

Tri-Borough Electronics, Manhattan, NY   1992 – 1993
Sales Associate
- Earned "Employee of the Month" award four times, working full-time while attending college.
- Sold over $4000 in products and services per month.

EDUCATION

Manhattan University, Manhattan, NY
Bachelor of Science, 1993. GPA: 3.5

AWARDS AND RECOGNITION

"Manager of the Year," 1999, McKenzie Communications, New York, NY
"Employee of the Month," four times, 1993, Tri-Borough Electronics, Manhattan, NY

STEP 6: AWARDS AND RECOGNITION SECTION

If you've earned any awards or honors at previous positions or at your current job, such as "Manager of the Year" or "Employee of the Month," you should create an Awards section. This section should immediately follow the Education section.

Although this part of your resume is optional, as many job seekers have not won awards, professional recognition demonstrates a strong work ethic and the ability to produce great results. As with a graduate degree or a Ph.D., an award can set you apart from the competition. We recommend listing this information in two places: bulleted in the Summary of Qualifications or Professional Experience section and additionally in an Awards section. This is an ideal opportunity to demonstrate why you're the best candidate for the job.

Power Rules for Creating an Effective Awards Section

List your most recent awards, certificates, or honors first and work backward to the first applicable honor you received. List all pertinent awards or achievements next to the years in which they were received.

If you have a weak Education section, bolster your resume with an Awards section.

Awards Section Examples

AWARDS AND RECOGNITION
Cornerstone Award, 1999, TELLIOS COMPANY, NEW YORK, NY
Sales Engineer of the Year, 1998, TELLIOS COMPANY, NEW YORK, NY

HONORS
"Salesman of the Year," 1997, MANTACORE INDUSTRIES, NEWARK, NJ
President's Club for Outstanding Sales, 1995 – 1998, 2002, MANTACORE INDUSTRIES, NEWARK, NJ

AWARDS
Bronze Star • Army Commendation Medal (5) • Joint Service Achievement Medal • Good Conduct Medal (6)

John Doe

248 W. 35th Street • New York, NY 10001 • (800) 737-8637 • info@resume.com

Award-winning retail sales professional with demonstrated background managing business operations and creating successful in-store promotions

SUMMARY OF QUALIFICATIONS

- Continually recognized with positions of increasing responsibility for outstanding work ethic.
- Strong communicator with dynamic training and management abilities.
- Selected by corporate headquarters to lead six-member team that trained and updated computer system for 17 stores nationwide.
- Team leader who establishes goals and motivates employees to achieve objectives.
- Excellent contributor to corporate sales and success.

PROFESSIONAL EXPERIENCE

McKenzie Communications, New York, NY   **1998 – Present**
Manager
Train and manage sales staff of leading national cellular company with $26 million in annual revenues.
- Oversee in-store promotions, including displays, point-of-sale, and general retail operations.
- Received "Manager of the Year" award in 1999.
- Oversee seven cash registers, verify receipts, handle all bank deposits, and monitor daily balances.
- Establish and maintain professional, clean, and well-stocked store.
- Continually educate staff on key products and current consumer trends.

Tralfama Digital Express, Lynbrook, NY   **1996 – 1998**
Assistant Manager
Oversaw growth of start-up store from four-employee operation to 11-employee business with $1.5 million in annual revenue.
- Established multiple sales programs, creating database of repeat customers and offering special incentives-rewards to guarantee referral business.
- Created innovative merchandise displays and promoted in-store specials and events.
- Hired and trained seven employees, monitoring performance and creating schedules.

Regional Phone Service, Manhattan, NY   **1993 – 1996**
Assistant Manager
Monitored 11 employees and handled office banking, including cash deposits and daily balances.
- Established morning and evening shift schedules for employees.
- Introduced in-store displays that increased wireless product sales 65%.

Tri-Borough Electronics, Manhattan, NY   **1992 – 1993**
Sales Associate
- Earned "Employee of the Month" award four times, working full-time while attending college.
- Sold over $4000 in products and services per month.

EDUCATION

Manhattan University, Manhattan, NY
Bachelor of Science, 1993. GPA: 3.5

AWARDS AND RECOGNITION

"Manager of the Year," 1999, McKenzie Communications, New York, NY
"Employee of the Month," four times, 1993, Tri-Borough Electronics, Manhattan, NY

COMPUTER SKILLS

Windows 95/98/2000/ME, MS Office Suite (Word, Excel, Outlook, PowerPoint), Internet-savvy

STEP 7: COMPUTER SKILLS SECTION

Over the last decade the demand for job applicants with strong computer skills has skyrocketed. Technology is now the engine that drives the global economy, and the effect it has had on almost every job opening in every industry has been palpable.

You should list all the computer programs in which you are proficient directly after the education and awards sections. Whether your experience is limited to writing a letter using Microsoft Word or you have an extensive background working with computer applications, any and every program you know how to use should be listed on your resume. This includes software, operating systems, databases, and networking tools, as well as familiarity with the Internet and e-mail programs.

For information technology specialists, technical skills are an essential part of the resume. Clearly list this section immediately after the Summary of Qualifications or at the end of the resume.

Computer Skills Section Examples

COMPUTER SKILLS

MS Windows, MS Word, MS Excel, E-mail Applications

COMPUTER SKILLS

Microsoft Office Suite, Outlook, Explorer, Adobe Acrobat, AS400, BOSS billing system, E-mail, Application Management

COMPUTER SKILLS

MICROSOFT WORD, EXCEL, LOTUS NOTES, SALESLINE, BIAS, AND INTERNET SEARCH ENGINES

COMPUTER SKILLS

Windows 95/2000/XP, MS Word and Excel, Lotus 1-2-3, IBM AS400, SAP (System Application Products) R/3

Information Technology Computer Skills Examples

Applicants with more complex computer skills should define this section as the primary selling point of the resume. For a more in-depth approach to computer skills for information technology (IT) professionals, see Chapter 12.

TECHNICAL SKILLS

O/S:	Windows 2000 Server, Windows NT 4.0 Server/Workstation, Novell 3x
Hardware:	Compaq Proliant Servers; IBM, Compaq, and Dell Laptop and PC
Software:	Concur Expense, MS Office 2000, MS Internet Information Server 5.0, MS SQL Server 7.0/6.5, MS MDAC

TECHNICAL KNOWLEDGE

Platforms: UNIX Administration (SunOS 4.1.X, Solaris 5.X, HP-UX, Interactive UNIX); VMS 5.X; MS-DOS 6.2; Windows 3.1/NT/3.51/NT 4.0 /95/98/2000/ME/XP

Languages: C; UNIX Shell (C, Bourne, Korn); SQL and Embedded SQL; PERL.

Databases: Informix; Ingres; Empress; Oracle 8.0

Software: MS Office, Project, FrontPage, SECSIMPro (GW Assoc. Inc./Asyst Technologies Inc.), CCS Envoy (Brooks-PRI Automation Inc.), SECS/GEM, E4/E5/E30/E37/E84/E87/E90/E40/E94

Networking: TCP/IP for UNIX and Windows

Hardware: PCs; UNIX Systems

COMPUTER SKILLS AND CERTIFICATIONS

Java Expertise
J2EE 1.3+: ORBs, CORBA, RMI, Jini, EJB, JNDI, JDBC
JDK 1.3 & 1.4: Reflection, I/O, Dynamic Classloading, Security, Threads, Swing, Javadocs
GENERAL: JBuilder, Ant, CVS, jCVS, SourceSafe, Design Patterns

Professional Knowledge

OO Analysis & Design	Enterprise Application Integration
Performance Tuning	Unified Process/Iterative Development
Telephony/Telecommunications	MetaSolv TBS
Distributed Systems	Daleen Billplex & RevChain
Linux, Windows, OS X & Solaris	Shell Scripting

Certifications
Sun Certified Developer for Java 2 Platform, in progress.
Sun Certified Programmer for Java 2 Platform, 2000.

PROFESSIONAL AFFILIATIONS (OPTIONAL)

Professional affiliations are a great way to let employers know that you're committed to your profession and that your involvement in your industry extends beyond office hours. This section is optional and doesn't have to be the focus of your resume. If you want to include a Professional Affiliations section, list each of your affiliations under a single header. Dates are not necessary, but don't list expired or previous affiliations unless you are using the functional format. Here are some examples:

PROFESSIONAL AFFILIATIONS
New Jersey Investment Bankers Club
International Foundation for Global Economics

PROFESSIONAL MEMBERSHIPS
Bilingual Speakers Club, New York City
Yale Alumni Club

PROFESSIONAL ACTIVITIES
NORTH DAKOTA MUSIC AND ART SOCIETY
- Teach underprivileged youths music and art at local community center.
- Raise funds to purchase instruments for elementary school children.

PROFESSIONAL GROUPS
AMERICAN MEDICAL ASSOCIATION
DOCTORS WITHOUT BOUNDARIES

Activities and Community Involvement (OPTIONAL)

Community activities and volunteerism can be excellent ways to bolster a resume, especially for parents reentering the workforce and professionals pursuing employment at nonprofit organizations. However, if your resume is complete without this section and your community involvement does not support your career goals directly, exclude it. Your resume should be a concise overview of your best selling points; don't include every detail of your life.

Rules for Creating an Effective Community Involvement Section

- This section should follow your Education or Awards section.
- List the organization where you volunteered, your role, and the years of activity.
- You can bullet specific achievements in this section.

AFFILIATIONS
New York City Shelter for Homeless Women, 1990 – 2003
Meals on Wheels, 1991 – 2003

MEMBERSHIPS
New York Literacy Program	1999 – Present
National Federation of Reading to Children	2000 – 2003
Parent and Child Community Association	2002 – 2003

VOLUNTEER/COMMUNITY ACTIVITIES
Volunteer – Provide "Animal Assisted Therapy" to nursing home patients

VOLUNTEER ACTIVITIES
Colonies Pool, President, San Antonio, TX
- Advised recreational facility in marketing methods to increase membership. Suggested and oversaw development of promotional Web page.

Jimenez Thanksgiving Dinner, San Antonio, TX
- Served meals to needy families and individuals.

John Doe

248 W. 35th Street • New York, NY 10001 • (800) 737-8637 • info@resume.com

Award-winning retail sales professional with demonstrated background managing business operations and creating successful in-store promotions

SUMMARY OF QUALIFICATIONS

- Continually recognized with positions of increasing responsibility for outstanding work ethic.
- Strong communicator with dynamic training and management abilities.
- Selected by corporate headquarters to lead six-member team that trained and updated computer system for 17 stores nationwide.
- Team leader who establishes goals and motivates employees to achieve objectives.
- Excellent contributor to corporate sales and success.

PROFESSIONAL EXPERIENCE

McKenzie Communications, New York, NY   1998 – Present
Manager
Train and manage sales staff of leading national cellular company with $26 million in annual revenues.
- Oversee in-store promotions, including displays, point-of-sale, and general retail operations.
- Received "Manager of the Year" award in 1999.
- Oversee seven cash registers, verify receipts, handle all bank deposits, and monitor daily balances.
- Establish and maintain professional, clean, and well-stocked store.
- Continually educate staff on key products and current consumer trends.

Tralfama Digital Express, Lynbrook, NY   1996 – 1998
Assistant Manager
Oversaw growth of start-up store from four-employee operation to 11-employee business with $1.5 million in annual revenue.
- Established multiple sales programs, creating database of repeat customers, and offering special incentive-rewards to guarantee referral business.
- Created innovative merchandise displays and promoted in-store specials and events.
- Hired and trained seven employees, monitoring performance and creating schedules.

Regional Phone Service, Manhattan, NY   1993 – 1996
Assistant Manager
Monitored 11 employees and handled office banking, including cash deposits and daily balances.
- Established morning and evening shift schedules for employees.
- Introduced in-store displays that increased wireless product sales 65%.

Tri-Borough Electronics, Manhattan, NY   1992 – 1993
Sales Associate
- Earned "Employee of the Month" award four times, working full-time while attending college.
- Sold over $4000 in products and services per month.

EDUCATION

Manhattan University, Manhattan, NY
Bachelor of Science, 1993. GPA: 3.5

AWARDS AND RECOGNITION

"Manager of the Year," 1999, McKenzie Communications, New York, NY
"Employee of the Month," four times, 1993, Tri-Borough Electronics, Manhattan, NY

COMPUTER SKILLS

Windows 95/98/2000/ME, MS Office Suite (Word, Excel, Outlook, PowerPoint), Internet savvy

KEYWORDS

management training, customer service manager, retail sales manager, customer loyalty, in-store promotions, inventory control, loss prevention, merchandising, pricing

STEP 8: KEYWORDS SECTION

Keywords are a relatively new component in resumes, having appeared only in the last five years as technology has become an integral aspect of the hiring process. Keywords are now an essential element of a resume, however, and if you're not handing your resume directly to a friend, do not submit it without a keywords section.

The reason why Resume.com includes a keywords section is to ensure that your resume is not eliminated by computer scanning software. This is software that is used by many human resources personnel at large companies to eliminate your resume automatically before it is viewed by human eyes. Here's how the process works: Hirers gather nonelectronic resumes via fax and mail, as well as electronic resumes via e-mail and job boards. These resumes are stored in a database where hiring personnel can use individual keywords to sort them and eliminate those which do not meet the criteria, reducing a potential stack of a thousand applications to a select few. If your resume does not contain these keywords, you won't be called in for an interview.

You can use keywords to your advantage to maximize the chances of having your resume chosen by hiring managers. Chapter 7 provides an in-depth discussion of the importance of keywords and their role in all professional resumes.

Your keywords section can be formatted to resemble the other sections, but it can just as easily appear as a few lines at the bottom of the resume.

Keywords Section Examples

Keywords: Operations Manager, Supervisor, Coordinator, Administrative Manager, Program Manager, Analyst (examples of keywords for an operations manager)

KEYWORDS: Junior Mechanical Engineer, Junior Maintenance Engineer, Assistant, Associate, Technician (examples of keywords for a Mechanical Engineer)

KEYWORDS
Programming Director, Project Manager, Technical Lead, CRM, RDBMS, streaming media, broadband, marketing, e-commerce (examples of keywords for a Product/Project Manager)

7

What Is a Keyword?

If you're applying for a position at a medium-size or large company, the odds are that your resume will be sorted, preranked, and filed in an electronic resume database before a human being ever reviews it. A human resources professional will then enter certain keywords (such as **"Bachelor's Degree"** or **"Accounts Payable"**) into the electronic database, performing a **keyword search** to select only the resumes that match the specific, requested criteria. The documents with the right keywords will be retrieved and reviewed by a hirer; the rest usually will be eliminated.

This technology is used to expedite the hiring process, saving an employer both time and money by quickly rejecting hundreds, if not thousands, of candidates. At the heart of this process is optical character recognition (OCR) software, which sounds like something out of a science fiction movie but in reality is used to identify qualified candidates quickly whether their resumes are e-mailed, faxed, or mailed in.

OCR software reads the text on a resume and stores it in a database, usually saving it there for up to six months. One benefit of this process is that you may be eligible for certain positions for which you didn't apply. However, the key drawback is that if your resume does not contain the vital keywords established by the hirer, there's an excellent chance that you will be rejected.

Therefore, computer scanning software has become the first obstacle that many candidates must overcome to obtain an interview. Resume.com uses a **Keywords Section** to ensure that our candidates have every competitive advantage in the hiring process, and we strongly recommend that you incorporate this section into your resume.

HOW KEYWORDS WORK

Every time you use a word in your resume—such as "sales," "prospecting," "revenue," or "management"—the OCR software will read and store this information, and so in essence your resume is already packed with keywords. To a certain extent, consider every word that you put down on your resume as a potential keyword. However, let's say you're applying for an accounts payable position. A common search that may be entered into the database is "A/P," which is common industry jargon for "accounts payable." If you do not have "A/P" in your resume, you may be rejected even if you have 15 years of experience in this field.

ELECTRONIC RESUME DATABASES

A Boolean search is one way a potential employer can search for information in a resume database without reviewing each resume. Using the options "And," "Or," and "Not," a hirer can eliminate 500 candidates who don't have MBAs or BAs, are not bilingual, and are not experienced in sales or customer service. For example, if you've been an English teacher for 10 years, it's probably safe to assume that you have a strong understanding of grammar. However, if you don't include "grammar" as a keyword and it doesn't appear on your resume, a computer will not be able to make the correlation between your position as an English teacher and your grammar skills, and you won't get the proofreading job.

Multiple keyword searches may include terms covering your professional or educational background, previous job titles, action words, and industry terminology. They frequently include acronyms and words indicating specialized areas of knowledge. Industry jargon, memberships, and alternative terms and spellings for keywords, as was mentioned above, also should be included in your resume.

For example, the scannable resume of a professional journalist might contain some of the following **keywords**: Reporter, Writer, Staff Writer, Newspaper, Publishing, Published, Editor, Edit, Editing, Copy Editor, Copyedit, Copy Edit, Proofreader, Columnist, Column, Daily, Daily Newspaper, Journalism, Journalism School, and Journalist. This would cover a great deal of information, including areas that may not be covered in the candidate's resume.

As a rule of thumb, try to include at least 10 keywords, targeting what a hirer in your industry may be looking for. Be sure to write out as well as abbreviate any acronyms; if you're proficient with Microsoft Word, make sure to include "MS Word."

Where you include your keyword section will not affect the results, but as with the rest of the resume, appearances matter. Make sure that this section is aesthetically pleasing. We recommend placing the keyword summary at the bottom of the resume. Note: Keywords also play a vital role when you post a resume to job boards (see Chapters 7 and 9).

Below are some valuable keywords listed by industry. Our expert resume writers and editors find the most up-to-date keywords by conducting searches for help wanted ads on job boards and in newspapers. This is a great way to identify the most prominent keywords for the positions and industries for which you are applying. Review a job board or the help wanted section of a major newspaper to obtain alternative job titles and additional criteria that can be used as keywords in your resume.

ADMINISTRATIVE
Office Manager
Office Administrator
Office Coordinator
Administration Specialist
Administrative Coordinator
Administrative Assistant
Executive Administration
Executive Secretary
Word Processing
Administrative Support
Project Support
Project Coordinator
Project Assistant
Office Supervisor
Office Manager Assistant
Schedules
General Office Duties
WPM

ADVERTISING
Account Management
Prospecting
Client Management
Sales Representative
Account Development
Cold Calling
Negotiating
Ad Placement
Collateral
Research
Marketing
Design
Consumer Trends
Graphic Design
Copywriter
Copy
Production
Buying
Selling
Ad Time
Radio
Television
Internet

BUSINESS
Project Analyst
Operations Analyst
Process Modeling Tools
Documentation Training
Finance

BUSINESS (Cont.)
P & L
Profit and Loss
R & D
Research and Development
Operations
Debt
Restructuring
Reports
Accounting
A/P
Accounts Payable
A/R
Accounts Receivable
Process Improvement
Infrastructure
Forecasting
Supervisor

ENGINEERING
Mechanical Manufacturing
Optical Engineer
Technology
Components
Electronics
Computer
Controls
Project Management
Mechanical Engineering
Manufacturing
Engineer
Machine
Machinery

FINANCE
Financial Analyst
Finance Associate
Financial Advisor
Administration
Investment Trainee
Management Assistant
Payroll Associate
Investments
Research Analyst
Economics Analyst
ROI
Risk Assessment
Portfolio
P&L

HOSPITALITY
Hotel Manager
General Manager
Manager of Hotel Operations
Hospitality Management
Hotel Director
Executive Operations Manager
Assistant General Manager
GM
Assistant GM
Customer Service
Grounds Keeper
Restaurant Manager
Hospitality Manager

HR
Benefits Administration
Recruiting
Associate
Manager
Staffing
Hiring/Firing
OSHA
Worker's Compensation
Workman's Compensation
Employment
Best Practices
Director
Policies
Procedures

IT
Database Administrator
Systems Administrator
QA
Quality Assurance
Troubleshooting
Level I
Level II
Level III
Help Desk
Technical Support
Networking
Analytical
Problem Solving
Team Lead
Project Manager
Systems Analyst

IT (Cont.)
Software Development
Information Technology
Software Engineering
Technical Manager
Senior Network Engineer
VP of Engineering
IT Engineer
Programmer
Software Developer
Network Engineer
Software Engineer
Java Programmer

MANAGEMENT
District Manager
Manager
Management
Supervisor
Training
Mentoring
Marketing Director
Director of Sales
Account Manager
Product Manager
National Account Manager
Marketing Associate
Client Manager
Regional Sales Manager
Client Services
Marketing Director
Account Executive
Brand Manager

MANUFACTURING
Goods
Services
Technology
Assembly Line
Military
Inventory
Shipping
Receiving
Project Manager
Engineering
Machinery
Manufacturing Manager
Production Manager
Service Manager
System Manager
General Account

MANUFACTURING
(Cont.)
Operations Manager
Warehouse
Warehousing
Spreadsheets
Tracking

MARKETING
Advertising
Copy
Advertising Copy
Branding
Television
Radio
Internet
National
Regional
Programming
  Director
Sales Collateral
Project Manager
CRM
Clientele
Accounts
Database
Streaming Media
Broadband
e-commerce
B2B
Marketing Manager
Assistant Manager

PR
Account Executive
Publicist
Advertising
Promotions
AE

PR (Cont.)
Account Executive
Executive AE
Event Planning
Senior Publicist
Manager
Coordinator
Events
Branding
Special Events
Crisis Management
Goods
Services
Regional
National
Communications
Relationship
  Development

PUBLISHING
Editor
Writer
Assistant
Associate
Managing
Senior
Publications
Trade
Traffic
Copy Editing
Copy
Designer
Book
Magazine
Newspaper
Journalism
Research
Fact Checker
Proofreader

SALES
District Sales
Regional Manager
Channel Development
Territory
District Manager
Regional Sales
SALES (Cont.)
Operations
Operations Manager
Sales Director
Customer
Client
GM
General Manager
Product Sales
Accounts
Account Executive
Account Manager
Director
Group Project Manager
Marketing Manager
Quota
Percent
New Account

**TELECOMMUNICA-
TIONS**
Telecom
Engineering
Fiber Optics
Laser
Computer
Master's Degree
Sales
Technical Support
Customer Service
Supervisor
Team Leader

**TELECOMMUNICA-
TIONS** (Cont.)
Consultant
Telecommunications
Technician
Cable
Cable Technician
Wireless
Engineer
Technology
Sales
IT
Computer
Interface

TRAINING
Mentor
Procedures
Counselor
Team Leader
Skills
Manager
Assistant Manager
Assistant Director
Personnel
Personnel Manager
Operations Manager
Program Manager
Training Manager
Operations Coordinator
Training Coordinator
Consultant
Supervisor
Relationship Management
Relationship
Oversee
Manuals
Collateral
Process Improvement

8

The Internet Resume

The Internet has changed almost every facet of the job application process, creating a fundamental shift that affects not only the way job applicants research, apply for, and obtain new positions but also the way resumes are written. The Internet resume has had a profound impact on the job application process because of its defining characteristic: the lightning-quick transfer of information. This has created an ideal means for contacting hirers; unlike using a fax or mailing a resume, it's a relatively cheap and paper-free way to apply for a position.

There are drawbacks to using the Internet to apply for a job, however. The ease with which information is exchanged on the Internet has created a deluge of available candidates for almost **any** position listed online, and you therefore can expect to compete with hundreds, if not thousands, of applicants for any job. Some career-services companies even offer automated resume-submission tools that immediately submit your resume when a hirer first posts a job online. Hirers usually are inundated with candidates, and as the applicant pool increases, the cream does not always rise to the top. As we've discussed in the last chapter, employers have begun to use powerful software to eliminate candidates on the basis of predetermined criteria.

This chapter will walk you through the steps you should use to apply for a position by using e-mail and the Internet and what electronic pitfalls you'll have to avoid along the way. To ensure that your resume is not eliminated with those of the herd of applicants who aren't applying for a *specific* position so much as for *any* position, you should adhere closely to the following ground rules.

DON'T ATTACH YOUR DOCUMENT—AT FIRST, ANYWAY

In the age of job boards, resume distribution, and e-mail applications, the first step in applying for a position online is to adhere to the golden rule: Don't submit a resume as an attachment to an e-mail. Although every e-mail program has this option, the smartest way to apply for a job online is to cut and paste the resume into the body of the e-mail, using an ASCII conversion, which in lay terms is an electronic, text-only version of a resume.

Attaching a resume is usually a mistake because many companies have made it standard practice to delete e-mails containing attachments automatically, as it not only takes time to open an attachment, but, more important, an e-mail with an attachment may contain a virus.

Viruses can be hidden in attachments and, if downloaded, can wreak havoc and destroy data. You don't want to be grouped into the same category as Bill from accounting, who was fired last week and thinks that sending his former company a nasty virus is a great way to say thank you to the department. Remember, a potential employer can't tell you from Bill, and many companies automatically delete job applicants' e-mails if they contain attachments.

The threat of viruses, real or perceived, has resulted in programs that automatically delete attachments, and many hirers would rather delete a file than risk a virus. Cutting and pasting an ASCII version of your resume into an e-mail is a smarter way to apply.

THE ASCII RESUME

ASCII stands for American Standard Code for Information Interchange, and it's the industry standard for e-mailing or posting a resume online. As a result of its safety and plain-text readability, the ASCII (pronounced "as-kee") resume avoids the e-mail deletion problem when properly cut and pasted into the body of an e-mail. It also avoids the second biggest problem that job seekers encounter when applying for a position online: translation problems that can occur when a document is saved on one computer and opened on another.

Although most resumes created in a word-processing program use style traits to make a document aesthetically pleasing (such as bullets and bolding), not every e-mail program, operating system, and Web browser can read these documents without translation problems occurring.

An ASCII resume can be read by any of these systems and programs and ensures that a hirer is not reading an incomprehensible document. Although the ASCII format is not as pleasing to the eye as a nicely formatted Word document, what it loses in attractiveness, it makes up for in practicality. Whether an employer is using a Mac or a personal computer (PC), your resume will be read. You can create your own ASCII conversion by following a few simple steps.

First, make sure to save the document.

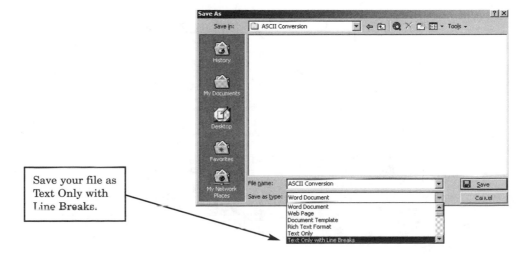

Then go into Save As... and go into Save as Type at the bottom of that window.

Then, choose Text Only with Line Breaks and save.

Save your file as Text Only with Line Breaks.

Next close the document and then open up the text version. Your new document will have lost most of its formatting and will look something like this:

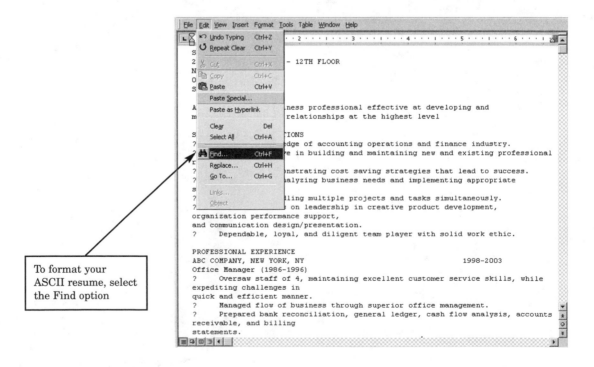

The first step in correctly formatting the ASCII version is to change all the bullets, which probably will have turned into question marks (?), into asterisks (*). You can do this by going to Edit and selecting the Find option. Then select Replace in this window. Then enter the question mark (?) to be replaced by the asterisk (the asterisk is shift-8) and choose Replace All.

To format your ASCII resume, select the Find option

Then select
Replace and enter
the question mark
(?) to be replaced
by the asterisk (*).
Then choose the
"Replace all."

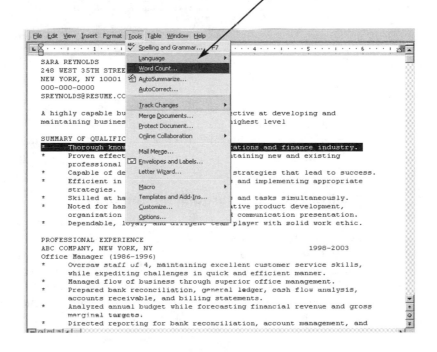

USE 65 CHARACTERS PER LINE

Make sure that each line of your ASCII resume does not exceed 65 characters.
(Each letter or space you type counts as one character.) To check this, highlight
a sentence, go to Tools, and select Word Count.

The character count will appear on the screen. In this case it has exceeded the 65-space limit.

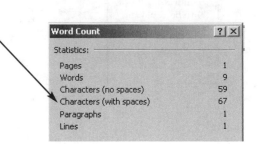

Make sure that all dashes are still dashes and that the dates are aligned. Now copy and paste the formatted ASCII resume into the e-mail you send to hirers. This formatted document should be cut and pasted directly below your cover letter.

Simply "cut" the ASCII resume from your Word program and "paste" it into the body of the e-mail. To do so, select Edit and then Cut. Then move your cursor to the body of the e-mail, and select Edit and Paste.

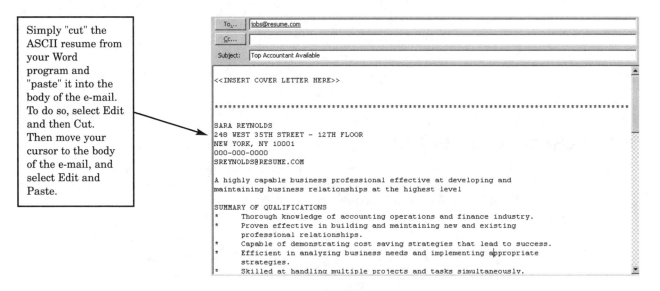

We recommend e-mailing the resume to yourself first to verify that the formatting is clear. This highly readable version, you'll notice, won't be as attractive as a nicely formatted resume, but sometimes it's a matter of form following function.

Optical Character Recognition and the ASCII Resume

Another benefit of the ASCII resume is its ability to be scanned easily by optical character recognition (OCR) software. As we indicated in the discussion of the keywords section in Chapter 7, job applicants often send resumes that can't be read by OCR software. To ensure that the content of your resume, which is the key to any interview, is reviewed, heed the words of communications theorist Marshall McLuhan: "The medium is the message." Make sure you're adhering to the rules of the medium, and the results will follow.

OCR software cannot read certain types of fonts or symbols commonly used in many resumes, and so it's best to have two versions of your resume: one for applying online and another for handing out at job fairs or giving directly to a potential employer.

Otherwise, you'll waste a lot of time sending out resumes that are not being read. And that's before the competition even starts.

The three most common methods of applying for an advertised position are by fax, e-mail, and the U.S. Postal Service. Although there's the story of the candidate who sealed his resume between two panels of glass and air-mailed it to an overseas architecture firm—and received an interview—most companies are looking for a fast, easy, and safe way to review resumes. Paste your resume into the body of the e-mail; if an employer likes it, he or she may print it out or request a revised, Word-formatted version. To be on the safe side, many candidates send two e-mails: one with the resume cut and pasted into the body of the e-mail and a second with a non-ASCII attachment.

Proper Font and Style for Scannable Resumes

When resumes are faxed or mailed to a hirer, they can be scanned and stored into a database automatically for later review using OCR software, as we discussed in Chapter 7. Sending in a resume that contains graphics, is photocopied or printed on dark paper, or uses certain fonts or characters (such as lines or bold) can result in a document that can't be scanned and will be passed over. Make sure to save your resume in a serif-free font, remove any visual interference, and align the document to the left margin.

Internet Cover Letters

Every resume needs a strong cover letter, and whether you're applying for a job online or offline, this is a rule that should never be broken. Compared with a standard cover letter, an Internet cover letter can be a bit shorter. As with all cover letters, you should target the position by researching the company you are applying to and discussing the qualifications that you possess that are directly related to the job opening. For a step-by-step overview of creating cover letters, see Chapter 16.

ASCII Resume Example

The following example shows what an ASCII resume should look like. This candidate is in the information technology (IT) field.

Jared Blake
78 Bob Builder Way
Juneau, AK 99811
(800) 737-8637
jblake@resume.com

Experienced, knowledgeable IT Professional with superior Systems
Administration and Data Center Management skills

SUMMARY OF QUALIFICATIONS
*   Eleven years of Information Technology experience, with
        specialization in system management, design, maintenance and
        support.
*   Excellent business acumen with demonstrated expertise in
        developing and administering budgets, contract negotiation,
        and vendor management.
*   Strong troubleshooting, installation and configuration
        proficiency.
*   Exceptional focus and follow-through abilities, with a track
        record of efficiency and productivity.
*   Able to succeed in fast-paced, chaotic business
        environments.
*   Committed team player with excellent interpersonal and
        communication attributes.

COMPUTER SKILLS
Servers/Hardware: Dell Servers, Laptops, Desktops, SANs, Compaq
                       Servers, EMC & Dell San Hardware, Dell Open
                       Manage, FM200, AC & Noc systems, IIS 5.0
Applications: HP OpenView, Generator, UPS, Windows 2000
                       Active Directory, Veritas Backup Exec,
                       Microsoft Office, Microsoft Exchange
Networking: TCP/IP, F5/Big IP Load Balancers, Network
                       Appliance N.A.S., Advocent & Freevision KVM
                       Switching
Languages: SQL 7.0

CERTIFICATIONS AND COURSES
MCSE NT 4.0, TCP/IP and IIS 3.0 (Windows 2000 in progress)
SQL Server 7.0/2000
Server Management and Backup Software
PC LAN/WAN Environments
Microsoft Exchange 5.0
Microsoft System Management Tools

PROFESSIONAL EXPERIENCE
Boston Computers, Juneau, AK   2002 - Present
IT Consultant
Handle variety of full and part-time consulting jobs, including
IT Manager for Cain Technology.
*   Upgraded Cain office to Windows 2000 Active Directory,
        implemented LAN and WAN configurations and directed system
        upgrades.

AAA Wiring, Juneau, AK   1994 - 2002
Data Center Operations Manager & Senior Systems Administrator
Managed staff of eight System Administrators and Server Technicians,
hired personnel and performed annual reviews.
*   Directed design and construction of four data center facilities.
*   Oversaw management of 24/7 facilities and operations (HVAC,
        FM200, UPS, Generators); planned and supervised purchase and
        implementation of equipment installation with Facilities and
        Operations.
*   Monitored and upgraded all server standards and
        configurations as required.
*   Formulated strategy regarding capacity planning for
        acquisition consolidations.
*   Designed, built, and maintained several Windows 2000/SQL
        2000 database clusters while overseeing deployment of 750
        corporate servers.
*   Upgraded entire system from NT 4.0 to Windows 2000;
        successfully installed Windows 2000 Active Directory
        structure.
*   Created data mining operation for daily updates to Website,
        following move to newer facilities.

Triple Crown Circuits, Juneau, AK   1991 - 1994
Customer Service Manager
Managed nationwide technical support call center; serve as
Technical Lead to telephone support group of 46 technicians.
*   Troubleshot complex computer hardware problems for end
        users; provided exemplary levels of customer service and
        satisfaction.
*   Designed test environments to duplicate problems and
        failures with customer hardware.
*   Promoted to Customer Service Manager to manage 24/7 customer
        service group.

EDUCATION
Electronic Institute of Science, Juneau, AK
Computer Science/Technology Technical Degree, 1990

KEYWORDS
Programmer, Senior Programmer, Engineer, Consultant, Applications
Developer, Technical Support, Help Desk Coordinator, Technical
Help Desk, Technical Computer Technician, Network Support, PC
Technician, Systems Support Engineer, Systems Analyst, Network
Administrator, Help Desk Manager

Note that the ASCII format does not produce the most aesthetically pleasing document. There is neither formatting nor styling elements in this sample. However, an ASCII-formatted resume is an important tool in your job search, and this pared-down document will pass through e-mail accounts that may not accept attachments and will be clear to hirers that use varying computer platforms. Even if you are not technically savvy, the bottom line is that the ASCII format is the best way to guarantee that hirers will read your resume. (Always bring a formatted resume to an interview.)

THE FUTURE OF THE ONLINE JOB

Many recruiters now use the Internet as the sole source for finding new hires, and the reliance of companies on this medium is growing. It is relatively easy to transform your resume from an aesthetically pleasing Word document to an ASCII resume, and in the global job market you should always have two resumes available. Most important, be prolific! Perseverance is key. The more resumes you send out, the better chance you'll have of hearing from an employer. Don't count on one resume doing the trick; remember that following these tips will allow your resume to be seen.

9

The Inside Scoop on Job Boards

The job board is one of the most popular avenues for advertising new positions, and it also has allowed job seekers (both employed and unemployed) to post their resumes for all hirers to see, democratizing the job process to some extent. The efficiency and ease job boards have brought to the hiring process have allowed employment sites such as HotJobs.com, Monster.com, and Careerbuilder.com to get a foothold in the marketplace and expand rapidly. With incredible volumes of posted resumes and with employers finding the process easier and cheaper than the standard newspaper, this option has proved to be a success for job applicants in the global economy. However, this democratization process also has resulted in a steady increase in competition, meaning that professionals now must navigate a new horizon.

NEWSPAPERS VERSUS THE JOB BOARD

Whereas $150 might have bought an employer four lines in a newspaper five years ago, that amount now allows an employer to post a help wanted ad online for a month, reaching 500,000 visitors a day as opposed to the daily circulation of a single newspaper. More companies are departing from traditional media and posting job openings with interactive media, and the employment market continues to see dramatic shifts in the ways job seekers find job openings and apply for them. This also means that their resumes must adapt to the requirements of modern hiring practices or face elimination.

In today's electronic job market hiring managers can scan thousands of resumes in seconds, employers can send out job openings to thousands of applicants instantaneously, and job seekers can target entire industries or a single position at the click of a button. As Sunday help wanted ads yield to keyword searches, 1,000 applicants can now be rejected by a computer without a human being ever seeing one of their resumes, as we discussed in Chapter 7.

Ten years ago the hiring process was radically different. Whereas job seekers mailed in or even physically handed over resumes to prospective employers, the advent of the Internet has made virtual communication the norm.

Targeting Job Boards

Job boards are listings of career openings posted by employers, recruiters, headhunters, and marketing and advertising agencies. Many job boards also provide the option of posting your resume online, where thousands of employers can view it and contact you with potential job openings that match your background. This resource has been used widely and is an invaluable tool for job seekers.

There are many different types of job boards online, and a great tip is to find out what types of job boards are available in your industry. Although the large job boards are extremely valuable resources that should be a first step for every job seeker, don't stop there. Job boards that are listed on less known sites may have less competition because they cater to smaller audiences. Some organizations tend to target boards that are highly specialized, seeking employees who do not fit the "general" mold. Whenever possible, use job boards dedicated to your industry and geographic location. There are numerous job boards that cater to both select cities and industry-specific positions. Using any search engine, type in your city, industry, and job title and see what results you receive. Many times this small effort can yield great results.

ALTERNATIVE SOURCES

Associations

Many companies use the websites of industry associations to post information on new events and job openings. These are excellent resources that can keep you abreast of trends in your particular industry, and most of those associations do not charge a fee. Use a search engine to locate the online addresses of professional associations and groups that are prominent in your field and area.

Online Newspapers

Major newspapers also have their own career channels with original content geared to helping you develop your career. Some recent hot topics include the most popular jobs and industries in today's market, taking advantage of summer jobs and internships, and how to plan and take vacations without worrying about your work. These major newspapers also include articles from today's paper as well as free original content and weekly newsletters that are sent directly to your e-mail address.

Chat Rooms, Message Boards, and Community Forums

People are flocking to career-specific chat rooms and discussion forums for multiple reasons. Smart professionals know that online forums provide an excellent opportunity to network with industry representatives around the globe. As it has become increasingly important to build contacts and get word-of-mouth referrals, online chat rooms have facilitated the process of meeting peers without leaving the computer. Web forums are also great ways to find insider news, events, and job openings that are advertised only internally. Industry-specific job boards and associations, as well as career channels featured on popular Web browsers such as MSN, AOL, and Yahoo!, associations, newspapers, and chat boards, are some of the most valuable free resources available on the Internet. Whether you are hunting for a job or are interested in furthering your career, these services can provide an inside look at the changing face of today's job market.

A Word of Caution about the Internet

The job services industry historically has attracted people who care greatly about the needs of job seekers. However, as with any industry, the Internet has spawned numerous companies that take advantage of unsuspecting customers. The major job boards are well respected and have attracted a significant audience because of their strong business practices, but be cautious of a company guaranteeing employment for a price. Use the same smarts that you would use when dealing with a company offline. Research any company that you may do business with before committing to any for-fee service on the Internet. There are a lot of great organizations dedicated to helping job applicants, but use a measure of caution for safety.

10

Resume Presentation

Manufacturers invest millions of dollars each year to create attractive wrappers and packaging that entice consumers to buy their products. They present their products with various colors, sizes, and graphics that grab a consumer's attention. The same laws of marketing and advertising apply to a resume. To ensure that your resume creates a strong impression, you should invest in high-quality paper that will demonstrate your commitment to your job search and leave a good impression with prospective employers.

PAPER TYPE AND SIZE

Walk through any office supply store and you'll be inundated with a plethora of bold colors and patterns of resume paper. However, you should always choose a conservative color for printing your resume. White, gray, and ivory shades are safe bets. Avoid bright colors such as orange or yellow and darker tones such as blue. The **weight** of your resume paper should be 20-pound stock or heavier, and make sure to buy only watermarked bond paper. These tips should be followed if you are going to a job fair where you will be meeting company representatives who will be handed hundreds of resumes. If you are mailing your resume, use the standard 8½- by 11-inch letter size.

ADDITIONAL MATERIALS

If you are applying for a creative field that calls for samples of your work, be sure to include a portfolio or bring clips of your strongest work to give during an interview or drop off with a prospective employer. Additionally, we recommend keeping electronic e-mailable versions of your work in case a prospective hirer requests this information during the application process.

DON'T USE GRAPHICS

The golden rule in professional presentations is to create an aura of professionalism. Do not include "creative" graphics on your resume unless the position you are applying for requires them.

INTERVIEW PREPAREDNESS

With the great variety of computer software and platforms to choose from these days, it is rare that your prospective employer will have the same program you used to create your resume. Bring along a few copies of your resume and a list of references to job interviews, along with any other items that may be applicable to the position (writing samples, portfolios, etc.). You should prepare for the interview by researching the prospective company, its products, and its customers. A little homework demonstrates your interest in the company and the position.

ATTITUDE

The hirer you are contacting probably is inundated with resumes. Projecting a friendly tone is a valuable suggestion that we recommend implementing in all communications you have with a hirer. All good salespeople know that half the sale is connecting with the person as an individual. The same rule holds true for the job seeker. If you contact a hirer and demand to know the status of your application, 99.9% of the time this will be the first step to being eliminated from consideration. An abrasive tone probably will foreshadow your ability to get along with coworkers, and if you alienate the person making the first decision about your application, you're facing an uphill battle.

Do not, however, misinterpret this as a call to be passive. You must be aggressive in your job search, but your tone is the unwritten rule that many career services organizations do not discuss. Be friendly and optimistic. Hiring managers are generally very busy, and a kind tone will go a long way. Although your qualifications are the first and most important areas of consideration, all other things being equal, attitude *will* be factored into your evaluation.

11

Industry-Specific Examples

You've got the cream of the crop in the resumes that follow. The editors and writers at Resume.com have compiled their most effective samples, giving you a comprehensive overview of the kinds of resumes that impress hirers. We've provided samples for the most popular industries and each one is divided into three different levels:

- The entry-level candidate (with less than three years of experience)
- The midlevel candidate (three to six years of experience)
- The experienced candidate (seven or more years of experience)

Ritu Patel

8298 Lexington Avenue • Montgomery, AL 36103 • 800-737-8637 • info@resume.com

Experienced accounting professional with degree in finance and excellent managerial skills

SUMMARY OF QUALIFICATIONS
➢ Experienced in diverse accounting functions, including payables, receivables and payroll.
➢ Trustworthy and reliable with confidential information.
➢ Superior communication and organizational skills; adept at completing tasks on time.
➢ Quick-minded, eager to learn, detail-oriented.
➢ Accurate, dependable and dedicated to doing best possible job.
➢ Proactive in recognizing problems and implementing solutions.
➢ Stable work history.

PROFESSIONAL BACKGROUND
Apple Financial, Montgomery, AL   2001 – present
Accountant for restaurant with $1.2 million annual revenue and 15 employees.
Direct and perform all financial aspects of business, such as receivables, payables, payroll, advertising, inventory and year-end accounting.
• Implemented computer system to provide cost-effective inventory management and restaurant operations.
• Systematized financial management of business for smoother operation.
• Closely monitor food and liquor pricing to maintain appropriate profit margins.
• Negotiated for and obtained capital improvement financing.
• Successfully managed transition from sole proprietorship to corporation.
• Recruit, hire, train, develop and maintain staff of 45.
• Significantly increased revenue with new advertising strategies and updated menus.

EDUCATION
Western Connecticut State University, Danbury, CT
B.B.A. in Accounting, 2001. GPA: 3.2

Relevant Coursework: Statistics, Microeconomics, Macroeconomics, Accounting Principles, Calculus, Business Management

COMPUTER SKILLS
Proficient in a variety of Windows programs; familiar with DOS.

COMMUNITY SERVICE
Regular Volunteer for Regional Hospice of Western Connecticut since 1996.

KEYWORDS
Accounting, finance, closings, budgets, forecasting, P&L, profit and loss, manage, supervise, bank, ledger, journal, account reconciliation, verification, analysis, audits, taxes, billing.

BRETT MATTHEW

754 Emerald Way • Topeka, KS 66121 • 800-737-8637 • bmatthew@resume.com

An experienced accounting professional with solid financial background and expert analytical skills

SUMMARY OF QUALIFICATIONS

Utilize knowledge of accounting functions to optimize telecommunication systems. Manage multi-million-dollar monthly budgets. Proactive and highly analytical; demonstrated use of advanced computer skills to identify problems and create effective solutions. Successful at breaking down and restructuring processes to improve results, efficiency and cost-effectiveness. Resourceful and determined in removing obstacles to achieve results. Excellent verbal and written communication skills; bilingual in English and Spanish. Master's degree in IS Management.

ACHIEVEMENTS

- **Reduced expenses by $490,000** by noticing excessive charges related to conference cancellations and unnecessary usage of call conferencing feature. Implemented new reporting process to track and quantify unnecessary usage and aid in renegotiating contracts.
- **Designed and implemented effective cost allocation and charge-back system** for teleconference and toll-free number expenses. Played key role in migration of teleconference reservation system to the Web.
- **Identified $189,000** in vendor billing errors and made refund requests.

PROFESSIONAL EXPERIENCE

Bank of Kansas, Topeka, KS

Senior Financial Analyst   5/2002 – Present
Provide budgeting and financial reporting support to Corporate Administration and business partners.
- Manage intercompany account and business services charge-back.

Oz Financial Ltd., Topeka, KS   5/1996 – 4/2002
Financial Analyst (1/2000 – 4/2002)
Managed analysis, reconciliation and monthly review of inbound and outbound expenses for $45 million budget.
- Prepared profit and loss (P&L) statements and variance analysis by location and product.
- Partnered with operations and business units in development, review and modification of $6 million telecom budget.
- Compiled month-end accrual reports. Supervised the timely submission and correction of ledger entries.
- Conducted monthly audits of DID and 800-number database.
- Hired, coached and supervised two accountants and one assistant financial analyst.
- Prepared monthly reports with cost per minute, volume and trend analysis of expenses for management review.
- Evaluated, designed and implemented new reporting requirements.
- Collaborated with internal business units in evaluation of internal business processes.
- Created ad hoc reports and special projects as requested by management.

Assistant Financial Analyst (7/1997 – 1/2000)
Accounting Reviewer (Temporary Assignment) (5/1996 – 7/1997)
Performed monthly reconciliation and charge-back of all voice telecom expenses for four locations. Assisted in reconciliation and variance analysis of departmentwide expenses and revenues.
- Developed MS Access applications that significantly reduced data entry, minimizing human errors in processing and conversion of financial data from different sources.

COMPUTER SKILLS

Advanced knowledge of MS Access, Excel, Word, PowerPoint, Outlook and Lotus Notes, Quickbooks, Smart Stream, Hyperion and Khalix. Basic knowledge of SQL and DB2.

EDUCATION

Masters of Science in Information Systems Management, Kansas State University
Key courses in Financial Management, Analysis and Development of Information Systems, Project Management, Data Management, Enterprise Systems Management and Human Side of Project Management.

Bachelor of Science in Finance and Business, New York University, New York, NY

Keywords: Accounting, CPA, A/P, A/R, payroll

MINROSE LEE

66 Glendale Avenue #9A • Chicago, IL 62706 • 800-737-8637 • mlee@resume.com

SUMMARY

Detail-oriented Accountant with over eight years of experience in international business industries. Managed accounts payable and accounts receivable, general ledger entries, and bank reconciliation; prepared trial balance with eye on improving company's bottom line. Developed monthly financial statements and reports for management and auditing teams. Exceptional communication and organizational skills with ability to work both independently and as team member. Advanced educational and training background includes CPA designation and BA in Accounting. Willing to travel and relocate.

PROFESSIONAL BACKGROUND

ABC Financial, Springfield, IL   1998 – 2003
Accountant
Handled all banking and billing for offshore Canadian oil drilling company. Prepared tax submissions for Price Waterhouse to process.

- Played major role in implementing new software package that decreased company expenditures and manpower.
- Conducted field audits and processed all invoices and vendor queries.
- Performed journal entries and account reconciliation for monthly closings.
- Performed daily, weekly and monthly bank reconciliation.
- Covered three positions, saving company significant expenses in overhead.
- Successfully cleared up major backlog in accounts payable upon first joining company.
- Ensured all payments were timely, thereby eliminating late payment penalties.
- Established and maintained excellent working relationships with supervisors at company headquarters.

Buckley and Sons, Chicago, IL   1997 – 1998
Accountant
Accurately maintained records of receivables due from foreign clients.

- Settled accounts. Handled customer inquiries.

Rex Bank, Chicago, IL   1996 – 1997
Staff Accountant
Reconciled and organized inventory management records using proprietary system.

Bay Corporation, Schaumburg, IL   1994 – 1996
Staff Accountant
Administered payables, receivables, bank accounts, petty cash. Prepared spreadsheets using LOTUS and financial statements and balance sheets on ACCPAC.

- Played major role in helping maintain five-company conglomerate that was facing serious cash-flow problems.

EDUCATION and TRAINING

CPA, National Institute of Certified Accountants
Bachelor of Arts in Accounting, University of Chicago, Chicago, IL

COMPUTER SKILLS

Microsoft Excel, Word, Access, Lotus 1-2-3, Quick Books, Financial Stream Payables

Keywords: CPA, Accountant, Accounts Manager, Accounting Supervisor

HOWARD BLAKE

57 Jefferson Street ♦ Bismark, ND 58505 ♦ (800) 737-8637 ♦ hblake@resume.com

A highly motivated self-starter with advanced secretarial skills and over two years of professional experience in diverse environments

SUMMARY OF QUALIFICATIONS

❑ Three years of experience in clerical field supporting executive staff.
❑ Effective problem solver, able to multitask and handle multiple positions in fast-paced positions.
❑ Team player, able to build strong rapport with diverse range of coworkers, management, and clients.
❑ Exceptional verbal and written communication skills. Consistently create flawless documents.
❑ Fast learner, adept at quickly learning new procedures and implementing best practices in numerous departments.
❑ Awarded "Employee of the Month," January 2002.
❑ Computer and Internet savvy.
❑ Type 60 wpm.

PROFESSIONAL EXPERIENCE

OFFICE SUPPLY EQUIPMENT, INC., BISMARK, ND   10/01 – 12/03
Secretary
Managed phone lines and attracted new customers by being helpful and personable.
- Created company motto, "Where every customer is our favorite customer."
- Performed bookkeeping services, including accounts payable and expense reports, as well as maintaining petty cash.
- Named Employee of the Month, January 2002.

PFE, LTD., BISMARK, ND   06/00 – 09/01
Payroll Clerk
Organized administrative process and reduced errors by accurately entering data in computer system.
- Assisted on-site employees in completing I-9 and W-4 forms.
- Compiled weekly payroll and generated paychecks.

COMPUTER SKILLS

Microsoft Windows 95/98, Internet-savvy

EDUCATION

United States Academic Preparatory Academy, **3.75 GPA**

Keywords: administrative assistant, banking, teller, office skills, data entry, typing, filing

Sara Dulay

7608 West Falls ▪ Jefferson City, MO 65102 ▪ Telephone: 800-737-8637 ▪ E-mail: sdulay@resume.com

Highly responsible administrative assistant with eight years of legal experience

PROFESSIONAL HIGHLIGHTS

➢ Over eight years of administrative, legal, and executive-level experience.
➢ Excel in problem solving, project management, decision making, and office supervision.
➢ Strong communication skills, both written and verbal.
➢ Competent in bookkeeping and accounting.
➢ Ability to handle simultaneous projects and meet deadlines effectively.
➢ Efficiently schedule business travel and coordinate meetings and events.

EXPERIENCE

Rarebaum Associates, Jefferson City, MO   06/02 – Present
Secretary
♦ Secretary for Group Commander with 11 executives located throughout Germany.
♦ Currently working on joint effort with corporate headquarters to consolidate expenditures.
♦ Direct administrative responsibilities for all executives, including travel, finance, and housing.
♦ Answer correspondence and reroute incoming calls to appropriate management.

Waller, Smith, and Lee, St. Louis, MO   11/01 – 5/02
Secretary - Commercial Litigation Division
Responsible for administrative, secretarial, and automation services for six attorneys.
♦ Handled incoming calls and greeted visitors in professional, friendly manner.
♦ Distributed mail, reviewed correspondence, and composed administrative documents and reports.
♦ Arranged conferences and meetings for attorneys, clients, and opposing counsel.
♦ Scheduled travel, hotel accommodations, itinerary, requests for orders, and travel reimbursement.
♦ Maintained office files and suspense control.

American Red Cross, St. Louis, MO   05/98 – 10/01
Office Manager
Responsible for reconciling monthly ledgers and reviewing all computer-generated reports.
♦ Supervised office volunteers.
♦ Handled bookkeeping for field office, monitored annual budget, and prepared monthly budget reports.
♦ Maintained cashbook records, accounts payable, and accounts receivable.
♦ Coordinated with headquarters to ensure data was maintained in accordance with regulations.
♦ Worked as liaison with military, ensuring prompt notification of all Red Cross messages.

Mart Fashions, St. Louis, MO   04/96 – 04/98
Administrative Assistant
Responsible for recruitment and staffing for administrative positions.
♦ Maintained personnel records, conducted orientation and training for new employees, handled leave of absence and attendance records, and reviewed personnel records for departing employees.
♦ Delegated all overflow work to clerical and support staff.

COMPUTER SKILLS
PC, Mac, Windows 95/98/2000, PowerPoint, Access, Excel

KEYWORDS
Administrative assistant, human resources, manager, supervisor, computer skills, communication skills, accounting skills

SEAN CARNEY

55 North Boulevard • Raleigh, NC 27603 • (800) 737-8637 • scarney@resume.com

Talented Executive Assistant with exemplary track record and strong management,
administration, and customer service skills

Summary of Qualifications

- ❑ Proven success planning and directing executive-level administrative affairs and providing support to Corporate Officers, including Vice President and Director.
- ❑ Organized, efficient and precise, with exceptional communication skills. Adept at building strong business relationships with diverse range of customers, coworkers, and management.
- ❑ Demonstrated expertise in diverse areas, including data entry, telephone support, scheduling, human resources, bookkeeping, reporting, and customer service.
- ❑ Able to coordinate and complete multiple projects in deadline-oriented environment.
- ❑ Adapt quickly to challenges and changing environments.
- ❑ Technically proficient in MS Office, MS Windows, E-mail and Internet.

Professional Experience

MATTRESS EXPRESS, Raleigh, NC   2000 – Present

Executive Assistant (2001 – Present) promoted within 11 months of hire to provide executive-level support to director and vice president of Mergers and Acquisitions Group. Interface extensively with corporate clientele.

- ❑ Manage confidential correspondence, appointments, and meetings for group.
- ❑ Arrange and coordinate travel itineraries, including airfare, accommodations, and dining.
- ❑ Plan, schedule, and administer office operations, overseeing data entry, telephone support, mail distribution, scheduling, filing, and reporting.
- ❑ Monitor and secure approval of all expenses.
- ❑ Assist Vice President with recruiting and hiring sales associates and analysts for group.

Office Coordinator (2000 – 2001) responsible for assisting with administration of day-to-day office operations for Technology Corporation Group. Provided administrative support to office manager, assistant business manager, and administrative coordinator.

- ❑ Supervised and coordinated all special events, including catering, invitations, and guest list.
- ❑ Maintained and updated all vendor accounts and files.
- ❑ Supported assistant business manager in analyzing financial investments and producing reports.
- ❑ Administered all office functions, such as data entry, telephone support, filing, and scheduling.

JAVA EXPRESS, Raleigh, NC   1990 – 2000

Office Manager accountable for managing operations for $7 million coffee import/export company. Responsible for client contact, arranging inventory shipment, accounts payable and receivable, billing, employee supervision, correspondence, customer service, sales, and marketing. Directed all operations in lieu of proprietor. Reported directly to owner.

- ❑ Collaborated with sales and marketing teams in designing strategic business development strategies. Instrumental in increasing revenue from $4 million to $7 million within one year.
- ❑ Planned and executed customer service initiatives, resulting in increased customer satisfaction.
- ❑ Analyzed and automated bookkeeping functions, enhancing both efficiency and quality.
- ❑ Represented company at SCAA conventions and seminars.

Education

University of San Francisco, San Francisco, CA
Bachelor of Business Administration Degree, 1989. Concentration in Management.

Computer Skills

MS Word, Excel, Outlook

KEYWORDS: executive assistant, executive support, executive office support

Lucia DiVenti

7619 Grand Oak Blvd. • Salt Lake City, UT 84114 • (800) 737-8637 • ldiventi@resume.com

Enthusiastic business management trainee with diverse skills in finance,
administration, and customer service

SUMMARY OF QUALIFICATIONS

- Decisive, personable, goal-driven management style, able to build and nurture productive teams.
- Self-motivated, creative problem solver with strong oral and written communication skills.
- Solid educational background includes Bachelor's Degree in Business Management with extensive coursework in finance, marketing, and human resources administration.
- Honest, hardworking and responsible; dedicated to meeting both short- and long-term goals.
- Strong customer-service orientation; apply exceptional customer service skills to develop rapport with potential and existing clientele.
- Fast learner, capable of hitting the ground running.
- Willing to travel and relocate.

EDUCATION

BRIGHAM YOUNG UNIVERSITY, Salt Lake City, UT
BS in Business Management, *May 2002*

Key coursework in Finance, Business Administration, Marketing, Management, Information Decision Systems, Business Law and Human Resource Management.

WORK HISTORY

Fine Prints, Corp., Salt Lake City, UT   June 2001 – Present
Assistant Business Manager responsible for reevaluating and developing contracts with suppliers, informing clients of new product lines, and providing office support.
- Skilled in handling sales accounts, closing sales, informing clients of product line and reviving dormant accounts.
- Quickly mastered position's responsibilities and sought additional opportunities within and outside of salaried hours.
- Perform human resource generalist tasks and act as liaison between upper management and personnel.
- Implemented computer networking and two-way radio communication between satellite offices, resulting in savings to company and increased productivity.
- Meet with accounting department to expedite billing and inventory tracking.
- Raised 1999 after-market sales.
- Successfully completed Strategic Sales Training course for top product line.
- Conducted job task analysis for each of the company's 15 job classifications; then designed new position classification system that defined employee responsibilities, requirements, and core competencies.
- Built productive teams through motivation, training, and accountability measures.

COMPUTER SKILLS

Proficient in PC-compatible platforms, Microsoft Word, Works, ACT, WordPerfect, Lotus Notes, Excel, PowerPoint, HTML, Norton Utilities.

FRED EAGLE

89 Summit Drive #4R • Cheyenne, WY 82002 • (800) 737-8637 • feagle@resume.com

*A Columbia Business School graduate with excellent quantitative and computer skills
including financial analysis and modeling as well as equities trading experience*

SUMMARY OF QUALIFICATIONS

- ❑ Thorough understanding of risk management and financial analysis.
- ❑ Strong mathematical knowledge and aptitude. Competence in numerical analysis.
- ❑ Wide range of computer skills. Experienced programmer-analyst. Designed own computer.
- ❑ Creative problem solver. Adept at improvising in problem-solving process.
- ❑ Articulate communicator with exceptional presentation and negotiation abilities.
- ❑ Able to relocate and travel as needed.

EDUCATION

Columbia Business School, New York, NY
MBA in Finance, 1995
   Key course: Analytical Modeling for Financial Markets and Operations Research
   Additional courses: Computational Models in Analytical Finance, Corporate Finance, Financial Statement Analysis, Securities Analysis, Investment Management, Options Markets.
   Project: Built computer program to price options and calculate options.
   Activities: Small Business Consultant Group, American Finance Association, Derivatives Club, Investment Management Club.

MMS International, New York, NY
Internship, June 1993 – May 1994 at division of S & P that provides online market commentary.
   Built mathematical computer models:
   (1) To forecast general direction of stock market based on economic indicators.
   (2) Option pricing model based on modified Black-Scholes formula and five inputs used by options traders to help structure option strategies.
   (3) To calculate implied volatility based on historical stock price data using numerical techniques.
   Conducted research project:
   Statistical study between stock market and presidential election campaigns.

Northwestern University, Evanston, IL
BS in Electrical Engineering, 1989, specializing in computer architecture and design
   Activities: Volunteer tutor in electromagnetics, control systems theory, calculus, signal processing theory; president, Amateur Radio Society; founding member, Filipino Students Association; Debating Team; Sailing Team.

PROFESSIONAL ACHIEVEMENTS

- Four years of experience in equities trading, managing over $300,000 in client funds.
- Performed financial analysis of numerous companies yielding average annual return of 42% over past three years.
- Two years of experience working on information systems for major financial services companies; designed, built, tested and integrated module to process costs and revenues for prestigious private banking clients.

EMPLOYMENT HISTORY

Equities Trader, Financial Limited, New York, NY, 1995 – 2002
Information Systems Analyst, Trader.com, New York, NY, 1994
Systems Professional, On Your Mark, LLC, Chicago, IL, 1988 – 1989

COMPUTER SKILLS

Windows 95, 98; Macintosh, C, BASIC, COBOL, Assembly, Pascal, MS Excel, MS Word, Mathematica, Macsyma

KEYWORDS

Business Analyst, investment portfolios, financial analyst, business development, trading, finance analyst, portfolio management, banking

Anita Larssen

51 State Road, Apt. 7C • Providence, RI 02903 • (800) 737-8637 • alarssen@resume.com

SUMMARY

Senior-level manager with proven track record of turning around struggling business units. Well-rounded skills in development and execution of business plans, financial analysis and integrated sales and marketing management. International experience. Certified Public Accountant with an MBA in Finance.

PROFESSIONAL BACKGROUND

Fine Fiction, Inc., Providence, RI   1994 – present
A publishing firm with $180 million in annual revenue.

Vice President (2000 – present)
Assigned to turn around underperforming unit of four B-to-B trade publications and several conferences and exhibitions.

- Implemented new sales approach, leveraging strength of core brands to create new products.
- Reorganized staff to maximize skills and develop mature workforce.
- Launched magazine supplement to boost circulation.
- Spearheaded conference and exhibition to promote brand recognition.
- Hired new financial team to control costs and monitor competitiveness of unit's revenue growth.

Vice President, Business Development (1998 – 2000)
Assigned dedicated Marketing Consultants to key customers.

- Consolidated two business units and grew synergy. Doubled revenue in two years.
- Successfully revamped and repackaged key products. Created extensions of several brands and developed and launched new products. Brought costs under control.
- Originated idea of packaging advertisers' needs across multiple media in a single vertical industry, establishing company as leader in field.

Associate Vice President (1995 – 1998)
Hired dynamic new sales force and marketing team. Put effective cost controls in place.

- Took business unit of five publications from a $200,000 loss to $700,000 profit in one year.
- Implemented package selling across magazine lines.
- Cross-marketed the unit's publications with conference and exhibition businesses from another unit to leverage customers into more products.
- Relaunched failing magazine. Recognized need for, hired and set up dedicated UK-based staff. Magazine is now #1 in market share, with revenues that have more than tripled.

Senior Manager (1994 – 1995)
Assigned to protect company investment in disastrously unprofitable trade show. Established advisory board.

- Developed separate marketing campaigns for exhibitors, sponsors and attendees.
- Contracted with industry experts to develop top-quality content for changing market.
- Created over $500,000 profit in show's first year. Hired new sales, marketing and conference staffs.

EDUCATION

MBA in Finance from New York University, New York, NY
BBA in Accounting from Manhattan University, New York, NY
Intramural Chairman of Sigma Alpha Epsilon Fraternity

COMPUTER SKILLS

Proficient in Microsoft business applications including Excel, Word, PowerPoint, Access and Outlook.

KEYWORDS: executive, business development, business manager, operations, sales, marketing, senior executive, strategic planning, division head, budgeting, profit and loss, analysis

PETE TROUPOLIS

33 Old Riverhead Way • Salem, OR 97310 • (800) 737-8637 • ptroupolis@resume.com

An experienced building superintendent with solid experience in multifamily complexes

SUMMARY OF QUALIFICATIONS

- ❑ Three years of successful experience as superintendent of a four-building complex.
- ❑ Exceptionally broad range of handyman skills.
- ❑ Quick learner who rapidly becomes familiar with new types of hardware and equipment.
- ❑ Strong sense of public relations on behalf of building management.
- ❑ Friendly, outgoing personality.
- ❑ Take pride in quality of work. Strong sense of professionalism.
- ❑ Effective problem solver. Go out of my way to meet tenants' needs.
- ❑ Excellent work history as regards work ethic, dependability and willingness to go the extra mile.

PROFESSIONAL EXPERIENCE

ABC Furniture, Portland, OR   *10/00 – 12/03*

Finish Carpenter for apartment renovation project.

Cut, coped and successfully installed crown moldings on difficult, slanted walls.

- Accurately and carefully hung doors. Worked quickly and yet more effectively than team of two others.
- Put in extra time to complete job on schedule and within budget.
- Noted for keeping work areas clean and well organized.

RS Management Co., Salem, OR   *01/01 – 10/00*

Superintendent of two-building, 84-apartment complex.

Effectively managed all general maintenance, including cabinet installation, roof repairs, plumbing, plastering, electrical work, ceramics and floor tiling, electric garage doors, and operation and maintenance of Ray 200-hp oil boiler.

- Noted for prompt, neat and careful work.
- Demonstrated excellent customer service orientation toward tenants to uphold company's image.
- Suggested changes to save money, such as more efficient boiler motor.

EDUCATION

Georgetown College, Portland, OR
Associates Degree, 2000

SPECIAL SKILLS

Cabinet installation, microzinc roof installation, read blueprints

KEYWORDS

Supervisor, Grounds Keeper, Building Manager

ADRIENNE GONZALES

8 Blackberry Road, Apt. 2A • Austin, TX 78711 • (800) 737-8637 • agonzales@resume.com

Talented Journeyman and Maintenance Mechanic with expertise in millwright work

Summary of Qualifications

- ❑ Seven years of experience in manufacturing, including machining work and maintaining manufacturing equipment.
- ❑ Especially skilled at manual machining-mill and lathe work and welding fabrication.
- ❑ Solid reputation for quick, innovative troubleshooting and repair as well as high-quality machining work.
- ❑ Intense pride in workmanship. Consider work reflection of self.
- ❑ Outgoing, friendly person with good sense of humor.
- ❑ Intense interest in and enthusiasm for CNC operations/programming.

Professional Background

Glendale Production, Inc., Austin, TX   *1996 – Present*

Maintenance Mechanic/Millwright for manufacturing firm employing 180 production staff.
Maintain all mechanical equipment, performing troubleshooting, diagnosis and repair, as well as major preventive maintenance. Rebuild critical equipment, noting what is wearing out and installing parts.

- Rebuilt No. 2 laminator, which was highly praised by machine crews and management.
- Voluntarily performed in-house manual machining, resulting in 75% more machining done on site, saving company time and money.
- Machined wedge-style adjuster for shaft alignment, resulting in company-requested alignments for other equipment.
- Fabricated numerous parts for specific applications, such as shaft loading.
- Improved existing designs for clearance problems on the robotic palletizers and conveyor system.
- Unplugged and repiped starch delivery system when clogged.
- Designed a faster, easier method of shimming and gapping coating rolls, as well as safer and easier-to-remove guarding for numerous machines.

Education

Ongoing courses in machine fabrication and welding fabrication/layout,
Austin Technical Institute, Austin, TX

Journeyman Millwright Degree (GPA 4.0)
Houston Technical College, Houston, TX

Computer Skills

Microsoft Windows 95/98/2000, MS Word, Excel, Internet, e-mail

References

Available on request.

Keywords

Problem identification, technology design, installation, testing, operation monitoring, operation and control, product inspection, equipment maintenance, repairing, brazing

MARTIN BHATT

80 East Wilshire Blvd. • Hartford, CT 06106 • (800) 737-8637 • mbhatt@resume.com

PROFILE

Over 10 years of experience in construction industry. Developed skills through hands-on fieldwork experience. Keen business savvy developed as a result of 12 years of business entrepreneurship inclusive of all aspects of day-to-day operations, staffing, equipment and material maintenance, and front and back office operations. Superior project management abilities. Strongest suit is building relationships with all parties involved in job process from inception to completion. Commitment to excellence is exemplified in client servicing expertise resulting in only the highest levels of customer satisfaction.

EXPERIENCE

General Manager
Gebhart Construction, Hartford, CT, 1990 – 2000
Premier Paving, Stamford, CT, 1978 – 1990

Noted for:
- Training and expertise in construction bidding, project management, outside operations, paving operations, and paving sales.
- Built Gebhart Construction from a five-employee company to present day volume of 300 employees.
- Presently ranked as the fifth largest general construction company in greater Connecticut.
- Effectively handle singular jobs from $1 million to over $25 million.
- Consistently meet deadlines.
- Build strong and long lasting relationships with clients, vendors and subcontractors.
- Involved in community as member of Advisory Committee for Salvation Army of Connecticut and youth sports programs.

Construction Projects:
- Heavy Highway Construction
- Bridge Construction and Maintenance
- Utility Installation
- Vertical Building Construction
- Paving: Airports, Highways, Parking Lots

Clients include:
- Federal Government
- State Governments
- Municipalities
- Private Sector Industries

EDUCATION
Bachelor of Science in Civil Engineering
University of Connecticut, Storrs, CT

COMPUTER SKILLS
Microsoft Office, AutoCAD

KEYWORDS
Construction Supervisor, District Manager, GM, Contractor

Janet VanDyck

19 Derby Court • Baton Rouge, LA 70804 • (800) 737-8637 • jvandyck@resume.com

Hardworking, enthusiastic, tenacious professional with exceptional interpersonal skills

SUMMARY OF QUALIFICATIONS

➢ Contagious charisma paired with ability to work well with varying personality types.
➢ Determined, motivated professional; strive for success with each task and challenge.
➢ Team player; quickly and easily establish professional rapport with coworkers.
➢ Superior communication, interpersonal, and presentation skills. Type 80 WPM.
➢ Problem solver who acquires new skills quickly and demonstrates can-do attitude when taking on new responsibilities.
➢ Willing to travel and/or relocate.

EDUCATION

Oklahoma State University   2000
Bachelor of Science in Business Administration
Major in Marketing, Minor in Management Information Systems
GPA 3.35/4.0

Honors and Activities:
President's and Dean's Honor Rolls
Golden Key National Honor Society
Member and Steward, Sigma Alpha Epsilon Fraternity

PROFESSIONAL EXPERIENCE

Medford Marketing Services, Baton Rouge, LA   2000 – Present
Customer Service Trainee
Use effective communication and interpersonal-relations skills to interact with employees and customers.
➢ Participate in customer and prospect project bidding process, including preparation and review of submittals.
➢ Develop professional rapport through face-to-face interaction with more than 100 clients on daily basis.
➢ Attend forecasting and management meetings.
➢ Continually resolve issues with clients whose requests can not be immediately handled by company.
➢ Use listening abilities to help clients identify and gauge needs.

COMPUTER SKILLS

Microsoft Office Suite 2000, DOS/Windows, Windows NT and Macintosh/COBOL, HTML and Java

KEYWORDS

Management Information Systems; marketing; management; sales; customer service; market researcher

References furnished upon request

Clifford Seymour Smith

6 Omaha Drive • Frankfurt, KY 40601 • (800) 737-8637 • csmith@resume.com

A responsible customer service manager with first-rate computer skills, organizational ability and bookkeeping know-how

SUMMARY OF QUALIFICATIONS:

- ❑ Five years of experience in customer service management within diverse industries.
- ❑ Capable and experienced in managing customer relations, order entry, and problem resolution.
- ❑ Able to oversee human resources and customer relations functions for multiple-departments company.
- ❑ Strong writing and proofreading abilities. Compose effective correspondence.
- ❑ Exceptional communication, interpersonal, and presentation abilities.
- ❑ Work effectively under pressure and demonstrate flexibility to meet deadlines.

PROFESSIONAL EXPERIENCE AND ACHIEVEMENTS:

Customer Service

- Liaison with clients, inspectors and others to maintain and promote business relationships.
- Handled general office management, including mail, daily record keeping, and scheduling of customer and executive appointments.
- Generated client contract agreements for general construction vendors.
- Implemented spreadsheet applications to track items with unique record-keeping requirements.
- Successfully resolved problems with New York State agency.
- Supervised human resources functions for construction and building maintenance firms.

Marketing Assistance

- Research all necessary paperwork and created effective brochures, flyers, and other promotional material using desktop publishing software.
- Prepared proposal presentations on services and products offered to clients.
- Submitted successful bids for construction projects in both private and public sectors.

WORK HISTORY:

Customer Service Manager, Capitol Products, Frankfurt, KY, 1999 – 2003
Customer Service Manager, Henry and Sons Distribution, Elizabeth, KY, 1998 – 1999
Customer Service Manager, Flowers Express, Frankfurt, KY, 1997 – 1998

EDUCATION:

University of Illinois, Chicago, IL
Certificate in Business Administration

COMPUTER SKILLS:

Microsoft Office Suite (Word, Excel, PowerPoint, Access)

KEYWORDS:

Customer Service Manager, Office Manager, Department Manager, Senior Manager

BEN GREENE

9282 Silver Mine • Carson City, NV 89710 • (800) 737-8637 • bgreene@resume.com

Experienced Customer Service Professional with superior management
and interpersonal skills

SUMMARY OF QUALIFICATIONS

- Over seven years of customer service experience within telecommunications industry.
- Diverse professional development, including customer relations, office management procedures and personnel issues.
- Gifted communicator with proven ability to form strong relationships with, and gain trust of, colleagues and clients at all levels.
- Superior troubleshooting, problem solving and conflict resolution skills, with exceptional focus and follow-through abilities.
- Popular, tactful team player who thrives within group environment.

PROFESSIONAL EXPERIENCE

SILVER SMITH COMPANY, Las Vegas, NV   09/96 – Present
CUSTOMER RELATIONS SUPERVISOR for major telecommunications corporation with over 30,000 employees.
Responsible for management of personnel, processes and operations in busy customer service call center.

- Maintain highest standards of customer service, with emphasis on customer satisfaction levels and prompt resolution of customer problems or concerns.
- Direct and implement training programs for new and existing staff to ensure proper adherence to company procedures and policies.
- Increase efficiency by monitoring staff service levels, operational expenses and productivity.
- Assisted in creation of customer support team to improve levels of customer service.
- Awarded **Team Performer Award** for quality of contribution and achievement in customer service.

GRAND MOTEL INC., Las Vegas, NV   06/94 – 08/96
ASSISTANT HUMAN RESOURCES MANAGER
Responsible for accurate and proper handling of medical specimens for special accounts.

- Provided comprehensive training for new personnel.
- Improved efficiency by improving and refining existing procedures.

PAPER PRODUCTS INTERNATIONAL, Carson City, NV   09/86 – 05/94
HUMAN RESOURCES PROFESSIONAL

- Supervised three staff members with billings and collections for over 1,500 accounts.
- Managed all aspects of office operations, including accounts, billing, training and payroll.
- Directed implementation and administration for entire employee benefits system.
- Responsible for customer service, including setting up customer accounts, answering customer questions, problem solving and resolving account billing inquiries.

COMPUTER SKILLS

PC, Microsoft Word, Excel, PowerPoint

CERTIFICATIONS

Certificate in Basic Supervision, Silver Smith Products, 2001

KEYWORDS

Customer Relations Manager, Operations Manager, Customer Service Manager

LIZA SALEMMI

50 Mountain Crest Vista ▪ Helena, MT 59620 ▪ (800) 737-8637 ▪ lsalemmi@resume.com

Driven and self-motivated Computer Engineering graduate with two years of UNIX Administration experience seeks entry-level opportunity as network engineer/programmer/administrator

SUMMARY OF QUALIFICATIONS
- ◆ Strong educational background in computer engineering.
- ◆ Excellent computer skills. Working knowledge of UNIX operating system.
- ◆ Ambitious and hardworking, committed to excellence.
- ◆ Enthusiastic self-starter who enjoys working in team environments.

EDUCATION
UNIVERSITY OF CALIFORNIA, Irvine, CA   Graduated: 2003
Bachelor of Science in Computer Engineering
Dean's Honor List: Spring 1998 and Winter 2001
G.P.A.: 3.16/4.0

Key Courses	Computer Networks, System Programming, System Software, File and Database Management, Signals and Systems, Electronics, Microprocessor Interface Techniques
Involvement	Self-funded 30% of education

COMPUTER SKILLS
Software:	Microsoft Word, Microsoft Excel, Microsoft PowerPoint, Visual Studio (C++), Symantec Visual Café (Java)
Operating Systems:	Linux (Red Hat), UNIX (Solaris/Sun operating system), Windows 9x and ME, Windows NT and 2000
Languages:	C, C++, Perl, Java, OpenGL, SQL, VHDL, 80x86 and MIPS Assembly

EXPERIENCE
Teaching Assistant   04/01 – 06/01
Helena Middle School, Helena, MT
Responsible for proctoring exams and proofreading assignments prior to distribution to students.
- Provided educational support to undergraduate computer engineering students.
- Trusted to sublecture classes when professor was unavailable.

Consultant/UNIX System Administrator   09/99 – 03/01
Data Solutions, Helena, MT
Assisted with development of database, organizing end-user support procedures via e-mail.
- Completed documentation UNIX "procmail," eliminating unwanted e-mail for users.
- Promoted to UNIX Systems Administrator.
- Created Perl program, monitoring campus computer system performance.
  - ➢ Program assists system administrators with overload issues to date.
  - ➢ Attended staff meetings offering suggestions regarding computer and software purchases.

Research Intern   06/99 – 08/99
Red Roof Software Products, Stanford, CA
Responsible for hands-on nanofabrication research involving chemistry, electronics, materials science, optics, and physics.
- Designed microchips for bioanalytical device applications, including DNA sampling and analysis.
- Successfully interpreted collected data.
- Presented findings to National Nanofabrication Users Network.

Keywords: network analyst, network administrator, network engineer, computer engineer, network

Keesha Jones

627 Cocapelli Drive ▪ Santa Fe, NM 87503 ▪ (800) 737-8637 ▪ kjones@resume.com

Seasoned Construction Manager with expertise in civil, structural, mechanical and electrical segments

Profile of Qualifications

➢ Extensive experience in commercial, residential, industrial and institutional construction management.

➢ Supervise various high-end project budgets in excess of $50 million.

➢ Proven track record of meeting aggressive deadlines ahead of schedule and under budget. Skillful at fostering relationships with clients, vendors, designers and other industry professionals.

➢ Effective communicator and presenter of comprehensive documents, reports and presentations.

➢ Looking to relocate to Midwest or Southeastern states.

Professional Experience

Santa Fe Construction, Santa Fe, NM   1998 – Present
Project Manager
Oversee construction of exclusive residential gated community, consisting of 10 to 15 homes ranging in cost from $1 million to $3 million.

• Successfully completed comprehensive $30 million renovation of British historic hotel.

• Converted 100,000 square feet of hotel rooms in Modern English Center of Commerce into corporate suites and retail space with $6 million budget.

• Managed $15 million mechanical, cosmetic, and life safety systems upgrades to American-British Hotel in Nassua, Bahamas.

Holt Construction, Santa Fe, NM   1997 – 1998
Construction Manager
Supervised contracts, cost estimates, schedules and inspections for hotel and residential development firm.

• Successfully completed development and construction of residential subdivision of 150 single-family homes in nine months within strict budget.

• Worked exceptionally well with existing clients while researching prospective accounts.

Greenwood Engineering, Santa Fe, NM   1995 – 1997
Senior Project Engineer
Responsible for civil and structural division operations for top 100-ranked development contractor.

• Drafted and built 16,000-square-foot home for company president, winning favorable media and local recognition.

• Managed water and waste management facilities, underground utilities and general site development.

• Expanded and supervised various business ventures, includng Building Creation Corporation.

• Vital contributor to integral decisions involving mechanical, electrical, and fire protection.

Education and Certifications

University of Chicago, Chicago, IL: Construction Management & Architectural Design and Drafting courses
B.O.C.A. Certification in Code Administration for Mechanical and Structural Inspection, U. of Chicago
B.O.C.A. Certification in Structural Plumbing, Electrical, HVAC Inspection Code, U. of Chicago
EPA Certification

Memberships

City of Santa Fe Housing Commission
Santa Fe County Re-Development Commission

Keywords: public sector, private sector, asbestos detection, environmental, safety, administration, commercial, institutional, industrial

Yu-Ting Chang

7 Westwood Circle • Jackson, MS 39205 • (800) 737-8637 • ytchang@resume.com

Summary

Talented printed board circuit design specialist with 20 years of experience empowering engineers to build effective solutions. Extensive history in computer-aided engineering and program design, with demonstrated expertise in printed circuit board design, production, and testing. Fluent knowledge of complex circuitry board applications and processes. Skilled tool administrator; adept at improving development efficiency through modernization and education. Effective team leader, able to train and mentor professionals in tools, processes, and procedures. Experienced information technology specialist overseeing databases, libraries, software, and hardware for multiple engineering teams.

Engineering Skills

CAD/CAE Programs:	Cadence (PCB Design), Innoveda, Allegro, Remedy
Platforms:	UNIX, SUN operating systems, SUN Solaris 2.8, Windows 95/98/2000/NT 4.0
Languages:	UNIX Shell Script, HTML, JavaScript, SQL
Software:	Agile, Interleaf, Vantive, Microsoft Office (Word/Excel/PowerPoint), Adobe FrameMaker and Acrobat

Certifications

Reproductive Arts A+ Certification
Network Certification
Agile Administration
SUN 2.x System Administration I and II
SUN Microsystems Shell Programming
Remedy Administration/User
SUN System Administration, OS 4.1.3

Professional Experience

Filigree Construction and Engineering, Jackson, MS   2000 – 2002
CAE/CAD Librarian
Provided support to several printed circuit board engineering centers, requiring expert knowledge of Innoveda and Allegro computer-aided design tools.

- Increased quality, insured integrity, and improved efficiency by modernizing and standardizing existing libraries.
- Administered all computer-aided design and computer-aided engineering programs, databases, processes, and procedures for entire company.
- Created and published Library Process Manual utilizing ISO certification knowledge.

DEF Company, Jackson, MS   1998 – 2000
Software Support Engineer
Fully maintained all Cadence and Fujitsu tools for integrated circuit designers and developers throughout company.

- Generated quality assurance program for all computer-aided design software and hardware using standardization, modernization, and education.
- Proved proficiency in Remedy systems by increasing efficiency of departmental trouble-ticket operations.
- Researched, selected, and implemented next generation of engineering design applications.
- Created course materials, conducted training, and provided postimplementation support on new tools and procedures.
- Managed all tool manufacturer relations, licenses, and purchasing.

Cadmon Company, Jackson, MS   1995 – 1998
CAE/CAD Tool Support
Lead administrator for databases and documentation control program. Evaluated next-generation computer-automated design tools, from interface and scripting to support.
* Generated and maintained library symbols for computer-aided design tools for electrical engineering department.
* Increased quality assurance by analyzing, creating, and implementing standards, processes, and procedures for tools.

Interstar Company, Tidewater, MS   1994 – 1995
EDA Analyst
Reviewed and improved software development cycle processes and procedures.
* Increased companywide efficiency by creating global output file, empowering multiple engineering departments to use same design.
* Unified library design standards, increasing effectiveness and alleviating confusion in design centers.
* Generated computer-aided design symbol processes local and remote library design teams, employing expert knowledge of Cadence tools.

ABC Company, Chicago, IL   1985 – 1994
MIS Programmer/Analyst
Administered logical and physical CAE/CAD symbols tool set for entire engineering staff using Cadence Tools.
* Directed customer contact and resolved escalating technical issues for 450 customers over three years.
* UNIX administrator for two years, utilizing communication and troubleshooting skills.
* Database administrator for engineering staff providing configurations, resolutions, and general upkeep.
* Designed, tested, and supported all in-house and third-party software written on UNIX and Windows NT 4.0.
* Conducted in-house training on emerging tools and procedures.

Education
University of Illinois-Chicago, Chicago, IL
Bachelor of Science Degree in Computer Design. GPA 4.0

Keywords: PCB, Printed circuit board designer, CAD, CAE, Computer-aided designer, engineer, computer-aided engineer, drafting, integrated circuit designer, EDA, engineering development administrator

KRISTIN K. RUEK

668 Blueberry Hill • St. Paul, MN 55155 • (800) 737-8637 • kruck@resume.com

A well trained, skilled Event Planning Coordinator with excellent academic credentials

SUMMARY OF QUALIFICATIONS

- ❑ Completed registered training and certification program for **Professional Wedding Consultant** credentials.
- ❑ Able to manage both day-to-day and long-term operations for private and corporate events.
- ❑ Strong organizational skills. Highly detail-oriented.
- ❑ A good listener. Communicate well with diverse range of coworkers and clientele.
- ❑ Excellent budget management skills.
- ❑ Creative thinker and problem solver. Readily offer suggestions and solutions.
- ❑ Provide a calming presence and unflinching support in times of pressure and stress.
- ❑ Highly flexible. Available to work within a 150-mile radius.

EDUCATION

Association of Certified Professional Wedding Consultants, St. Paul, MN
Certificate of Completion

- Comprehensive 50-hour course covering all aspects of planning weddings, meeting clients' needs, and working with other professionals in the wedding industry.

University of Boca Raton, Boca Raton, FL
B.A. in Human Relations with Minor in Psychology
Honors: Dean's List
Key Courses: Management, Public Relations, Communications, Organizational Management, Marketing I, Marketing II, Marketing III, Graphic Design, Psychology, Human Resources Management, Sociology

PROFESSIONAL ASSOCIATIONS

Association of Bridal Consultants, St. Paul, MN
Gorgeous Weddings Worldwide, St. Paul, MN
Association of Certified Wedding Planners, St. Paul, MN

RELEVANT EXPERIENCE

Wedding Coordinator, Wedding of Heather Willard, July 1999 (125 guests)

Arranged	Hotel	Florist
Musicians	Dresses	Tuxedos
Bakery	Rehearsal	Rehearsal Dinner
Chair Covers	Favors	Honeymoon Planning

COMPUTER SKILLS

MS Word   Web-savvy

KEYWORDS

Special Events, Planning, Coordination, Event Coordinator
Promotions Coordinator, Party, Parties

Stanley J. Riccobono

5 Port Smith Key • Columbia, SC 29211 • (800) 737-8637 • sriccobono@resume.com

Seasoned Events Coordinator with proven track record of successfully managing events
from initial concept to execution and follow-up

ACHIEVEMENTS, SKILLS & ABILITIES

■ **Events Coordinator:** Manage all aspects of three annual yacht shows in Charleston area, including selection and transportation of yachts on display, setup of all communications for sales team, and provision of pre- and postsales support through marketing promotions.

■ **Recognized Leader/Project Manager:** Skilled at working under tight deadlines while coordinating countless details. Independent and competent demeanor allows parties involved in events to trust that work will be thorough and completed according to strict quality standards.

■ **Effective Communicator:** Exceptional interpersonal relations skills. Provide single point-of-contact during shows so all parties involved are kept informed.

■ **Problem Solver:** Flexibility paired with creativity quickly resolves issues. Use diplomacy to handle communications problems among employees with competing interests working at shows. Streamline show staffing processes to ensure appropriate resources are readily available at all times.

EXPERIENCE

Special Events Coordinator   1998 – Present
Tanner & Associates – Yacht Brokerage   Charleston, SC
Spearhead all aspects of three annual, large-scale boat shows for this 30-year veteran of yacht brokerage industry. Establish and administer relationships with outside vendors involved in the shows. Oversee pre- and postshow sales efforts for 12 brokers and clientele, including developing marketing campaigns to generate show attendance and managing relationships with customers throughout the sales process.

• Acquired additional responsibilities throughout process to allow company owner and salespeople to dedicate more time to sales efforts.
• Set up relationships with key industry players to help shows operate smoothly.
• Streamlined communications processes at the shows by serving as go-to person for all questions, thus removing this responsibility from the company owner.
• Efforts resulted in the execution of yacht shows that helped create satisfied clients and owners, that were fun to attend and participate in, and that required minimal effort given by the sales force working the show.

Coordinating Assistant   1997 – 1998
Maritime and Company   Columbia, SC
Assist Chamber's President and Director of Events in successful planning and execution of Chamber of Commerce-sponsored events. Communicate with local businesses to generate participation.

• Regularly communicated with Chamber members to ensure they were informed of meetings, events, committee meetings, and special opportunities.
• Handled ordering and transportation of supplies for events, including budgetary responsibility.
• Developed new system to store Chamber's electronic files in an efficient and easily accessible format, in addition to a new system for interacting with each Chamber event's advertisers.

EDUCATION and TRAINING
BA in Communications
University of Charleston, Charleston, SC, 1996

COMPUTER SKILLS
Microsoft Word 2000 / Adobe PageMaker 6.5 / Microsoft Publisher

Keywords: Event Planning, Specialty Shows, Manager, Coordination Consultant, Special Events Manager

Svetlana Burske

8A Trapper Trail • Pierre, SD 57501 • (800) 737-8637 • sburske@resume.com

SUMMARY

Veteran Events Planner with demonstrable skill planning special events from start to finish. Adept at coordinating large-scale events on tight deadlines while adhering to budget. Proven interpersonal skills: outgoing and positive with ability to work well with diverse people. Strong professional presence. Exceptional communication and presentation skills. A self-starter who can identify a need and step in to meet it. An enthusiastic, effective supervisor—able to motivate others to do their best.

MAJOR AREAS OF ACHIEVEMENT

Event Planning

- Raised $55,000 net in one event as Volunteer Auction Chair for an elementary school. Wrote and sent 1000 solicitation letters, recruited and managed 20-person volunteer staff, designed invitations, adhered to tight budget by securing donations of wine and flowers, found celebrity auctioneer, and implemented profit-boosting innovations such as advertising T-shirts, complimentary tickets to potential high bidders and a kickoff event to ensure parental involvement,
- Arranged essential image-building parties for advertising agency.
- Led the coordination of meetings for 600 area Junior League members, including scouting and negotiating for locations.

Administration

- Relied on for direct contact with major advertising clients. Created effective written communications.
- Arranged cost-effective, smooth-running travel.
- Sourced and handled details of medical insurance.
- Throughout work experience, interacted with employees at all levels, in many different departments.
- As Training Director for Junior League, interviewed and hired professional trainers on a national basis and designed a training continuum still in use.

WORK HISTORY

Senior Special Events Manager, Party-24 Company, Pierre, SD, 1984 – 1988
Director of Promotions, Big Bang Circus, Pierre, SD, 1982 – 1984
Promotions Manager, Weddings and Things, Pierre, SD, 1981 – 1982

EDUCATION

Pierre College, Pierre, SD
BA in Marketing

COMPUTER SKILLS

Windows 98, Macintosh, FileMaker Pro, Microsoft Word, Word Perfect and Internet navigation.

KEYWORDS

charity event planner, business event planner, entertainment, vice president

References provided on request

Scott Hunter

248 Forrester • Columbus, OH 43215 • (800) 737-8637 • shunter@resume.com

Talented finance student with strong management skills and demonstrated record of academic success seeks position in business and financial industry

SUMMARY OF QUALIFICATIONS

- ❑ Outstanding financial training with strong experience in auditing, as well as diverse economic fields, including mutual funds and life insurance.
- ❑ Member of student chapter, Certified Internal Auditors; graduated with BS in Finance, 5/2003.
- ❑ Demonstrated background effectively supervising people and processes.
- ❑ Strong interpersonal and communication skills. Adept at building business relationships with coworkers, clientele, and management.
- ❑ Highly motivated, with strong work ethic.
- ❑ Able to thrive in fast-paced, deadline-oriented environments.

EDUCATION

OHIO UNIVERSITY, Columbus, OH
Bachelor of Science Degree in Finance, May 2003
Coursework in Internal Auditing; 3.2 GPA

Activities: Student Finance Association
Student Chapter, Certified Internal Auditors (CIA)

EXPERIENCE

Columbus Capital, Columbus, OH   08/01 – 12/03
Financial Intern
Assisted with strategic planning and technical support of financial database of 150 to 200 clients.
- Supported staff with development of marketing plans focused on locating new clientele.
- Teamed with staff in designing management seminars.
- Received extensive training on mutual funds and life insurance.

Bank of Ohio, Columbus, OH   05/01 – 08/01
Financial Intern
Coordinated inventory and delivery, ensuring accuracy and matching incoming and outgoing stock with invoices.
- Reconciled financial information to computer files and made periodic deposits.
- Communicated with customers via telephone; served as information source.

ADDITIONAL EXPERIENCE

Smith's Restaurant and Bar, Columbus, OH   1999 – Present
Manager
- Supervised and directed 120-member staff for largest catering company in Ohio.
- Effectively assisted with numerous facets of operations for high-end clientele.

COMPUTER SKILLS

MS Word, MS Excel, MS PowerPoint, MS Access, MS Money, ACT 2000

KEYWORDS: Financial Analyst, Financial Advisor, Marketing, Training

SHEILA MCMULLEN

35 Southeast Boulevard • Augusta, ME 04330 • (800) 737-8637 • smcmullen@resume.com

Award-winning financial professional with strong financial planning,
business development, and project management skills

SUMMARY OF QUALIFICATIONS

- Over five years of financial management experience within Financial Services field.
- Diverse professional development, including strategic planning, budgeting and forecasting, financial analysis, and business profitability reporting.
- Committed team player, with proven ability to meet and exceed set goals and deadlines.
- Exceptional focus and follow-through abilities, with record of efficiency and productivity.
- Detail orientated multitasker, with exemplary organization and project management skills.
- Strategic thinker and planner, skilled in design and execution of financial, administration, and business programs.

PROFESSIONAL EXPERIENCE

GIANT BLUE DATA, INC., Augusta, ME   04/01 – Present
STRATEGIC ANALYST
Analyzed business line profitability and performance as related to initial plan. Made presentations to senior management from division and parent regarding strengths/weaknesses and suggested strategies.

- Developed and implemented annual planning processes; collected necessary financial data via internal budgeting process.
- Played key role in conversion of two major loan systems and migration to new loan and accounting system.
- Oversaw bank reconciliation, accounts payable processing, general ledger account analysis, proof and control functions, and closing activities.
- Established strategic partnership between accounting department and loan operations area. Coordinated implementation of daily cash settlement model as related to customer loan accounts and daily company funding requirements.

INCOMING SOLUTIONS, Bath, ME   09/98 – 04/01
JUNIOR ANALYST (01/99 – 04/01)
Analyzed and reported business line financial performance results to CEO and senior management; coordinated between business line and finance division regarding all performance-related issues.

- Directed gathering of all relevant financial data elements from six major Corporate Banking divisions to support annual planning process, monthly and quarterly forecast, and monthly staffing analysis.
- Developed internal reporting formats and spreadsheet systems for profitability analysis, planning and forecasting, loan pipeline, and staffing analysis.
- Awarded for identifying opportunities to enhance revenue and increase efficiency of internal processes, 1998.

ASSOCIATE JUNIOR ANALYST (09/98 – 12/98)
Supervised collection of all necessary data and participated in preliminary and final meetings for each company and senior management.

- Coordinated quarterly and annual planning forecasting with various subsidiary companies.
- Played key role in preparation of annual Corporate Banking budget and business review.
- Developed in-house process for approval and tracking of purchase lease requests for major capital expenditures.

EDUCATION

BOWDOIN COLLEGE, BRUNSWICK, ME
BS, Accounting, 1997

COMPUTER SKILLS

PC, Windows, Excel, Word, PowerPoint, Lotus 123

KEYWORDS

Financial Executive, Financial Consultant, Financial Director, Business Development Executive

LEE AKIRA WALLACE

3 Platinum Circle • Nashville, TN 37243 • (800) 737-8637 • lawallace@resume.com

EXECUTIVE SUMMARY

Results-oriented professional with over 20 years of experience in sophisticated international and domestic financial markets. Expertise in derivatives, currency arbitrage, and spot, forward, and medium-term currency trading. Demonstrated strategic planning and business development talent. Excellent rapport building, developing, and maintaining strong business relationships with CFOs, Presidents, Chief Dealers, and diverse high-net-worth individuals. Proven track record in foreign and domestic markets. Experienced in European and Asian business cultures; conversational in German and Japanese.

PROFESSIONAL EXPERIENCE

LA Wallace, Inc., Nashville, TN   1994 – Present
Vice President
Developed financial strategies for corporations and high-net-worth individuals. Conducted due diligence for clientele seeking new venture/existing company investments.
- Aided clients in franchising and licensing of services and products.
- Advised clients in corporate restructuring; represented entrepreneurs and established corporations in all stages of funding, from acquisition to implementation and management.
- Worked with diverse private and publicly held companies.
- Matched large corporate clients with suitable buyers, managing all stages of financing and development.

Indo-America Trading, Co., New York and Hong Kong   1989 – 1994
Vice President
Served as interest rate markets broker, specializing in cross-currency interest rate swaps.
- Managed top-tier banking clients in USA, Asia, and Europe.
- Specialized in derivatives, medium-term forwards, and euro-currency arbitrage.
- Utilized aggressive but exceptionally detail-oriented style to acquire, retain, and manage high-net-worth clientele.
- Managed complex transactions from conception to conclusion.

Trident Financial, New York, NY   1982 – 1989
Manager
Trained new associates in forward and medium-term currency trading.
- Forward Currency Broker, specializing in Japanese Yen, German Marks, and Pound Sterling.
- Specialized in new business development, including acquiring new business in Pacific Rim and European markets.

EDUCATION

Hofstra University, Garden City, NY
Bachelor of Arts in Finance

LANGUAGE SKILLS

Conversational in Japanese and German

PIERRE ARNAUD

13 June Street • Oklahoma City, OK 73105 • (800) 737-8637 • parnaud@resume.com

Skilled professional with extensive experience in food services
specializing in payroll and personnel administration

SUMMARY OF QUALIFICATIONS

- Three years of experience in restaurant management with expertise in creating and overseeing successful new venues.
- Fluent understanding of creating attractive environments and exceptional food for diverse range of clientele.
- Strong computer software skills, including proficiency in Microsoft Excel, Word, Outlook, Lotus, and custom applications.
- Diligent worker with positive attitude and ability to learn new concepts quickly.
- Adept at instituting process improvements to increase efficiency and productivity.
- Independently financed 100% of education through part-time employment.

PROFESSIONAL EXPERIENCE

AMERICAN DINING COMPANY, Oklahoma City, OK   2000 – Present
Assistant Manager overseeing day-to-day operations for global dining business.

- Played a key role in creating three new chain restaurants for national organization, achieving profitability of all locations within 11-month period.
- Coordinate all aspects of catering events for business meetings and cocktail receptions.
- Improve operations by developing and maintaining worksheets to track daily account activity. Develop and distribute reports representing accounts payable, accounts receivable, sales, and payroll transactions to home office.
- Track and report pension fund allocations to union organizations on monthly basis.
- Administer personnel records, including employee attendance, vacation, and payroll information.
- Prepare and submit paperwork for disability and workers' compensation claims.

AWARDS

Culinary Arts and Restaurant Management

MEMBERSHIPS

NOT-FOR-PROFIT HOUSING COMMITTEE   1999 – Present
Work on team responsible for instituting building improvements for fund-restricted organizations such as academic institutions and low-income housing facilities on annual basis.

EDUCATION

AMERICAN CULINARY INSTITUTE, NEW YORK, NY
Degree in Fine Dining

COMPUTER SKILLS

Microsoft Excel, Outlook, Word, Lotus, and ARAMARK custom software applications

KEYWORDS

food service, office administration, office manager, administrative assistant, clerical, clerk, facility management, facility administration, bookkeeping, payroll, compensation, benefits, reporting

Maryellen Simon

59 Grappelle Road • Montpelier, VT 05609 • (800) 737-8637 • msimon@resume.com

Energetic and self-motivated management professional with strong devotion to food, wine, and restaurant industries

QUALIFICATIONS SUMMARY

➢ Over five years of experience in various phases of food and wine industries enhanced by dual degrees in Culinary Arts and Business Administration.
➢ Strong organizational, management, and leadership qualifications.
➢ Superior communication and public relations skills; fluent in French and Italian.
➢ Effective problem solver and decision maker with ability to handle stressful situations.
➢ Excellent planning, project management, and marketing abilities.
➢ Proven ability to train and motivate others with positive disposition.
➢ Experience in inventory, purchasing, bookkeeping, and generating cost savings.

EDUCATION

CULINARY INSTITUTE OF AMERICA, Long Island, NY
Associate of Occupational Studies, Culinary Arts, 1998

GEORGE WASHINGTON UNIVERSITY, Washington, D.C.
Bachelor of Business Administration, Foreign Service, 1996

CERTIFICATIONS
Fine French Wines, Level I
Court of Master European Wines, Level II
Global Wine Foundation, Certification
New York State Food Safety Certificate

PROFESSIONAL EXPERIENCE

Consultant   2000 – Present
Design and institute wine programs and seminars for restaurants lacking in-house sommeliere.
▪ Manage inventory and purchasing operations, including food costs/profit ratios and beverage costs/profit ratios.
▪ Develop and implement staff training programs for variety of establishments.
▪ Write descriptions of items for gourmet food catalogue/retail store; devise menus for promotional food/wine tasting dinners.
▪ Create recipe/cooking instruction cards for Behelio, a New York City dining establishment.

BLUE ANGEL DINING, Montpelier, VT   1999
Chef
Oversaw successful operations in preparation of retail and catered cuisine.
▪ Managed hot line, grill, and garden manager stations.
▪ Maintained quality of food product and ensured consistency in food delivery and standards.
▪ Created daily specials.
▪ Responsible for presentation of display case.

KEYWORDS

Restaurant Consultant, Food Critic, Food Journalism, Executive Chef, General Manager, Restaurant Editor, Management Consultant, Fine Dining, Hospitality Management, Wine Specialist, Hotel Management, Food Director, Sommelier, Teacher

Excellent References Available upon Request

Avery Handel

9653 Washington Avenue • Madison, WI 53707 • 800-737-8637 • ahandle@resume.com

PROFILE

Extensive experience in fine dining. Expertise in dining room service. Hands-on leader with ability to build cooperative, productive teams. Innate understanding of customer needs, with talents to meet those expectations. Ability to lead servers in friendly manner, without sacrificing quality. Strict attention to detail, presenting exquisite table layout and food delivery. Excel in sophisticated atmosphere. Provide superior dining and celebration events for many high-profile celebrities.

PROFESSIONAL EXPERIENCE

Captain
- Oversee waiter and bus persons, ensuring customer accommodation.
- Manage station and occasionally entire dining room, coordinating front- and back-of-the-house personnel, enabling smooth service.
- Increase revenue through suggestive selling, utilizing extensive knowledge of fine wines.
- Display expert carving of meat, bonefish, and fowl.
- Prepare and present flaming dishes and desserts tableside with professional style.
- Work closely with customers, creating excellent dining experience.
- Gained valuable skills and knowledge serving elite social and political clientele in European hotels.

EDUCATION

Culinary School, Budapest, Hungary
Concentration in fine food, dining room service, and safe food handling

WORK HISTORY

CAPTAIN, EMMANUELLE RESTAURANT, Madison, WI	1987 – Present
CAPTAIN, LES HUEVO RESTAURANT, Madison, WI	1986
CAPTAIN, AMBERLINE RESTAURANT, Madison, WI	1985
CAPTAIN, CLARKS, Madison, WI	1974 – 1985

LANGUAGES

English, Hungarian, and German

KEYWORDS

Banquet Manager, Hospitality Manager, Lead Server, Dining Room Manager, Maitre d'

References Available upon Request

Selena Roberts

76 Arctic Circle • Juneau, AK 99811 • (800) 737-8637 • sroberts@resume.com

A dedicated customer service and hospitality professional seeks a position as a flight attendant

SUMMARY OF QUALIFICATIONS

- Three years of successful experience in hospitality occupations, such as spa and salon.
- Dedicated to providing personalized services until customer is completely satisfied.
- Flexible. Easily adapt to various work settings.
- Enjoy challenging environments.
- Friendly with a good sense of humor.
- Effective communicator, both written and oral.
- Fluent in Spanish. Working knowledge of Italian.
- Able to travel/relocate.

PROFESSIONAL EXPERIENCE

Personal Services

- Provide one-on-one consultations for clients at Americana Hotel.
- Asses client needs and effectively meet them with company products and services.
- Fill in when other stylists are out, making sure clients are fully satisfied.
- Take extra step to build relationships with clients by being concerned with the total person and not just sale.
- Promoted from Assistant to Colorist to Senior Consultant due to volume of revenue.

Food Service/Hospitality

- As waiter, arranged parties from two to 200 persons at Jackson Club, making sure food was served in timely manner and seating and table arrangements were in order.
- Consistently provided courteous and prompt service.
- Promoted to front desk.

Administration

- As front desk clerk, made reservations and checked guests into club.
- Completed nightly auditing duties for monies and inventory.
- Prepared checkout statements for departing guests.
- Trained assistants in all aspects of salon operations.
- Monitor and maintain inventory at Americana Hotel.

LANGUAGES

Spanish: Read, write and speak fluently. Italian: Speak and write to some extent.

EMPLOYMENT HISTORY

Americana Hotel, Juneau, AK	3/03 – present
Roberts Salon, Juneau, AK	3/02 – 3/03
Jackson Club, Juneau, AK	4/01 – 3/02

EDUCATION

Santa Monica School of Cosmetology, Santa Monica, CA

COMPUTER SKILLS

Internet-savvy, Microsoft Office Suite, proprietary software

KEYWORDS

Hospitality, Hotel Management, Attendant, Corporate Hospitality, Conferences

PHILLIP ROTHCHILD

89 Gold Nugget Road ▪ Denver, CO 80203 ▪ (800) 737-8637 ▪ prothchild@resume.com

SUMMARY

➢ Over nine years of significant managerial leadership in hospitality.
➢ Hands-on manager with proven track record in operations, marketing and computer technology.
➢ Effective at team building and staff retention with first-rate communication and training skills and ability to work well with diverse, multilingual staff.
➢ Promote and maintain team morale, yield management skills and "can-do" attitude.
➢ Commitment to excellence in guest services and quick resolution of problems.
➢ Exceptional communication skills. Acute business acumen.

PROFESSIONAL BACKGROUND

AB Harbor Inn & Suites, Denver, CO   1996 – present
General Manager
Evaluate daily operations, develop forecast and strategic planning, update computer PMS programs regarding daily occurrences; oversee marketing, disaster and financial crises, guest issues and complaints.
- Directed financial turnaround and positioned hotel, domestically and internationally, to upscale status.
- **Hotel won Best Service Award** (Inn Key Award, nominated by peers in Greater Denver and The Ski Hotel Association) out of 900 hotels and cruise lines, 1999.
- **Increased occupancy by 45%. Maintain 47% repeat business.**
- Oversaw renovation of entire hotel property. Resulted in enhanced services and doubled revenues.
- Computerized all hotel functions and installed new systems to enhance services in Room Division.
- Developed food and beverage department, including restaurant and banquet facility.
- Travel overseas to meet with prospective clients and agents, resulting in global positioning of hotel.

AB Hotel and Resort, Denver, CO   1994 – 1995
Assistant General Manager for 225-room hotel and resort.
- Supervised staff of 85 employees. Promoted from Room Division Manager, 1994.
- Introduced corporate accounts and diversified client base, resulting in increased revenues.
- Maintained 93% year-round occupancy. Marketed hotel to conventions, increasing client base.
- Increased transient bookings by 36%. Doubled percentage of upsales.
- Created standards of operations utilizing forecasting and analysis for Room Division. Resulted in 17% decrease in payroll while maintaining quality and productivity.
- Computerized Reservation Department, increasing efficiency and guest satisfaction.

PROFESSIONAL AND VOLUNTEER ASSOCIATIONS

Hospitality, Sales and Marketing Association International (HSMAI), 1997 – present
Greater Denver and The Ski Hotel Association, 1996 – present
Denver Development Association, 1996 – present
Volunteer, Travel and Tourism Academy of Denver Public Schools, 1996 – present

EDUCATION

University of Colorado, Denver, CO
B.S., Hotel Management, 1992

COMPUTER SKILLS

Microsoft Office Suite

KEYWORDS

Hotel Management, District Manager, Corporate Hospitality, Operations, Vice President

Janell Jones

62 Wayne Street ▪ Boise, ID 83720 ▪ (800) 737-8637 ▪ jjones@resume.com

QUALIFICATIONS PROFILE

A highly experienced, customer-satisfaction-oriented manager in casino, food and hotel industries. Over 10 years of experience in hospitality industry. Highly organized team motivator with enthusiastic, hands-on management style. Roll up sleeves and pitch in as needed. Hired and managed 120-person staff. First-rate communications skills, both oral and written. Effective planner and problem solver with proven history of developing creative, logical solutions that increase efficiency. Strong commitment to customer satisfaction. Friendly, outgoing team player with good sense of humor. Noted for reliability and getting the job done.

PROFESSIONAL EXPERIENCE AND ACCOMPLISHMENTS

Grand Marquee Hotel, Boise, ID   *1985 – 2002*
General Manager of 120-employee hotel casino, restaurant and motel.
Surveyed all employees and wrote job descriptions based on knowledge, skills and aptitudes required. Maintained high employee morale, resulting in low employee turnover and greater productivity. Established open-door policy for all employees.

- Responsible for most recent yearly profit, nearly $2.5 million. Analyzed, selected and implemented new payroll software enabling accounting department to work more efficiently and save time.
- Managed five checking accounts, savings account and company vault.
- Implemented and conducted meetings with department heads on regular basis to improve communications and efficiency.
- Instituted and promoted policy of active community involvement, resulting in excellent public relations for company.
- Served as liaison between owners and attorneys. Assisted legal counsel in resolution of issues facing the company.

Motel   *1987 – 1990*

- Developed new pricing structure, resulting in 30% increase in revenues.
- Investigated and addressed guest complaints and concerns. Successfully resolved problems to maintain customer satisfaction.

Restaurant   *1985 – 1987*

- Implemented point-of-sale system to track food sales, increasing profitability.
- Arranged and coordinated group meetings, banquets and conventions.
- Planned meals and daily specials. Purchased food and equipment. Prepared employee schedules.

COMPUTER SKILLS
Familiar with PC and Windows 98

AWARDS AND COMMUNITY ACTIVITIES
Friend of 4-H Award, Pershing County 4-H, 1998

EDUCATION
University of Nevada, Reno, BA in Business Administration

KEYWORDS
Hospitality Management, Senior Manager, Vice President, Operations Manager

Elisa Rembrandt

228 Lincoln Street • Des Moines, IA 50319
800-737-8637 • erembrandt@resume.com

**Talented Human Resources assistant, knowledgeable in payroll, benefits,
and governmental assistance rules and regulations**

SUMMARY OF QUALIFICATIONS
- ❑ Certified Professional in Human Resources.
- ❑ Over three years of experience in personnel industry with progressive responsibilities.
- ❑ In-depth understanding of federal and state rules and regulations.
- ❑ Adept at providing exceptional benefits administration and support.
- ❑ Excellent written and oral communication skills.
- ❑ Fluent in Spanish.

PROFESSIONAL HISTORY
Brennerman Finance, Des Moines, IA   2002 – Present
Benefits Representative
Prepare and validate numerous administrative bills, including health EAP, dental, LTD, and life insurance.
- Coordinate and instruct benefits orientation classes for new representatives.
- Create, revise, and maintain total human resource files; make system adjustments for 500 employees.
- Solely responsible for enrollment, termination, and payroll deductions of welfare programs.
- Administer COBRA notifications and HIPAA certificates for entire personnel.
- Manage all aspects of short-term disabilities and enrollments of multiple insurance plans.
- Guide staff in problem resolutions.

Financial Equity Group, Mount Vernon, IA   2001
Human Resources Assistant
Assisted in all stages of recruiting new hires, including tracking, administering, and preparing postoffer applications, as well as physical and aptitude testing.
- Preserved daily attendance records and originated and validated monthly insurance payments, in addition to processing hourly employee compensations.
- Secured union discipline letters and updated reports.
- Acknowledged personnel verification forms and letters.
- Revised 401K elections through payroll and investment companies.
- Processed benefit revisions and claim enrollments.
- Utilized PeopleSoft systems to maintain accurate employment records.
- Administered OSHA 200 and applicant flow logs.
- Documented employee daily times and processed payroll of absentees.
- Controlled plant site badge authorization and photo identification systems, ensuring proper flow of traffic.

EDUCATION
Bachelor of Science Degree in Human Resources Management, 2000
University of Iowa

COMPUTER SKILLS
Microsoft Office Suite, Windows, PeopleSoft, Report Writer

KEYWORDS: Employee Relations Coordinator, Personnel Director, Hiring Manager, Recruiter

Jan Johnson

2481 Peach Grove, Apt. 4 • Atlanta, GA 30334 • (800) 737-8637 • jjohnson@resume.com

Skilled health and welfare consultant with four years of experience empowering corporations with efficient and cost-effective benefits packages

SUMMARY OF QUALIFICATIONS

Accomplished benefits consultant with demonstrated track record of success in health and welfare industry. Talented and dedicated employee repeatedly awarded by superiors with positions of increasing responsibility. Skilled analyst and negotiator, creating effective, successful plans for companies with changing needs. Adept at developing strong, long-term relationships with customers and vendors. Exceptional attention to detail; researched and wrote contracts and booklets with error rate of only 4%.

PROFESSIONAL EXPERIENCE

Glowing Health Solutions, Atlanta, GA   02/02 – Present
Health and Welfare Consultant
Analyze and restructure numerous facets of employee benefit programs for multiple corporations, enhancing effectiveness and reducing costs.

- Using expert knowledge of Consolidated Omnibus Budget Reconciliation Act of 1985, Women's Health and Cancer Rights Act, and Employee Retirement Income Security Act, ensure company compliance and troubleshoot problems.
- Conduct vendor negotiations using innovative techniques and industry knowledge to define and procure appropriate solutions.
- Improve insurance plans through postimplementation reporting and analysis.
- Coach and mentor peers in health and welfare industry policies, restrictions, and programs.
- Communicate policy and program changes to benefit holders by employing written and verbal skills.

Atlanta Social Work Solutions, Atlanta, GA   08/00 – 01/02
Health and Welfare Consultant
Reviewed, analyzed, and offered innovative solutions to health and welfare plans for numerous companies.

- Ensured compliance and resolved issues regarding benefit acts, preventing major legal costs.
- Procured successful benefits programs tailored to client requirements and budgets.
- Informed customers of plan changes and compliance issues through effective communications.
- Quickly and effectively resolved employee and vendor issues.

Atlantis Products, Atlanta, GA   09/97 – 07/00
Marketing and Proposal Analyst (02/98 – 07/00)
Membership Analyst (09/97 – 01/98)
Organized, compiled, and wrote key elements of proposed solutions utilizing excellent communication skills and attention to detail.

- Generated tailored responses by carefully analyzing and researching incoming requests for proposals, resulting in increased number of contracts awarded to company.
- Created and maintained new membership database containing valuable marketing and sales information.
- Produced revenue-generating reports matching potential customers to company providers.

COMPUTER SKILLS

Microsoft (PowerPoint, Word, and Excel), GeoAccess, Windows 95/98/NT 4.0/2000

EDUCATION

University of South Carolina, Columbia, SC
Political Science Major/Business Minor; completed 115 credits (GPA 3.4).

Keywords: benefits analyst, health and welfare consultant, benefits program administrator, benefits manager, health-care administrator, health insurance consultant, welfare insurance manager

CATHY DENNIS

6097 Governor's Drive • Phoenix, AZ 85007 • (800) 737-8637 • cdennis@resume.com

Successful, accomplished Human Resources Professional with excellent planning, organizational and interpersonal skills

SUMMARY OF QUALIFICATIONS

Over 15 years of Human Resources experience within major financial corporation. Diverse professional development including accounting, corporate procedures and personnel issues. Proven ability to form strong relationships with and gain trust of colleagues and clients at all levels. Detail-oriented, with extensive analytical, organizational and management skills. Superior troubleshooting, problem-solving and conflict-resolution skills, with exceptional focus and follow-through abilities. Popular, tactful team player who thrives within group environment.

PROFESSIONAL EXPERIENCE

Cactus International, Phoenix, AZ   1987 – Present
Assistant Vice President, Human Resources (1996 – present)
Personnel Manager (1991 – 1996)
Administrative Assistant (1987 – 1991)
Responsible for management of personnel, payroll, secretarial, receptionist and mail staff within major financial corporation.

- Conducted annual performance appraisals and seminars while providing conflict resolution and management/employee benefit coordination for employee population of over 500.
- Direct responsibility for implementation and administration for entire employee benefits system, including life, medical, dental, vision, flexible spending, FMLA, COBRA and Workers' Compensation disability insurance programs.
- Effectively coordinated with brokers/vendors to resolve employee claim issues.
- Developed and streamlined HR systems and procedures, providing greater efficiency.
- Recognized for tactful, delicate and successful handling of difficult individual employee issues, gaining trust of colleagues throughout company.
- Responsible for all aspects of prospective employee interview and hiring process.
- Coordinated random drug testing program, with recovery techniques designed for treatment needs of individuals.
- Worked with company attorney on immigration issues, ensuring efficient and timely documentation handling for current and future employees.

COMPUTER SKILLS

PC, Internet knowledge, Microsoft Word, IBM AS400

EDUCATION

NORTHERN ARIZONA UNIVERSITY, SCOTTSDALE, AZ
BA IN BUSINESS ADMINISTRATION

KEYWORDS

Personnel Manager, Human Resources Manager, Office Manager, Administrator, Employee Relations Specialist, Operations Manager

LATRELL CURTISS

34 Harvard Drive • Wilmington, DE 19801 • (800) 737-8637 • lcurtiss@resume.com

Highly motivated recent graduate with expertise in insurance, human resources and customer service

Summary of Qualifications

- Exceptional knowledge of health insurance and social services with strong customer service and organizational background.
- Highly trainable, fast learner. Willing to undertake new and exciting challenges.
- Independent; also capable of performing as team member.
- Innovative and flexible in approach to problem solving.
- Excellent communicator, effective mentor and tutor.
- Able to interact with people from all walks of life.
- Dedicated and hardworking; proven ability to work in fast-paced environment.

Professional Experience

Winegardt Associates, Wilmington, DE   1999 – Present
Enrollment Specialist (2000 – Present)
Establish and maintain member eligibility records for various health insurance programs.
- Update member account information by processing changes, additions and terminations.
- Record and process premium payments, adjustments and refunds.
- Interact with human resource departments and medical providers regarding eligibility issues.
- Investigate and resolve eligibility inquiries through intervention and effective follow-up procedures.

Claims Clerk (1999 – 2000)
Coordinated and distributed daily, weekly and monthly medical billing reports to appropriate departments.
- Recovered disputed claim data from microfiche, enabling efficient investigation and resolution.

Media in Delaware, Wilmington, DE   1997 – 1998
Interviewer
Complied and analyzed data obtained during interviews.
- Contacted clients and conducted telephone interviews on various issues.
- Collaborated with supervisors on interview processes and data collection.

Office Temps, Wilmington, DE   1996 – 1997
Clerk
Documented and revised computerized client information files.
- Determined and budgeted requirements for welfare recipients.

Education

THE CITY UNIVERSITY OF DELAWARE   1996
Bachelor of Arts in Sociology, with a minor in Psychology

Keywords: Carrier Liaison Assistant, Human Resources Assistant, Financial Administrator, Case Technician, Service Coordinator

Sandy Shu

8 South Reinhold Blvd. • Indianapolis, IN 46204 • (800) 737-8637 • sshu@aol.com

SUMMARY OF QUALIFICATIONS

Over 20 years of experience in insurance industry. Proven performer, earning highest quality and production awards four consecutive years. Trained in medical terminology and medical coding. Proactive "doer" able to identify problems and find solutions, face challenges head-on. Quick and eager to learn; conscientious and detail-oriented. Referred to in recent review as "great resource and wealth of knowledge." Trustworthy and dependable with access to confidential information. Outgoing and personable; able to satisfy customers while meeting company objectives.

PROFESSIONAL BACKGROUND

Commitment Health Company, Indianapolis, IN   **1988 – present**
Senior Claims Analyst
Research, investigate and process complex claims in timely manner. Assist in training and auditing.
- Use broad knowledge of medical terminology, COB, Medicare, CPT 2000 coding, CRVS, ICD-9, HIAA coding, short-term disability and dental insurance to ensure validity of claim.
- One of company's top producers, consistently achieving highest quality.
- Work directly with agents and insurance representatives.
- Communicate effectively with customers regarding claim-processing complaints, including researching complaint and adjusting where appropriate.
- Trusted with high dollar limit for release of payments to providers.
- Updated training and auditing procedures to address claims-processing concerns missed in audits.
- Suggested computer system enhancements to improve claim-processing efficiency.

City of Indianapolis, Indianapolis, IN   **1986 – 1988**
Medical/Dental Claims Examiner
Manually reviewed and processed complex claims with substantial research and investigation.
- Communicated directly and effectively with customers.

First Rate Processors, Indianapolis, IN   **1983 – 1986**
Claims Processor/Examiner
Manually coded claims using CPT-4 and ICD-9.

EDUCATION

Indiana State University, completed 3 years; GPA: 3.7
Continuing Education Courses
- LOMA Certificate for Fundamentals of Life and Health Insurance
- CPT-4 Coding
- Medical Language

COMPUTER SKILLS

Operating Systems: Windows 98, Mac, CPT
Applications: Excel, WordPerfect, Word

KEYWORDS

Insurance analyst, claims adjuster, medical insurance, dentist insurance, claims investigator

Jonathan Lang

1A Bishop Court • Lincoln, NE 68509 • (800) 737-8637 • jlang@resume.com

Talented management information systems student with exceptional academic record and strong experience achieving company objectives while enhancing growth

PROFILE OF QUALIFICATIONS

➤ Strong experience in multiple facets of E-Commerce, including researching and analyzing E-Business, E-Market and B2B companies, examining consumer habits and evaluating competition.

➤ Able to effectively apply E-Commerce knowledge to compile and evaluate statistical data.

➤ Adept at designing and enhancing information management systems to ensure optimum productivity rates and maintain both quality and cost-effectiveness.

➤ Exceptional communication skills; able to develop and maintain strong business relationships with clientele, managers and coworkers.

➤ Skilled in analyzing and identifying potential markets and strategic partnerships.

➤ Excellent academic record.

EDUCATION

Nebraska State University, Lincoln, NE
BS, Business Administration/Management Information Systems, December 2001

- GPA: 3.62/4.0
- Member, Golden Key National Honors Society. Dean's List, six of eight semesters
- Volunteer computer support consultant, United Way

State University of Nebraska, Omaha, NE
Bachelor of Commerce in Management, December 1997

COMPUTER KNOWLEDGE

Programming Languages:	Visual Basics 6.0, SQL, HTML
Software Applications:	MS Office 2000, Visio2000
Operating Systems:	Windows 95/98/NT
Additional:	Web Design

PROFESSIONAL EXPERIENCE

Transactions.com, Lincoln, NE   2001 – Present
E-Business Analyst
Evaluate E-Market/E-Business transactions impacting company's four industry segments.

- Assess E-Business activities of targeted accounts, including supply and demand.
- Research and analyze competition, including tracking E-Business initiatives and activities.
- Examine service providers and Internet companies to define partnerships and explore new markets.
- Design, develop and reengineer E-Monitoring systems.
- Created customer segmentation reporting system using weighted-average adjusted-value multiplier.
- Developed MS Excel spreadsheet tool to analyze client product portfolios.
- Designed internal-contact tool and maintenance support system.
- Successfully supported B2B marketing team in executing targeted marketing plan.

Lincoln North Trust, Lincoln, NE   1996 – 2000
Assistant Manager
Recruited, trained and supervised personnel.

- Monitored inventory/supplies and maintained customer/employee database.

Smith Townshend and Partners, Omaha, NE   1992 – 1996
Assistant
Created written documents and reports, coordinated schedule and provided executive support.

Keywords: Information Systems, Systems Management, Systems Administration, Support, User Support, Data Management, Data Analysis, Internet

Wini M. Fountain

87 Bluebird Circle • Concord, NH 03301 • 800-737-8637 • wfountain@resume.com

Award-winning IT professional with demonstrable analytical, problem resolution,
and technical support expertise

SUMMARY OF QUALIFICATIONS

- Solid professional and academic experience in **project management**.
- Able to utilize technical skills and problem-solving abilities to assess end-user needs, develop solutions and track progress. Supported by Bachelors Degree in **Management Information Systems**.
- Experience in **administrative support**, documentation management and resolution of complex issues; demonstrate professionalism, attention to detail and collaborative nature.
- **Strong communicator** exhibited by skill in working closely with customers to identify and resolve problems; ability to convey technical concept to nontechnical audiences.

AREAS OF EXPERIENCE and ACADEMIC PREPARATION

Help Desk Support	Project Management	Staff Supervision
Troubleshooting	Analysis, Design	Staff Support
Problem Resolution	RF Flow, Visual Analyst	Health Services
E-commerce	System Development Life Cycle	Documentation
Windows 95 / 98 / 2000 / XP	Java, HTML	Website Design

EDUCATION

M.B.A.   Master of Business Administration Degree, Troy State University, Troy, AL, May 2003

B.S.   Bachelor of Science in Management Information Systems, Auburn University, Auburn, AL

B.S.   Bachelor of Science in Health Services Administration, Auburn University, Auburn, AL

Certification: Fundamentals of Project Management, Villanova University, Villanova, PA

WORK HISTORY

Technical Solutions, Inc., Concord, NH   1998 – present
Help Desk Technician at e-commerce department (2002 – present)
Call Center Supervisor (1998 – 2002)
Troubleshoot e-commerce teleconferencing products.
- Utilize technical and problem-solving skills to identify glitches and quickly implement solutions.
- Work closely with internal sales representatives and customers to optimize Web-conferencing software.
- Trained employees, sales representatives and customers in product/service features and use.
- Effectively resolved employee conflicts and issues.
- Received Employee of Month Award and award for Outstanding Performance in Customer Service.

Analysis and Design Project (through Auburn University), Auburn, AL   2000
Project Lead
Led team of five to assess business needs, build, test and implement website.
- For senior project, utilized System Development Life Cycle to work closely with E-commerce business and create new Website to enhance online services.
- Scheduled and facilitated meetings to track and discuss progress.

Northern Georgia Hospital, Jones, GA   1998
Assistant Project Lead
Provided technical support to all departments.
- Resolved system and network problems.
- Ensured operations ran smoothly.

ADDITIONAL EXPERIENCE

Auburn University, *Help Desk Consultant,* Auburn, AL 20000

Keywords: QA, Quality Assurance, Help Desk I and II, Database administration, System administration

Franklin Heverless

39 Socrates Lane • Raleigh, NC 27603 • (800) 737-8637 • fheverless@resume.com

SUMMARY:

More than 10 years of senior-level Information Technology management experience. Proven ability to direct teams, projects, and departments. Experienced at reengineering and department development. Consistently recognized for outstanding technical and management performance. Skilled in hardware, software, and client system evaluations. Highly knowledgeable in systems design, programming, and data management. Able to create and implement technical and operational plans and strategies. Familiar with Software Development Life Cycle methodologies, including waterfall, spiral, and MS Solutions Framework. Ability to liaison between management, clients, and technical personnel. Able to manage budgets and resources. Strong communication and presentation skills.

TECHNICAL SKILLS:

Operating Systems:	Windows 95/98/2000, NT Server/Workstation, MS-DOS, MVS/XA, MVS/ESA
Applications:	Visual Studio, IIS, Visio, MS Office, Project, Windows Sockets, Crystal Reports, IBM JCL and Utilities, TSO/ISPF, ADW, SQL, Oracle, MS Access, IDMS, DB2
Networking:	TCP/IP, LAN/WAN, SQL Server, MS Site Server
Languages:	ASP, HTML, XML, VBScript, Visual Basic, Transact-SQL, SQL Plus, CICS, COBOL, COBOL II, IBM Assembler, FORTRAN
Access Methods:	ODBC, ADODB, ADO, DAO, RDO, VSAM, IAM, QSAM
Certifications:	Certified Project Management Professional by Project Management Institute

PROFESSIONAL EXPERIENCE:

Project Construction, Raleigh, NC   1998 – 2004
Senior Project Manager
Oversaw system design and Internet development projects for key clients, including Nutrail, Global Sources, FleeTrap, and State of Washington. Worked closely with clients, to determine needs and requirements.

- Managed teams of technical personnel and consultants. Worked in conjunction with senior management and sales teams on project development, presales meetings with clients and definition of enterprise architecture.
- Led team of developers in completion of Phase 1 of project involving design, construction, and deployment of new Website for client. Originated requirements, formulated data model, and prepared all documentation.
- Oversaw development of support system encompassing management reporting, payment approval, and accounting interfaces for FleeTrap project.
- Responsible for repair order and parts inventory systems construction. Established requirements, carried out design activities, and managed testing and implementation. System enabled client to recoup more than $5M.

Construction Design, Raleigh, NC   1997 – 1998
Senior Consultant
Conducted system upgrades, database conversions, client systems analyses, and creation of design specs.

- Performed project planning for major human resource projects, such as upgrade of CSS Horizon system and conversion of PeopleSmart applications to Horizon.

ABC Solutions, Raleigh, NC   1994 – 1997
Vice President, Information Technology
Directed all IT operations and activities for start-up company. Responsible for designing and implementing departmental infrastructure and technology development. Created and established policies and procedures. Supervised all hardware and software selection and acquisition.

- Led yearlong project involving reengineering of company systems from Windows for Workgroups and Access to SQL Server, Visual Basic, Crystal Reports, and NT.
- Developed and implemented CARE Mechanization Process, designed to manage data entry, data uploading, and reporting for customers. Later carried out total rewrite of this system as part of change from Access to other data management systems.

EDUCATION:

BS in Computer Science, North Carolina State University

TRAINING:

Microsoft's Solutions Framework, Unified Modeling Language, Supporting Microsoft Windows NT, Networking Essentials, Supporting Microsoft SQL Server, Project Managers Workshop, EDS System Life Cycle

Keywords: Senior Consultant, Senior Project Manager, Senior IT Manager, Technology Management, Project Development Manager, Director of Technology Development, Technology Officer

Brad Lowell

11 Green Acres Drive ∎ Richmond, VA 23219 ∎ 800.737.8637 ∎ blowell@resume.com

Driven, dedicated, and professional Police Academy graduate possessing training and experience in Law Enforcement, with superior leadership, emergency management/reporting, and communication skills

SUMMARY OF QUALIFICATIONS

✓ Demonstrate positive attitude, strong work ethic, loyalty, and dedication. Consider impact of decisions on department, its members, and community.

✓ Extremely personable, utilizing logic and sound judgment, as well as obtaining cooperation from others in multiple-demand situations. Strength in working with colleagues and community at diverse levels.

✓ Proven record of responding and working well in extremely high stress environments.

✓ Experienced in identifying problems and executing decisions. Exemplary record of conduct/productivity.

✓ Strong oral/written skills in communication information, producing complete, concise, and reflective data.

EDUCATION & PROFESSIONAL DEVELOPMENT

Police Academy, Richmond, VA
State Certified. Date of Completion: October 2002

► *Firearm Techniques*	► *Investigative Process*
► *Patrol Operations*	► *Defensive Driving*
► *Personal Fitness*	► *Criminal Law*
► *Report Writing*	► *First Aid/CPR*
► *Traffic Enforcement Investigations*	► *Military Customs and Courtesy*

Achieved certificate for Outstanding Performance in Military Customs and Courtesy
Performed voluntary duty as part of Cleaning Crew

Richmond Community College, Richmond, VA
Law Enforcement Coursework / 70 Credit Hours toward Bachelors Degree in Criminal Justice

RELEVANT EXPERIENCE

Security Services, Richmond, VA
Protective Services Officer   **July 2000 – May 2003**
Worked directly under Sergeant providing patrol and physical security to County Welfare Building, County Courthouse, and Juvenile Detention Centers.
- Responded to alarms, provided safety to county employees, and patrolled during and after building closings.
- Interacted with Richmond EMS and Police Department and held police commission. Assisted in arrests.
- Worked closely with community, maintaining positive, caring, and supportive demeanor.
- Consistently produced and distributed all reports and documentation in timely manner.

Safety First Company, Richmond, VA
Security Safety Officer   **November 1996 – July 2000**
Maintained high-rise security/fire and life safety for over 7,000 tenants, with 57 floors and 1,000-car parking garage.
- Responsible for building surveillance and safety of federal park located on building premises.
- Monitored and oversaw operation of FS 90 Fire System, as well as closed-circuit TV.
- Upheld positive interaction with Richmond Police, Fire and EMS departments in response to fire and theft.
- Assured confidence to tenants, visitors, and the community. Efficiently completed all report writing.

CERTIFICATE TRAINING

Police Academy: ADAP Certified and ASP Tactical Baton Certification
City of Richmond: Auxiliary Police Officer Training
Ohio Peace Officer Training Council: Private Security Training Course, 160 Hours

References Available upon Request

SUCHERA SANGMIN

9263 Mount Rainier Road ◊ Olympia, WA 98504 ◊ (800) 737-8637 ◊ ssangmin@resume.com

Well-respected, experienced Investigator with solid record of accomplishments and excellence

SUMMARY OF QUALIFICATIONS

- ❑ More than five years of investigative experience in United States Armed Forces.
- ❑ Conduct in-depth military criminal investigations for U.S. Army.
- ❑ Interview subjects, victims and witnesses; prepare cases for prosecution.
- ❑ Prepare detailed reports of investigations.
- ❑ Recipient of numerous awards for professionalism and competency.
- ❑ Awarded noncommissioned officer of the year in 1999.

WORK HISTORY

Secure and Safe Organization
123rd Military Police, Bldg. 4567, Olympia, WA 98504, U.S.A
Military Police Officer   2002 – Present
Supervisor: Lt. John Donn
Carry out law enforcement duties as Patrol Supervisor; responsible for 15 patrol officers.

- Investigate crimes at Fort Hood, including conducting interviews, fact gathering, and compiling reports.
- Member of Protective Service mission during presidential visits.
- Accountable for performance of highly sensitive equipment valued at more than $300,000.
- Trained and supervised soldiers.

State of Washington
Camp Hungry, US, APO, AP 11111, Olympia, WA 98504
Military Police Investigator   2001 – 2002
Supervisor: Marin Ford
Conducted criminal investigations; interviewed victims and witnesses and interrogated subjects.

- Cultivated skills to identify and analyze nonverbal actions, facilitating the ability to recognize merit of responses during interviews.
- Supervised Protective Service missions for dignitaries and celebrities.
- Trained and supervised more than 300 military police working at Camp Allegiance.
- Increased conviction rate 25% from extensive surveillance and investigations on black marketing.
- Maintained fleet of 13 vehicles valued at more than $200,000.
- Received no discrepancies during annual inspection of evidence room.

Hamilton Airforce Base, Olympia, WA 98504
Military Police Investigator   1997 – 2001
Supervisor: John Doe
Canvassed neighborhoods to conduct interviews with victims and witnesses.

- Conducted interrogations on subjects, interviewed personnel, and investigated Fort Meander crimes.
- Wrote detailed reports of investigations, submitted final reports to Commanders, Staff Judge Advocate and U.S. Criminal Records Center.
- Managed $20,000 annual budget; provided training to military police and more than 500 soldiers.
- Participated in community DARE program interacting with more than 600 children.

EDUCATION

LMNO Community College, Elmira, NY, U.S.A., Associate's Degree, 2001
72 Semester Hours. Major: General Studies

Freeman State University, Freeman, NY
25 Semester Hours. Major: Business Administration

Keywords: Investigator, Security, Law enforcement, criminal justice

BORIS ALLEGHENY
5 Wright Avenue • Charleston, WV 25305 • (800) 737-8637 • ballegheny@resume.com

PROFILE
New York City Sergeant providing security, management, and investigative expertise. Over eight years of award-winning experience in law enforcement, including four years in security services. Certified Security Guard Instructor. Excellent interpersonal skills with fellow officers, supervisory personnel, and the public at large. Strong follow-thorough skills. Gets the job done. Friendly outgoing personality, yet firm and in charge. Accustomed to remaining calm, maintaining self-control, and thinking clearly while under duress. Stable work history and career path.

PROFESSIONAL EXPERIENCE
Protection Services, Charleston, WV   1993 – 1998
Special Patrolman/Sergeant (1994 – 1998)
Provided protective services in complex of 46 high-rise buildings, as well as power plant, community center, garages, and mall. Licensed to carry gun and authorized to make arrests. Managed scheduling of officers.
- Effectively led team of 25 peace officers and dispatchers.
- Conducted investigations. Maintained close working relationship with WVPD.
- Trained newly hired potential officers in eight-hour preassignment course, 16-hour on-the-job training course, and eight-hour annual in-service training.
- Attended and addressed tenant meetings to identify concerns and maintain good public relations.
- Promoted and put into practice concept of community policing in Star City.
- Assisted in making arrests including cases involving attempted murder and drug dealing.
- Star City saw 35% decrease in crime during this time.

Charleston Special Patrolman/Corporal (1993 – 1994)
Led group of six officers. Conducted investigations, arrested offenders, wrote reports.
- Acted as tour supervisor in absence of lieutenant. Promoted to Sergeant after 10 months.

Armed Security Officer   1991 – 1993
Rendered security services in assigned area. Promoted to Corporal after two years.

Patrol and Protect Products and Services, Charleston, WV   1987 – 1991
Operations Manager for security company providing P.I. services.
Successfully resolved problems with clients in order to maintain loyalty and satisfaction.
- Promoted from Security Officer to Operations Manager within one year.
- In charge of staff of 300 under owner of company.
- Proposed that company seek out and bid on government contracts.

AWARDS
Honor Board Letter of Commendation, 1992
Three Departmental Recognition Awards (Meritorious) – 1991 (2), 1992
Seven Departmental Recognition Awards (Excellent) – 1991, 1992 (2), 1993, 1994, 1995 (2)

EDUCATION
State Mandatory Reporters Course
Security Supervisors Training Program, Star City
General Law Enforcement Course
West Virginia State Security Guard Instructor
WVS Municipal Police Training Council, Firearms and Deadly Physical Force
WVS Municipal Police Training Council, Basic Peace Office Course
WVS High School Equivalency Diploma

CERTIFICATION
West Virginia State Division of Criminal Justice Services
General Topics Security Guard Instructor, through March 2000

Keywords: Law enforcement, police officer, security guard

ROSARIO CLEESON

598 North Face Road • Madison, WI 53707 • (800) 737-8637 • rcleeson@resume.com

Motivated, high-energy, and reliable Law Student with enthusiasm for criminal law and challenge of working in district attorney's office

SUMMARY OF QUALIFICATIONS

■ **Knowledge & Experience**: Cum laude graduate offering more than three years of practical experience as legal advisor in student resource center and as trial paralegal for prestigious firm.

■ **Proven Performer**: Respond positively in crisis situations; consistently rise to occasion. Played key role in mounting successful case against major manufacturer.

■ **Organizational Expertise**: Simultaneously managed 40 to 50 active files and two cases. Able to analyze and prioritize daily routines and project tasks to meet deadlines. Envied by staff attorneys for having best-organized office in firm.

■ **Outstanding Communicator**: Articulate and persuasive; write with strength, clarity and style. Easily relate to people from diverse backgrounds and all walks of life with tact and diplomacy. Mediated many rancorous wills/family settlement matters in probate cases.

■ **Computer Skills**: Proficient in applications of WordPerfect, Microsoft Word and Access, Lexis Nexus, and West Law.

RELATED EXPERIENCE

Trial Paralegal   1999 – 2001
STONE AND ROBERTS COMPANY   Madison, WI

Worked with two senior partners. Processed trial cases from inception through closing arguments for this firm specializing in civil litigation. Conducted interviews and developed intake memos. Ordered records, set up depositions, and prepared witnesses. Conducted library research. Wrote and filed interrogatories and motions.

- Contributed to a case against major manufacturer in which court awarded $1.5 million in compensation and $50 million in punitive damages.
- Successfully conducted client settlement agreements.
- Selected to directly assist the firm's senior partner.
- Prepared critical trial documents and other legal materials.

Legal Resource Center Staff   1999
GOLDEN GATE MANAGEMENT   San Francisco, CA

Advised on landlord-tenant disputes and small claims issues. Interviewed clients to ascertain relevant facts in each case. Researched legal precedent and consulted senior staff members to provide sound legal advice and/or strategies for resolving conflicts.

- Collaborated effectively with the Center's staff attorney.

EDUCATION

Law Program, 1999
Golden Gate University Law School – San Francisco, CA
Law Review Member

Bachelor of Arts in Political Science, 1996 • *Cum Laude, Dean's List*
San Francisco State University – San Francisco, CA

KEYWORDS: legal assistant, paralegal, law clerk, legal intern, legal secretary, law office assistant

Arthur Clarke

53 Piedmont ♦ Secaucus, NJ 08624 ♦ 800-737-8637 ♦ aclarke@resume.com

A highly experienced Attorney skilled in family law, divorce, bankruptcy and foreclosures with substantial courtroom experience and special aptitude for client interaction

Summary of Qualifications

- ❑ Over five years of intense experience in and solely responsible for all matters of family law, divorce, bankruptcy and general practice at extremely busy law firm.
- ❑ Abundant courtroom knowledge and familiarity with judges and court personnel in Federal Bankruptcy Court, District Courts, local Circuit Courts and Criminal Courts.
- ❑ Fluent in motion practice, mediation, settlement conferences, foreclosures, and drafting various Family Law and Bankruptcy pleadings, discovery papers, motions and petitions.
- ❑ Key ability to communicate with clients and devise beneficial solutions resulting in significant increases in referrals.
- ❑ Reduced problematic cases and increased office productivity by revising and streamlining long-standing office procedures.
- ❑ Successfully identify with and relate to needs of local communities and retain significant number of new and former clients.

Professional Experience

FILBURN AND SONS, Newark, NJ   2001 – Present
Family Law and Bankruptcy Attorney
Represent high volume of clients independently at five-member law firm with emphasis on family law, divorce, bankruptcy and all related matters.

- Attend various hearings, including 341 and Chapter 13 confirmation hearings in United States Bankruptcy Court for Eastern District New Jersey, appearing before trustees and creditors to examine viability of bankruptcy claims.
- Conduct family law trials and divorce proceedings before judges, including motion practice, mediation, and settlement conferences in Oakland County Circuit Court and other District Courts.
- Prepare and draft foreclosure petitions and associated documents to assist troubled clients in saving homes and possessions.
- Spearhead personal initiative to increase productivity and enhance services to clients by spending extra time and delineating all options and creative solutions to legal matters.
- Decisive and organized with strong capacity to think quickly and present facts rationally.
- Successfully entrusted with vast responsibility under little direction with proven results; numerous referrals and satisfied clients.

WATERS, MEYERS, AND LARSON, Orange, NJ   1997 – 2001
Criminal Defense Attorney
Represented defendants in criminal matters focusing mainly on activities for felony cases.

- Assisted sole practitioner in preparation for oral arguments and pretrial motions; conducted legal research using Lexis and Westlaw.
- Reviewed reports and testimony and helped prepare defendants and witnesses for trial.

Education

Juris Doctor, Detroit College of Law at Michigan State University, Detroit, MI, 1998
Dean's List: Spring 1996, Winter 1996, Fall 1997

Oakland University, Rochester, MI
Bachelor of Arts, History, 1993

Internships

Misdemeanor Defender's Office
Represented defendants charged with misdemeanors at downtown local courthouse; received job offer.

Bar Admission

Admitted, New Jersey State Bar, November 1998

KEYWORDS: attorney, lawyer, family law, divorce, bankruptcy, foreclosure, criminal, courtroom, motion practice, mediation, settlements, felony, misdemeanor, manager, customer service, Lexis, Westlaw

Melissa T. Wesson

28 West 25th Street ♦ New York, NY 10003 ♦ (800) 737-8637 ♦ mwesson@resume.com

Top-notch Legal Secretary with experience in estate planning and administration, workers' compensation and family law

SUMMARY OF QUALIFICATIONS

Over 10 years' experience as legal secretary with expertise in family law and general practice. Skilled in processing documents for such diverse areas as personal injury, social security disability and corporate law. Effectively manage calendars, dockets and files, ensuring administrative efficiency. Excellent communication skills. Able to interface with clients and attorneys at all business levels.

PROFESSIONAL EXPERIENCE

Legal Defense Organization, New York, NY   8/01 – Present
Legal Secretary
Prepare estate planning and administration documents for three senior partners.
- ❖ Employed dormant case management system, increasing ability to track file contacts and possible disputes.
- ❖ Administer government estate taxes, utilizing knowledge of policies and procedures.
- ❖ Perform all office operations, including processing mail, operating switchboards and scheduling appointments.
- ❖ Prepare agendas and record minutes for corporate meetings; type all correspondence and legal documents.
- ❖ Accurately and efficiently transcribe dictation from lawyers.

Johnson Rule, Jersey City, NJ   03/97 – 06/01
Legal Secretary
Processed documents pertaining to family law, real estate, estate planning and administration, social security disability, workers' compensation and criminal and personal injury.
- ❖ Referred significant number of clients to firm, increasing revenue.
- ❖ Utilized case management process to maintain calendars, dockets and files.
- ❖ Entered attorney time sheets into automated time records/billing system.
- ❖ Corresponded with clients, making collection attempts on delinquent accounts.
- ❖ Aided in recruiting extraordinary staff.
- ❖ Participated in yearly Christmas fund-raisers to benefit disadvantaged in community.

Meyers and Meyers, New York, NY   08/93 – 12/96
Legal Secretary
Managed attorney professional development files.
- ❖ Customized accounting and filing systems and organized administrative support tasks to improve effectiveness and continuity of office environment.
- ❖ Prepared all legal documents and maintained client files.
- ❖ Hired and managed staff of three employees.
- ❖ Performed accounting functions related to maintenance of accounts payable and accounts receivable.
- ❖ Oversaw benefits management and payroll, ensuring appropriate taxes and deductions were applied.
- ❖ Instrumental in deployment of advertising campaigns.

EDUCATION

Penn State, Ogontz, PA: Estate Planning and Administration coursework
Montgomery Community College, Blue Bell, PA: Business and Accounting coursework

COMPUTER SKILLS

Microsoft Office, Windows Operating Systems, Corel, Amicus Attorney, ProLaw

Keywords: stenography, litigation, legal assistant

JUANITA BOLERA

680 Bayside Drive • Orlando, FL 32985 • (800) 737-8637 • jbolera@resume.com

Talented student with strong understanding of operations management, including over three years of experience in retail industry

SUMMARY OF QUALIFICATIONS

- Proven track record working in competitive industries and providing key support to senior management professionals.
- Developed techniques for reducing expenses and improving profitability.
- Adept at creating and implementing successful marketing and promotional campaigns.
- Outstanding analytical, technical and problem-solving abilities.
- Successfully performed relationship and negotiation management with internal and external clients.
- Excellent oral and written communication skills.
- Result-oriented professional with solid work ethic.
- Team player who is able to relate to people at any level. Fluent in English and Spanish.

PROFESSIONAL EXPERIENCE

Saint Jude Fashions, Miami, FL   2002 – Present
Assistant Manager for retail clothing business with two stores in Florida.
Played key role in developing successful line of seven new products aimed at urban market.
- Utilized excellent customer service skills to achieve high degrees of client satisfaction.
- Implemented effective management techniques, including developing strong working relationships with coworkers, management, and clientele.
- Oversee employee time cards, including hours per week and overtime pay.
- Improved employee performance through implementation of effective motivational techniques.

Gregor Department Stores, Orlando, FL   2001 – 2002
Floor Manager
Designed in-store promotions and displays, ensuring that key merchandise with high profit margin was sold in important areas.
- Initiated frequent-purchase club, resulting in increase of 45% of blue jeans and jean jackets.
- Achieved increase in overall floor sales by over 10%.
- Installed in-store cameras, reducing shrinkage by 15% within seven months.
- Responsible for training and developing junior employees.

EDUCATION

Degree in Accounting & Administration, Barnard College, New York, NY, 2000

COMPUTER SKILLS

Microsoft Office (Word, Excel, PowerPoint), Peachtree, Explorer, Money

Keywords: general manager, regional manager, store manager, chain manager, inventory manager, sales manager, marketing, supervisor, staff manager, district supervisor, chief manager, director, food store manager, customer service manager

LEE M. SMITH

77 ½ JONES ROAD • SALT LAKE CITY, UT 84114 • 800-737-8637 • LSMITH@RESUME.COM

SUMMARY:

Over seven years of experience in store, district, and area retail management, including supervision of both local and regional operations. Proven ability to dramatically increase sales while decreasing both costs and losses. Adept at developing and implementing successful strategies, policies, and procedures. Exceptional relationship-building skills; able to lead, motivate, and develop successful sales and sales support teams. Familiar with all aspects of store, warehouse, and business operations, including store management, merchandising, and inventory control. Strong commitment to customer satisfaction and product quality.

PROFESSIONAL BACKGROUND:

ABC Company, Salt Lake City, UT   1999 – 2001
District Clearance Center Manager (2000 – 2001)
Performed budgeting, sales strategy development, forecasting, P&L, and loss prevention. Directed all advertising, marketing, and merchandising operations and campaigns.

- **Increased sales 136% in one year.**
- Oversaw clearance center operations for two locations, with total sales exceeding $900,000.
- Hired and trained sales staff. Managed all sales, budget, and inventory activities.
- Supervised inventory control and building maintenance.

Distribution Manager (1999 – 2000)
Directed warehouse activities and operations, managing distribution team of 14 employees.

- Oversaw inventory control for more than $3.5 million in stock.
- Performed budgeting and forecasting.
- Supervised all shipping and receiving, as well as deliveries.

Madison's Fine Furniture/Madison's Rent to Own, Boise, ID   1996 – 1998
Merchandise Manager (1998 – 1999)
Supervised and directed inventory movement and stock rotation.

- Implemented and managed sales strategy.
- Oversaw all floor activities, including displays and sales.
- Responsible for buying and merchandising activities.
- Performed budget analyses and development.
- Monitored sales and delivery personnel to ensure highest levels of customer satisfaction.

Operations Manager (1984 – 1998)
Directed operations for five stores and three warehouses, as well as indirectly overseeing five additional stores.

- **Increased gross and net profits each year for eight consecutive years by as much as 27%.**
- Grew rental business by 45% in one year through development and implementation of innovative corporate/commercial rental program. Program eventually served as model for new rental division.
- Designed and introduced new computerized system for management reporting.
- Formulated and established new management goals and employee incentive programs.
- Investigated and resolved legal issues and customer complaints.

TRAINING:

Business Management, Boise Business College
Effective Supervision and Management, ABC Institute for Professional Development
The Seven Habits of Highly Effective People, Manny Reynolds Coaching
The Attitude of Servitude, Manny Reynolds
Behavior Recruitment Studies, John and John Index Analyst

AWARDS AND RECOGNITION:

Four Employee of the Month awards

COMPUTER SKILLS:

Windows 95/98/2000, Word, Excel, PowerPoint, proprietary business applications

KEYWORDS:

Regional retail manager, regional manager, district manager, operations manager, territory manager, sales manager, senior store manager, area manager, area director, operations director, merchandise management

JERRY JOHANNES

48 Cleavert Court • Tucson, AZ 85742 • 800-737-8637 • jjohannes@resume.com

SUMMARY

Proactive, senior-level operations executive with over 14 years of profitable management experience. Strong record of achievement in increasing sales, developing and implementing new revenue channels, controlling expenses and enhancing customer service. Demonstrated strengths in analysis, negotiations, relationship management, project management, loss prevention and public relations. Extensive knowledge of leasing, labor relations and policy and procedure implementation. Excellent communication and interpersonal skills.

PROFESSIONAL EXPERIENCE

Southwest Clothing Company, Phoenix, AZ   **1999 – present**

Southwest Regional Director of Retail

Direct all operations of 24 retail outlets in five national parks. Recruit, develop and retain management team.

- Increased average sales 7%. Design and implement store policies and procedures.
- Control budget of over $43 million. Reduced shrinkage from 2.1% to 1.5%.
- Successfully transitioned retail operations from traditional to thematic.
- Integral player in successful renewal of 10-year contract with National Park Service.
- Reorganized long-standing "porch artists" operation, increasing revenues by 28.3%.

Rising Star Designs, Tucson, AZ   **1997 – 1998**

Regional Director

Directed operations of 10 costume jewelry stores in malls and casinos locations over three-state area. Established landlord relations and display policies.

- Created sales goals and incentives, which resulted in increased sales and overall profits.
- Significantly reduced management turnover.

Rainbow Sand Tours, Taos, NM   **1990 – 1997**

Regional Vice President (1995 – 1997)

Directed $67 million region of retail operations at 12 major U.S. airports and two tourist locations.

- Collaborated on program to put merchandise carts in airports, now multi-million-dollar revenue channel.
- Successfully acquired and managed new contracts and operations at major airports, casinos, and tourist attractions.
- Supervised construction and established management organization for 22 stores at major airport.

General Manager (1990 – 1995)

Directed all operations in various retail markets, including management training, landlord relations, profit and loss, new store openings, shrinkage and store policies and procedures.

- Established smooth union labor relations, upgraded merchandise, managed duty-free operations. Developed register and bank audit system, reducing shrinkage by 2.2 to 2.3%. Initiated sales goals contests and instituted job referral bonuses. Increased profit from 5.6% to 10% of sales.
- As GM of Casino Operations, reduced merchandise costs by 14%, managed construction projects, reduced overhead expenses and computerized replenishment system. Introduced new food operation and cigarette merchandising program, increasing tobacco and candy categories over $220,000 per year.

COMPUTER SKILLS

Proficient in MS Office and Internet applications

EDUCATION

BA Management/Human Behavior, University of South Florida, Tampa, FL, 1989

Professional Development Courses including Dale Carnegie Professional Development, Sean Delaney Leadership Training, Decker Effective Communications and Total Quality Management

COMMUNITY SERVICE

Former Vice President, Local Lions International

DENNIS DONAS

73 Apple Orchard Lane ● Albany, NY 13876 ● (800) 737-8637 ● ddonas@resume.com

High-energy marketing professional offering extensive expertise in advertising and sales

SUMMARY OF QUALIFICATIONS

➢ Proven record of success in new client development, account management, and marketing.
➢ Persuasive sales and presentation skills. Effective at pitching products/services. Adept at cold calls.
➢ Skilled negotiator. Able to make deals happen.
➢ Outstanding communication skills, both verbal and written.
➢ Excellent problem-solving/troubleshooting ability. Effective in crisis situations.
➢ Strong interpersonal skills. Easily establish rapport.
➢ Well organized with ability to multitask effectively. Solid time management skills.
➢ Computer proficiency includes Microsoft Word, Excel, PowerPoint; Internet-savvy.

EXPERIENCE

A1 INFORMATION, Albany, NY   2002 – Present
Account Executive
Foster, maintain, and grow media accounts in 32 markets. Develop new accounts.
❑ Act as central salesperson for clients, including station affiliates and agencies.
❑ Negotiate sale of advertising packages.
❑ Conduct ongoing research on potential markets.
❑ Meet and exceed goals.
❑ Follow up with clients to determine satisfaction.
❑ Supervise and direct staff.
❑ Retain over 90% of client base.

Sales Specialist
Developed and maintained key relationships and contacts.
❑ Provided assistance to Washington, D.C., sales team.
❑ Serviced political agencies in tristate area.

Administrative Coordinator
Managed coordination of assisting Senior VP and Director of Sales.
❑ Acted as liaison between affiliates, sales force, and senior management.
❑ Coordinated all written communication, scheduled meetings, conference calls, and affiliate visits.

BIG APPLE MEDIA, New York, NY   2001 – 2002
Account Executive
Solicited, recruited, and managed advertising; liaison between TV stations and ad agencies.
❑ Representative for major-market television advertising firm.
❑ As part of national team, sold airtime for key cities, including Miami, Tampa, and Raleigh.

FLUSHING MARKETERS, Flushing, NY   2001
Marketing Representative
Coordinated and organized major sporting events in New York.
❑ Developed effective corporate sales packages.
❑ Represented association with major clients, including National Football League.

EDUCATION

Bachelor of Science in Communications – St. John's University, Jamaica, NY

KEYWORDS: Broadcasting, Television, Advertising, Advertising Management, Network, New Client Development

Andy C. Smith

8 Henry Street • Boston, MA 02133 • 800-737-8637 • asmith@resume.com

Accomplished sales and marketing professional with power and drive to penetrate new markets, lead organized sales force, and deliver quota-shattering results

Summary of Qualifications

Over six years of experience expanding new territories, generating successful promotional campaigns, and overseeing professional sales teams. Repeatedly exceeded sales quotas and increased market share by capturing new clientele through innovative marketing techniques. Rewarded with promotions to positions of increasing responsibility for achievements at every level. Currently earning Masters in Business Administration in Organizational Behavior and Marketing to further contribute progressive ideas and effective solutions. Skillfully led sales and distribution force with excellent communication and organization skills.

Experience and Achievements

Boston Residentials, Boston, MA   1994 – Present
Residential Sales Representative (2000 – Present)
Route Operations Specialist (1997 – 2000)
Hiring Team Coordinator (1997)
Route Salesman (1994 – 1997)
Built talented sales and marketing force by overseeing all aspects of hiring, including recruiting, screening, interviewing, selecting, and training.

- Generated unprecedented sales growth in representative residential program, increasing revenue from 50% to over 120% of goal.
- Spearheaded most successful sales effort in company by partnering with parent-teacher organizations for school fund-raising.
- Penetrated new markets through product promotions and samplings at national and regional businesses.
- Developed and maintained largest customer base in Waltham, MA.
- Increased market territory and captured new customers at home improvement shows, health fairs, and business expositions.
- Managed delivery routes, schedules, and customer orders, requiring excellent communication and organization skills.

Education

Suffolk University, Boston, MA   2000 – Present
Masters in Business Administration, Organizational Behavior/Marketing

Eastern Nazarene College, Quincy, MA   1998 – 2000
Bachelor of Science in Business Administration

Licenses and Certifications

A+ Certification, 2001
Perrier Sales Training Instructor Certification, 2001
Perrier Sales Training, 1999
Target Selection

Computer Skills

Microsoft Office Suite, Internet-savvy

Keywords: sales management, marketing management, marketing coordinator, assistant manager, representative, field sales, agent, market, promotional, distributor

Linda Luvos

205 Roadrunner Road • Houston, TX 78734 • (800) 737-8637 • lluvos@resume.com

SUMMARY OF QUALIFICATIONS

Highly motivated marketing and public relations executive with over 15 years of experience focusing on radio, television, online, entertainment, music, and live events. Demonstrated ability to successfully identify incremental revenue streams, structure logistics, develop thorough and reliable marketing plan, and create and manage new profit centers. Proven track record of producing outstanding media campaigns that satisfy client needs. Strong negotiator handling exclusive rights and official licensing contracts.

ACCOMPLISHMENTS

- Dramatically increased revenue for Pluto Planet Media Entertainment by developing and implementing new marketing plan that successfully attracted sponsors.
- Increased SMT contracts by 32% within one-year period for Hevlo Worldwide.
- Negotiated over 500 live concert appearances for managed artists, grossing over $150 million with national promoters.
- Created and launched Authentic News Network for Rao Corporation, offering celebrity interviews, concerts, entertainment news, and multimedia Web programming to more than 1,000 radio stations nationwide.

PROFESSIONAL EXPERIENCE

Houston Media Specialists, Houston, TX   1999 – Present
Vice President Media Relations
Supervised staff of 15 media specialists, wire writers, and monitoring executives who wrote advisories, maintained media databases, pitched stories to national and local broadcasters, and tracked story placement.

- Managed diverse, high-profile clientele, including Hevlo Worldwide and Cereal Box Promotions.
- Developed daily report that allowed every department to identify status of media campaign planning, production, launch, and results.
- Negotiated distribution deals with California K Radio Networks.
- Advised corporate clients on broadcast strategies and creative approaches to attract maximum interviews, hits, and audience for publicity efforts.

Texas Educational Instruments, Austin, TX   1997 – 1999
Vice President of Marketing
Planned marketing strategy, developed content, and attracted sponsors for multiple television shows, including Bob Builder Hour, Numbers Tuesday Game, and Natural Adventures for Kids.

- Negotiated multi-million-dollar licensing and corporate sponsorship contracts, significantly increasing revenue.

Right-on Media, Corpus Christi, TX   1994 – 1997
Vice President of Entertainment and Marketing
Hired and supervised news staff of 14 reporters who wrote, produced, and booked talent for daily news feeds; satellite interviews broadcast nationwide to member stations.

- Conceived and implemented strategic marketing campaigns for initial launch, including all advertising collateral and publicity.

Farelli Entertainment, Austin, TX   1988 – 1994
Senior Director of Entertainment Programming and Marketing
Conceptualized and planned high-profile entertainment programming for member stations, attracting well-known advertisers and increasing revenue.

- Created and produced "Top 25 Cartoons" twentieth anniversary tour, attracting major corporate sponsorships.

COMPUTER SKILLS
Windows XP, WordPerfect, MS Word, MS Excel, Netscape Navigator, Explorer

KEYWORDS
Event Planner, Marketing Director, Nielson, Arbitron, Press Relations, Newswire Services, Satellite News Feed, Uplinks, Downlinks, Feed Coordinates

Jane Jackson

11 Oliver Way ▪ Portland, OR 97324 ▪ (800) 737-8637 ▪ jjackson@resume.com

Exceptionally talented video and film editor who will enhance your current workforce through creativity, quality, and effective project management

SUMMARY of QUALIFICATIONS

- Practical video and film editing experience.
- Committed to quality. Exceptional ability visualizing "the big picture."
- Proven ability to manage both people and projects.
- Effectively able to multitask.
- Solid interpersonal expertise and outstanding communication skills.

AREAS of EXPERTISE

Production Management

- Partnered with Amid editors to create 30-minute documentary.
- Organized productions into articulate tales.
- Originated and cultivated themes to produce graceful films.
- Formed appealing features with eccentric speed. Incorporated strong pacing and realistic cuts.
- Edited 30 to 60 story segments daily.
- Used communication skills to coordinate program enhancements; improved ratings to first place.
- Selected photographs used in four nightly newscasts.

Project Management

- Launched successful e-commerce business using cross-functional team management philosophy.
- Created detailed specifications for $200,000 request for proposal.
- Developed product plans and requirements using research and analysis techniques.
- Managed team of 40 volunteers and contractors to raise over $1 million.
- Increased fund-raising contributions by 44% in one year.
- Established new programs focused on increased support, donor retention, and contributions.

WORK HISTORY

Editorial Production Assistant	Blackbird Company	07/01 – Present
Video Editor/Coordinator	Oceanbreeze Films	04/00 – 06/00
Avid Editor	ABC Documentaries	08/00 – 03/01

EDUCATION

Bachelor of Arts, Scripps College, Claremont, CA

Avid Film Camp Graduate, Digital Media Education Center, Portland, OR
Completed: Avid Media Composer 101, 102, 201, 205, and 210

Bay Area Video Coalition and Film Arts Foundation, San Francisco, CA

COMPUTER KNOWLEDGE

Macintosh and PC
Microsoft Excel ▪ Microsoft Access ▪ Sony DNE – Version 1.41 ▪ Adobe PhotoShop
Avid Media Composer – Versions 5.5, 7.1, and 10.0

KEYWORDS

coordinator, production coordinator, general production, technology coordinator, production

Steven P. Lorenzo

28 West 56th Street • Philadelphia, PA 17115 • (800) 737-8637 • slorenzo@resume.com

Hardworking talented videographer and multimedia artist with solid background and education in design, photography, and film

SUMMARY OF QUALIFICATIONS
- Seven years of experience in photography and video journalism.
- Expert knowledge of media equipment, setups, and production.
- Created stunning multimedia art and footage using current Macromedia, Adobe, and MIDI tools.
- Responsible and flexible artist able to generate quality films and Web sites under tight deadlines and budget constraints.

EXPERIENCE AND ACHIEVEMENTS
Freelance Work, Center City, PA   2003 – Present
Multimedia Designer
- Generated innovative media solutions for accounting firm Website, including all video and graphics.
- Designed print collateral in keeping with corporate style using industry standard applications and protocols.
- Worked with company to enhance corporate image in both online and print media.
- Outstanding service resulted in callback to produce pro-audio Website.

Graphic Designer
- Generated eye-catching music label compact disc covers, stickers, and labels for Vinyllords Productions, NJ.

Videographer
- Competent videographer, editor, and motion graphic artist; produced complete 1-hour, 30-minute film and successful one-minute, 20-second commercial.
- Accomplished cameraman for numerous weddings, bar mitzvahs, and dance recitals, which required quick thinking, creative filming, and diplomatic customer service.

Quad Films Company, Philadelphia, PA   2002
Videographer
Played key role in filming, editing, and designing online demo film.
- Experienced Web designer; generated all graphics for promotional website using cutting-edge applications and languages.

Late Breaking News, Philadelphia, PA   1997 – 2001
Video Journalist and Videographer
Captured live footage of several newsworthy events occurring in and around Philadelphia. Prepared all video for television and Web broadcasts.
- Experience filming under diverse conditions in changing environments.
- Maintained all video and photography equipment, both on and off location.
- Used artistic skills to produce professional motion graphics for assorted films.
- Expanded knowledge of projections and alternative electronic-video positioning.

SKILLS
Platforms:	Windows95/98/2000/NT, Macintosh
Tools:	Adobe (Photoshop/Illustrator/After Effects/Premiere), Macromedia (Dreamweaver Ultra Dev/Fireworks/Director/Authorware/Macromedia Flash), MIDI Pro-Tools, MIDI Digital Performer, Logic Audio, Microsoft (Word/Excel/PowerPoint/FrontPage), QuarkXpress
Languages:	Lingo, Javascript, DHTML, HTML

EDUCATION
Art Institute of Philadelphia, Philadelphia, PA 1996
Associate Art Degree in Specialized Technology, Multimedia and Web Applications

Keywords: Designer, multimedia, graphic, creative, artist, videographer, video, director, design, cameraman

Janina Haggins

87 Mulberry Street, #3N ▪ New York, NY 10001▪ (800) 737-8637 ▪ jhaggins@resume.com

SUMMARY OF QUALIFICATIONS

More than 10 years of experience in Media Arts, Communications, Marketing and Sales. Expertise in Business Development, Information Architecture and Content Strategy. Extensive background in audience analysis, marketing and communications strategies, message development and project consultation. Results-oriented team player with proven capability to develop and execute both short- and long-term business plans. Strong understanding of creative and technical aspects involved in internal and external business development. Exceptional business writing, research, copyediting, proofreading and verbal communications skills.

PROFESSIONAL EXPERIENCE

Architecture Designs, New York, NY   6/00–Present
Director of Content and Information Architecture
Successfully manage team of Content Service employees to ensure world-class services to potential and existing clientele.
- Promoted from Content Specialist to Director of Content after four months due to demonstrated success in maximizing team performance and productivity.
- Build superior information structures for e-commerce and information-based Websites of Fortune 500 clients.
- Provide statistical analysis and documentation for content materials and client presentations.
- Increased company's revenue by more than $500,000 through effective operations management and focus on development of excellent Web content plans.

Communications Corp., New York, NY   7/99–6/00
Director of Corporate Communications
Created and implemented marketing and communications materials, including press releases, white papers, summaries, Web content and presentations.
- Created and executed highly successful business plan for New Media entertainment firm.
- Effectively led implementation of strategy through marketing, aggressive fund-raising, content development and strategic alliances.
- Sourced, evaluated and executed potential acquisitions/alliances in support of long-term business plan.

Marketing Development Ltd., New York, NY   3/99–6/99
Writer/Consultant
Evaluated marketing and content needs of clients in lieu of corporate priorities, channel objectives and initiatives to develop and implement business plans.
- Managed content creation of all programs and materials, defining client vision and strategy. Performed extensive industry research to achieve goals.
- Boosted effectiveness of sales and marketing programs through development of innovative business, marketing and research plans.

Self-Employed, New York, NY   5/93–3/99
Freelance Writer/Consultant
Played vital role in writing screenplays and providing script-consulting services for entertainment companies.
- Wrote and produced business plans and marketing materials, including presentations, training materials, press releases, brochures and Web content.
- Drove development and execution of incoming scripts, books and literary documents.

EDUCATION
University of California, Berkeley, Berkeley, CA
Bachelor of Arts, 1988

COMPUTER SKILLS
PC/Mac, Microsoft Office, Visio, Photoshop, Navigator, Communicator, Dreamweaver, FrontPage

Keywords: Communications Coordinator, Marketing Manager, Information Architect, Content Developer

Tracy White

612 Leonard Johnson Park ♦ St. Paul, MN 55155 ♦ (800) 737-8637 ♦ twhite@email.com

Personable, motivated medical professional with front-line patient experience
seeks position as Pharmaceutical Sales Representative

PROFESSIONAL SUMMARY

♦ Three years of experience in medical field, providing real-world experience and knowledge of pharmaceuticals on market.
♦ Fluent understanding of pharmacological products and their effects, including drug side effects, proper dosages, and contradictions.
♦ Adept at building strong business relationships with coworkers, management, and clientele.
♦ Strong background training employees to process Medicaid, Medicare, and private insurance claims.
♦ Enthusiastic, outgoing and take initiative to learn new things.

SKILLS & ACCOMPLISHMENTS

SALES & INDUSTRY BACKGROUND

♦ Achieved certification as respiratory therapist.
♦ Completed six hours of pharmacy college credits and receiving ongoing education in pharmacology and related subjects.
♦ Worked directly with patients and doctors and learned firsthand about various drugs and treatments.
♦ Experience as marketing representative selling gourmet foods on part-time basis.
♦ Sold business ads for local monthly newspaper.

MEDICAL

♦ As Certified Respiratory Therapist, assessed and cared for patients, participated on ER Code Team, and managed ventilators for ICU.
♦ Handled emergencies and helped with triage at medical clinic.

ADMINISTRATIVE

♦ Trained clinic personnel to process Medicaid, Medicare, and private insurance claims.
♦ Kept books for medical clinics and oil company; duties included managing accounts receivable, accounts payable, monthly profit and loss statements, and daily inventory.

PROFESSIONAL EXPERIENCE

Certified Respiratory Therapist
St. Paul Hospital, St. Paul, MN   2002 – 2003

Office Administrator and Part Time Triage
St. Louis Community Center, St. Paul, MN   2001 – 2002

EDUCATION

St. Paul College, St. Paul, MN
Associates Degree, Advanced Level Respiratory Care, 2000

Pharmacology Update for Respiratory Therapist, 2001 • Pulmonary Emergencies, 2002
Advances in Asthma Therapy, 2000 • Advances in the Treatment of Sleep Disorders, 2000

PROFESSIONAL MEMBERSHIPS

National Board of Respiratory Therapists, 2002 – Present
AARC American Academy for Respiratory Therapists, 2001 – Present

KEYWORDS: pharmaceuticals, salesperson, account executive, sales team, quota

TERRY WONG

914 Longfellow Drive • Bismark, ND 58505 • (800) 737-8637 • twong@resume.com

Enthusiastic and highly motivated bio-pharmaceutical professional skilled in developing and maintaining beneficial relationships and proficient in medical terminology

SUMMARY OF QUALIFICATIONS

- Strong educational background in Biology and Chemistry. Proficient in research procedures.
- Extensive prescription pharmaceutical sales; ensured maximum profits for store through recommendations. Effective sales techniques with proven track record.
- Exceptional talent in translating medical jargon for clientele.
- Proficient in pharmaceuticals, including OTC, prescriptions and dosage units.
- Fast learner; adapt well to changes and pressures in workplace.
- Ambitious and hardworking, with commitment to excellence.
- Effective communicator, both written and verbal. Working knowledge of Spanish.
- Friendly with positive attitude. Proven team player.

PROFESSIONAL SKILLS

Bio-Pharmaceutical

- Successfully prepare prescriptions under supervision of licensed pharmacist.
- Efficiently monitor patient profiles screening for allergies, therapeutic duplications, prescription interactions, noncompliance and identification of inappropriate therapies.
- Exceptional understanding of medical terminology.
- Skilled in basic emergency care techniques; trained in CPR and first aid.

Sales

- Strong sales experience dealing with diverse clientele.
- Persuasive sales ability, honed throughout years of experience, including phone, in-store and collegiate project work.
- Demonstrated ability to increase store profitability through both effective sales technique and outstanding product knowledge.

Instruction/Education

- Successfully create attention-grabbing presentations and course curricula.
- Recognized for providing effective teaching techniques and relating to students.
- Computer skills; MS Office Suite (Excel, Word, PowerPoint, Access) and Word Perfect.

EDUCATION AND CERTIFICATIONS

CPhT – Certified Pharmacy Technician, #00000000000000, 2000

NORTH DAKOTA UNIVERSITY, 1998
Bachelor of Arts – *Biology*

EXPERIENCE

BISMARK HOSPITAL SUPPLIES	07/2000 – present
Senior Certified Pharmacy Technician / Sales Associate	
BISMARK HIGH SCHOOL	08/1999 – 07/2000
Science Teacher	
BISMARK JUNIOR HIGH SCHOOL	01/1999 – 08/1999
Science Teacher	
PHARMACEUTICALS EXPRESS	09/1997 – 01/1999
Sales Associate	

KEYWORDS

Medical products, pharmaceutical industry, biotech, outside sales, biotechnology

DANIEL A. SAMSON

63 Palisades Park Drive • Sewell, NJ 08624 • (800) 737-8637 • dsamson@resume.com

SUMMARY OF QUALIFICATIONS

Extensive retail pharmacy experience. Expertise in management. Highly motivated, self-directed individual, oriented to fast-paced environment. Strong customer service skills; work well with public. Proficient leader; address needs with employees and motivate them to perform at their best. Efficiently manage budget and inventory, utilizing cost-saving measures. Exceptional listener and communicator; ability to effectively educate customers. Knowledgeable in pharmacy software and third-party insurance.

PROFESSIONAL EXPERIENCE

SEWELL PHARMACY, Sewell, NJ   06/98 – Present
Staff Pharmacist
Provide empathetic patient counseling, ensuring thorough understanding of medication.
- Fill prescriptions, guaranteeing accuracy.
- Oversee inventory, process orders, and return expired and recalled medication.
- Monitor drug interactions with prescription and over-the-counter medication, guarding safety of customers.
- Consult with patients on drug compliance.
- Supervise pharmacy lab.

SAMSON DRUGS, Pennsville, NJ   07/95 – 06/97
Retail Pharmacy Owner and Head Pharmacist
Managed daily operations, including accounting, inventory, compounding medications, and presenting patient consults.
- Pioneered idea for IV infusion franchise.
- Increased revenue through ostomy supply, prosthetic breast, and medical supply sales.
- Provided informative diabetic and asthma counseling, aiding in product retailing.
- Updated accurate data in pharmacy software.

PENNSVILLE DEPOT, Pennsville, NJ   10/91 – 07/95
Pharmacist in Charge
Directed retail environment, exercising competent leadership.
- Assured quality customer service through filling prescriptions and patient care.
- Participated in diabetic and asthma counseling, assisting clients with medication use and supply purchasing.
- Employed care and precision when compounding medication.

COMPUTER SKILLS

Zandall and T-Rex Pharmacy systems

EDUCATION

Flex Pharm D Program, University of the Sciences of Philadelphia, Philadelphia, PA
GPA: 3.0, *intensive coursework toward Doctor of Pharmacy Degree, 8/97 – 06/98*

Bachelor of Science in Pharmacy, Philadelphia College of Pharmacy and Science, Philadelphia, PA
GPA: 3.85, ranked 20th in class, Dean's List, *1989*

KEYWORDS

Staff Pharmacist, Clinical Pharmacist, Pharmacy Supervisor, Pharmacy Manager

References Available upon Request

Barbara LaClure

72 Winona Butte • Cheyenne, WY 82002 • (800) 737–8637 • blaclure@resume.com

Ambitious college graduate with demonstrated ability to coordinate and organize Public Engagements seeks position in Public Relations

SUMMARY OF QUALIFICATIONS
- Dean's List and National Honor student.
- Skilled in organizing professional engagements.
- Strong research and negotiation skills.
- Demonstrated ability to communicate effectively with executive-level personnel.
- Excellent organizer and manager.
- Goal-oriented individual with strong work ethic.

EDUCATION
University of Buffalo, Buffalo, NY
Major in Social Sciences, 3.4/4.0 GPA
Graduation: May 2003

Key Subjects: Psychology, Economics, and Sociology
Honors: Dean's List 1999 and 2000
International Honor Society
Activities: Studied abroad in Australia for one semester at ABC University.
Member: Golden Key International Honor Society, Omicron Delta Kappa National Honor Fraternity, Toastmasters International

EXPERIENCE
The Learning Company, Cheyenne, WY   7/03 – Present
Lecture Events Coordinator (4/01 – Present)
Coordinate and organize lectures, debates and forums, including speaker selection and discussion topics.
- Develop and manage $65,000 budget.
- Provide support to Executive Board and assist with projects as needed.
- Supervise 20 committee members.

Travel Events Specialist (7/00 – 3/01)
Researched and negotiated travel contracts; arranged travel plans.
- Participated in fund-raising campaign.
- Worked closely with Executive Board.

County Daily Times, Buffalo, NY   3/00 – 6/00
Marketing Coordinator
Placed advertisements and organized paper into clearly defined sections.
- Used numerous programs, including Quark, PhotoShop, and Adobe Acrobat.

EXPERIENCE
MS Word, Outlook, Quark, PhotoShop, Adobe Acrobat

KEYWORDS
Event Planning, Meeting Coordinator, Public Relations

Mary Rose Angello

18 Dutchess Rose Rd. • Spokane, WA 99218 • (800) 737-8637 • mangello@resume.com

SUMMARY OF QUALIFICATIONS

➢ Public Relations professional with outstanding background in diverse facets of marketing and communications field, including event marketing and management, product and name branding, media relations, collateral development, and advertising.

➢ Fluent understanding and practice developing successful press materials and marketing materials for corporate, commercial, and consumer clientele.

➢ Demonstrated record of managing and launching high-profile projects using expertise and fiduciary experience in budget allocation and negotiations.

➢ Visionary and strategic thinker recognized as distinguished leader in advertising industry.

PROFESSIONAL BACKGROUND

Senior Marketing Manager, A-List Inc., Seattle, WA   2002 – Present
Oversee all aspects of PR agency focusing on brand deployment, internal/external launch strategies, public relations.

- Devise internal and external communication strategies focused on achieving maximum media impressions with minimal campaign costs.

- Consistently provide exceptional public relations and media coverage via powerful communications devised to successfully align brand strategy with management's goals.

- Spearheaded internal and external communications and public relations initiatives to facilitate company's name change, as well as rebranding efforts.

Marketing Manager-US, DEF Entertainment Company, Seattle, WA   1999 – 2002
Revitalized company brand and improved business 12% for 107-year-old company, launching campaign focusing on four pillars of brand strength: history, technology, America, and quality.

- Achieved successful increase in both sales and recognition by deploying comprehensive business strategy that covered all aspects of company, from business strategy to long-term growth.

- Results included cleaner distribution network, clearer picture of customer segmentation and continual focus on growth and increased market share.

PR Account Manager, Cutting Edge Promotions, Seattle, WA   1996 – 1999
Oversaw and implemented strategic branding for high-range B2B and B2C clients.

- Targeted function and emotion impulse of customer segments to create successful marketing campaigns, analyzing consumer behavior, trends and competition.

- Generated new clientele represented up to 40% of performance goals; personally pitched and obtained multiple, high-profile accounts.

- Increased sponsor revenues 15% and obtained $80,000 of free media coverage after leading successful press conferences with nationally recognized supermodel.

- Grew brand awareness and product sales in excess of 40% with minimal program funding.

EDUCATION

University of Washington, Seattle, WA
Bachelor of Arts, 1993

Certificate of Completion in Communication-Public Relations and Japanese, 1989
Hakodate College, Hokkaido, Japan

COMPUTER SKILLS

Microsoft Office Suite (Word, Excel, PowerPoint, Access), WordPerfect, Desktop Publishing

LANGUAGES

Read, write, and speak Japanese and Thai

KEYWORDS

Communications, Promotions, Branding, Media, Director, Marketing, Account Director, Media Relations, Press Conference, Press Release, Assessment, PR, Strategy, Brand Deployment, Campaigns

Derek Wiseman

4B Palmetto Drive • Charleston, SC 29215 • (800) 737-8637 • dwiseman@resume.com

Exceptionally talented Public Relations and Marketing Professional with over 11 years of experience

QUALIFICATIONS

☐ Successfully created internal and external communications programs.
☐ Award-winning designer of effective marketing materials.
☐ Exceptional writing skills, improving both product and service visibility.
☐ Extensive experience managing both radio and television advertising campaigns.
☐ Generated marketing and public relations strategies, improving client image.

PROFESSIONAL EMPLOYMENT

Marketing and Community Relations Director
Johnson & Myers Company, Charleston, SC   1996 to 2000
Developed seminars, community relations campus plan, and public relations programs.
- Achieved profit margin of 30% by implementing new Center for Professional Education certificate program.
- Cut cost per lead to lowest in western region. Managed curriculum development.
- Controlled annual advertising budget of more than $500,000.
- Planned and coordinated annual commencement ceremony.
- Employed and trained faculty and curriculum developers.
- Created print, radio, and television advertising campaigns.

Senior Account Executive
Public Relativity, Columbia, SC   1994 to 1996
Built public relation plans and policies for telecommunications, adult education, high-end fashion retail, publishing, and special education clients.
- Accountable for media relations.
- Coordinated special events.

Consultant and Freelance Writer
Court Room TV, New York, NY   1994
Assisted high-technology start-up company by improving public relations outlook.
- Wrote feature articles and produced marketing materials for various companies.

Art Director and Business Manager
Camper Publications, New York, NY   1991 to 1993
Responsible for creation and presentation of monthly magazine, Happy Listener.
- Managed advertising contracts.

EDUCATION and TRAINING

Master of Art ♦ Journalism
New York University, New York, NY

Bachelor of Art ♦ English ♦ Magna Cum Laude
Charleston University, Charleston, SC

Communication and Leadership Seminar – 1998
Criticism and Discipline Skills for Managers – 1998
Supervisory Skills for New Managers – 1998
Sexual Harassment Workshop for Managers – 1997
Presentation Skills Workshop – 1997

KEYWORDS

Marketing Associate, collateral, advertising assistant, advertising associate, promotions

Regina W. Reddy

113 Bridge Rd. • Las Cruces, NM 85713 • (800) 737-8637 • rreddy@resume.com

Motivated, enthusiastic and personable Sales Representative with experience in Residential Real Estate

PROFILE

■ **Industry Knowledge**: Offer four years in housing industry. Sell Residential Real Estate and assisted with sales for housing developer.

■ **Sales Performer**: Effective in developing leads and determining client needs. Generate 50% of all sales for *Thurston Homes*. Sold $1.5 million within first 12 months.

■ **Skilled Closer**: Excellent communication and interpersonal skills, both articulate and persuasive. Successfully negotiated sales of *Thurston's* homes to individuals and to other real estate agents.

■ **Business Savvy:** Suggested and implemented "zero down" program with additional incentives, which contributed $250,000 in new sale revenues for *Thurston Homes.*

■ **Leadership Qualities**: Member of local Home Improvement Show Board. Managed staff of 22 and set record for performance. Accomplished Eagle Scout.

EXPERIENCE

Real Estate Associate   2002 – Present
Thurston Homes   Las Cruces, NM
Develop effective marketing strategy and drive sales production for this housing construction company. Prospect leads, contact realtors, and respond to individual homebuyers. Determine customer needs; select and present attractive properties and terms. Assist in arranging financing; ensure compliance with all company procedures and industry regulations.

- Significantly increased company sales revenues and market performance.
- Established reputation for providing quality customer service.
- Skillfully utilize computer system for daily accounting and administrative tasks.

Assistant Real Estate Associate   2000 – 2002
Trend Homes   Mesa, AZ
Provided key support to the construction superintendent for residential home developer. Executed walk-throughs of models and new construction with homebuyers. Motivated subcontractors to meet deadlines and performed detail work critical to the closing.

- Contributed to successful closing of eight to 10 homes a month.
- Raised to highest paid Assistant within eight months for consistently performing above and beyond scope of job description.

COMPUTER SKILLS

Microsoft Office Suite

EDUCATION

B.A. in Communications (Minor in Marketing), 2000
University of Arizona, Tucson, AZ

Additional courses, training and professional development include:
Team Builder Conference (2000)

KEYWORDS

Residential real estate, Realtor, realty, home sales, home construction, residential market, real estate development, marketing, sales, sales representative

REFERENCES AVAILABLE ON REQUEST

Scott MacDouglass

65 Bougainvillea Way • Carmel, CA 93287 • 800-737-8637 • smacdouglass@resume.com

Award-winning, experienced real estate sales professional with exceptional customer relationship skills

SUMMARY OF QUALIFICATIONS
- Broad knowledge of commercial and residential properties, including single- and multifamily properties, shopping mall complexes, and office buildings.
- Proven sales performer with expertise in prospecting and closing negotiations.
- Demonstrated administrative knowledge of phones, contracts, accounting, and marketing.
- Excellent communication skills, establishing relationships with management, peers, and clients.
- Good organizational, multitasking, and problem-solving skills.
- Willing to travel and relocate.

WORK HISTORY

ABC Homes, Carmichael, CA   2002 – Present
Real Estate Agent
Provide customer service to both buyers and sellers in real estate transactions.
- Closed over $4 million in property sales year to date.
- Developed and maintained lucrative relationships with key clientele.
- Source new residential clients utilizing newsletters, postcards, and cold calls.

A1 Residency, Sacramento, CA   2000 – 2002
Real Estate Agent
Researched and investigated residences for buyers. Marketed and sold property for sellers.
- Sold three $2.5 million homes annually, reviewing and completing all contract requirements.
- Obtained *Master's Club* designation by Sacramento Board of Realtors for over $2 million in sales.
- Received employee of the year award, 1999.

McMathers and Sons, Elk Grove, CA   1999 – 2000
Real Estate Agent
Facilitated purchase contracts for clients through every phase of sale, including showing property and negotiating loans.
- Achieved *Listing Agent of Year* six times. Earned *Top Selling Agent of Year* five times.

Forest Products, Inc., Sacramento, CA   1997 – 1999
Accounts Receivable Clerk
Researched misappropriated sums and posted payments to appropriate accounts.
- Promoted to Lumber Purchasing Secretary with similar duties in different department.
- Entered credit card charge data. Compiled and mailed monthly statements.
- Performed administrative functions, including receiving calls, filing, and copying.
- Earned *Employee of Month* four times.

EDUCATION and LICENSES
Bachelor's Degree in Business Administration, UC Davis, Sacramento, CA
Broker Certificate, Accredited Real Estate Schools, Fair Oaks, CA
Real Estate License, Anthony School of Real Estate, Sacramento, CA

MEMBERSHIPS
Carmel Board of Realtors, Membership Officer

COMPUTER SKILLS
Windows Operating Systems, WordPerfect, Microsoft Word & Works

KEYWORDS
Real Estate Sales, Sales Associate, Assistant Manager, Sales Manager, Account Executive

Michelle Zurcher

1176 Strawberry Hill • Trenton, NJ 08619 • 800-737-8637 • mzurcher@resume.com

SUMMARY

Highly successful senior manager with boutique real estate investment firm experience, specializing in acquisition and development of commercial and residential properties. Built start-up company from inception through successful operation. Completed four intensive graduate-level CCIM courses at most comprehensive educational resource in commercial real estate industry. Courses include financial, market, user decision, and investment analysis. Superior communication, negotiation, and presentation abilities.

PROFESSIONAL BACKGROUND

1999 – 2003   **Premier Properties,** Stamford, CT
Partner and Senior Vice President
Consultant to multi-billion-dollar corporation for $100 million corporate acquisition; analyzed over 50 commercial leases and performed disposition analyses for approximately 10 million sq. ft. of commercial property.
- Top producer for two consecutive years.
- Identified and targeted new business relationships with corporate office tenants to build and expand market presence.
- Interfaced with corporate executives and C-level decision makers to facilitate real estate transaction process, providing site research, demographic studies, space disposition, corporate budget estimates, and contract negations for clients.
- Screened all vendors, including architects, attorneys, and construction firms.
- Utilized proprietary and industry standard software to render financial analysis models. Managed and refined database daily.

Vice President
Key role in start-up of commercial real estate tenant representation firm.
- Instrumental in site selection, technology research and network construction.
- Actively participated in research and acquisition of employee insurance benefits and recruitment of brokers and administrative staff.
- Coordinated with senior partners to create company brochure; launched direct mail campaigns, achieving company name recognition in community.

1995 – 1997   **Commercial Land Associates,** Stamford, CT
Associate for corporate tenant representation firm.
Directed all aspects of commercial real estate office and warehouse brokerage.
- Made effective presentations to potential clientele, expanding business development. Managed and updated all corporate clients' databases.

1991 – 1995   **Consultant Solutions,** Seattle, WA / Southport, CT
Mortgage Loan Consultant for $40 billion banking institution.
Oversaw financial analysis, appraisals, title researches, and evaluation of credit reports and preunderwrote loans for applicants.
- Remained within top 15% of all producers throughout tenure.
- Originated loans for single- and multifamily homes.
- Developed cold calling campaign and direct mail initiatives to attract prospective borrowers. Established and maintained successful referral business with realtors.
- Successfully introduced portfolio loan concepts to new markets.

EDUCATION and LICENSES

Commercial Real Estate Institute, Stamford, CT, CCIM
Ithaca College, Ithaca, NY, Bachelor of Science, Business Management
New York University, New York, NY, Real Estate Law and Commercial Brokerage
Licensed Real Estate Broker in Connecticut and New York

KEYWORDS: director of operations, operations manager, operations management, developer

Adam Benjamin

3890 Westwood Lake Drive ♦ San Diego, CA 92117 ♦ (800) 737-8637 ♦ abenjamin@resume.com

Award-winning sales professional with exceptional background shattering quotas,
penetrating new territories and increasing both growth and revenue

SUMMARY OF QUALIFICATIONS

➤ Over three years of experience in diverse facets of sales industry, with demonstrated track record of exceeding quotas, effectively negotiating deals and prospecting and closing new clientele.
➤ Adept at increasing sales revenue in assigned territories, continually ranking in top 5%.
➤ Skilled communicator; able to build strong, effective rapport with diverse range of customers.
➤ Outstanding research and business development acumen. Capable of identifying new business opportunities by analyzing market needs and capitalizing on trends before competition.
➤ Motivated to continually create sales through persistence, dedication and resourcefulness.

SKILLS AND ACCOMPLISHMENTS

SALES AND ACCOUNT MANAGEMENT
- Outstanding experience building, developing and managing network of customers.
- Able to generate strong leads through cold calling, referrals and face-to-face meetings.
- Adept at analyzing sales trends and identifying new sales, up-selling and cross-selling opportunities.
- Planned and implemented marketing strategies to target territories effectively and increase business.
- Tracked, monitored and analyzed monthly sales performance data.
- Researched prospect, customer evolution and competitor information. Compiled findings into collateral for use in all sales and marketing efforts.
- Awarded with positions of increasing responsibility due to outstanding sales and management performance.

CUSTOMER RELATIONSHIP MANAGEMENT
- Implemented consultative approach to address clients' needs, continually assessing client relationships and allowing for optimal customer satisfaction.
- Closed sales by addressing client concerns and consistently moving the client toward commitment.
- Developed, trained and managed sales teams, building internal capabilities and ensuring personnel were effectively motivated and provided with key insight into the sales process.
- Managed client accounts from consultation to installation and delivery.

PROFESSIONAL EXPERIENCE

Johnson and Jackson, San Diego, CA   01/02 – Present
Sales Representative

Fine Imports and More, Santa Monica, CA   11/00 – 12/01
Sales Associate *(04/01 – 12/01)*
Assistant Sales Consultant *(11/00 – 04/01)*

General Foods, Los Angeles, CA   02/00 – 11/00
Assistant Sales Representative

COMPUTER SKILLS

Microsoft Word, Excel

EDUCATION

Bachelor of Science, University of California, San Diego

KEYWORDS: account manager, account supervisor, territory manager, strategic alliances, return on investment, ROI, profit and loss, P & L, outside sales, sales territory, customer service, customer relations

PAT ABENOJAR

7 Huntington Street, Apt. 13F • Lincoln, NE 68507 • (800) 737-8637 • pabenojar@resume.com

Award-winning senior account manager with excellent sales skills, extensive marketing experience and solid technical background

SUMMARY OF QUALIFICATIONS

- Proven ability to increase sales and revenue greatly.
- Adept at developing and implementing innovative marketing strategies.
- Strong initiative for expanding new territories and cultivating major accounts.
- Skilled in preparing and conducting presentations and product demonstrations.
- Outstanding quality account manager. Results- and detail-oriented.
- Excellent customer service and client retention standards.
- Technically knowledgeable yet highly self-motivated to learn new concepts.
- Willing to relocate and travel.

PROFESSIONAL EXPERIENCE

Global Networks, Inc., Lincoln, NE   1999 – Present
Senior Sales Engineer responsible for territory sales of over 100 accounts in two states for $90 million heating, ventilation and air-conditioning manufacturing company.
Accomplishments:

- Awarded "Salesperson of the Year" in 2001 for excellence in sales and customer service.
- Produced annual sales increase of 10% over quota to achieve highest revenue in last five years for assigned market.
- Led entire nation in sales for two of three new benchmark products introduced in 2002 and was one of top three sales representatives for third product.
- Excelled with minimal supervision, maintaining strong commitment to company and colleagues.
- Play key role in developing marketing and sales strategies for sophisticated electronic devices aimed at broad market.

Responsibilities:

- Identify and develop diverse client base, using advanced sales techniques and extensive knowledge of industry.
- Provide technical support and training to clientele regarding proper product usage to ensure greater customer satisfaction.
- Conduct successful product and service demonstrations to potential customers and their affiliates.

Access Engineering, Omaha, NE   1997 – 1999
Inside Sales Representative for national distributor of automated controls for HVAC equipment. Prepared sales quotes, documented transactions and filled orders quickly and accurately.

- Handled sales calls using detailed knowledge of product lines from over 40 manufacturers.
- Maintained high level of customer service with over 6000 distributors and wholesalers.
- Acted as NAFTA coordinator, facilitating business and ensuring proper customs documentation for clients in Canada and Mexico.
- Consistently among highest performers in sales volume and administrative skills.
- Promoted from warehouse position after only one year with company.

EDUCATION

Wesleyan University, Lincoln, NE
Bachelor of Science in Marketing and Management, 1996

COMPUTER SKILLS

MS Word, MS Excel, MS PowerPoint, MS Outlook, Internet

Keywords: outside sales representative, account executive, sales manager, director of sales, technical sales, sales engineer, technical account representative, senior account manager, sales coordinator, territory sales manager, regional sales manager

DRAKE BABBSON

9807 Oak Drive • Chagrin Falls, OH 44022 • 800-737-8637 • dbabbson@resume.com

SUMMARY

Results-driven sales manager with over 15 years of successful sales and account supervision experience. Exceptional communication skills; able to develop strong business relationships with coworkers and clientele. Demonstrated history of successfully building, motivating, and leading professional teams to exceed goals and beat deadlines. Strategic thinker with excellent market analysis and new product development experience. Able to anticipate and meet client needs. Outstanding interpersonal skills. Expert at developing human assets and encouraging employees to assume higher levels of responsibility. Authorized to make companywide decisions. Willing to travel.

PROFESSIONAL EXPERIENCE

BANKING ASTRA CORPORATION, Cleveland, OH   2001 – present
National Accounts Manager. Oversee top 10% of nonclient banks for regional ATM-environments corporation, including establishing and improving customer relationships. Ensure corporate profits are met. Authorized to respond to RFPs and other proposals. Assist ATM vendors with account strategies. Handled major vendors, including Diamond Company and Data Corporation.

- Grew company to $8 million in sales, with seven additional clients and projected $3 million in sales in 2003.
- Acquired account from competitor, enhancing sales. Increased gross margin by 74%.
- Closed deal on RFP for key account, with potential 70% gross margin and $4 million in annual sales.
- Implemented installation and service program for western region.
- Established competitive sales strategy and increased national sales presence. Encouraged corporation to anticipate client needs and provide choices in ATM housing design.
- Developed new up-to-date stylized enclosures for NCR and Diebold ATMs.

DELTA COMPANY, Cleveland, OH   1996 – 2000
Account Executive. Recruited and acquired new major accounts for family-owned ATM Delta Company. Created global presence with Website. Established field sales team.

- Increased sales by $4.4 million and company growth margin by 28%, identifying and introducing products to meet consumers' needs. Further increased sales by utilizing third party.
- Acquired and managed two major West Coast ATM developers.
- Designed, promoted, and implemented ABC program for wall-embedded surround products.
- Separated division start-up dedicated to building modular banking facilities. Designed floor plans and elevations and created initial marketing and strategic sales plans.
- Worked closely with various ATM services to create specialized fast-track developments for ATM through-the-wall units.

FINANCIAL SECURITY SYSTEM MANAGEMENT, Cleveland, OH   1975 – 1995
General Manager, Buffalo Task Force. Accountable for division operations for $75 million bank security system manufacturer. Ensured delivery of sales, accounting, and customer service.

- Moved division from last place among corporate status to consistent slot in top 5%.
- Brought in premier account, contributing $11 million annually to company.
- Member of new product development team. New products patented under corporate umbrella.
- Developed and implemented specialized account team to acquire large-volume consumers.
- Authored corporationwide national accounts program.
- Assisted sales engineers and managers in exceeding established goals.
- Provided electronic drawings for banking industry, improving product approval process.
- Introduced numerous computerized concepts to the facility, increasing productivity. Made computerized delivery and installation programs available for in-house and client use.

(Continued…)

COMPUTER SKILLS
PC, Microsoft ME Office Suite, Lotus 123, db3, multiple banking-industry platforms, including automation and system integration; skilled in base 2 and TCP/IP ATM Communication systems, Internet-savvy

AWARDS
Sales Leader, Delta Company, 1999 and 2000
Top Productive Region, Financial Security System Management, 1985, 1991, 1993
Top Automated Distribution Handler, 1994 through 1995

AFFILIATIONS
American Safe and Lock Mechanical Engineers
United Lock Safety Board of America
Mechanical Adjustments for International Banks

EDUCATION
HOW TO BE A SALES TRAINER. Certified Corporate Sales Trainer
LEADERSHIP SKILLS TODAY. Received first place course ranking

UNIVERSITY OF IOWA, Des Moines, IA
Bachelor of Science, Mechanical Engineering

PUBLICATIONS
Cash Withdrawal in a SAFE Environment, 1996
Locking Systems Applications, 1984

MILITARY SERVICE
U.S. ARMY, 1970 – 1974. Received numerous awards for conduct during combat.

KEYWORDS
Sales manager, account executive, senior manager, director, VP, Assistant VP, banking

Jennifer Kim

408 Oleander Road • Gainesville, FL 32602 • 800-737-8637 • jkim@resume.com

Ambitious and experienced Educator with detailed knowledge of international relations and nonprofit fund-raising needs

SUMMARY OF QUALIFICATIONS

- Over two years of international teaching experience through Peace Corps programs.
- Master's-level education in Diplomacy and International Relations.
- Successful grant writer able to coordinate multiple community programs and projects.
- Proficient at establishing educational curriculums, such as computer training workshops, English language classes, and pen pal programs.
- Proven self-starter; adept at adjusting to new situations and diverse groups.
- Excellent written communication and oral presentation skills.

WORK HISTORY

ABC ORGANIZATION, Egypt   *10/01 – 012/03*
Community Development Volunteer (10/02 – 12/03)
Collaborated with village community center staff and members to implement humanitarian projects sponsored by several international development groups.
- Increased funding by interpreting proposals to English and submitting appropriate documents to philanthropic organizations.
- Secured grant to establish computer-training center, which strengthened marketable skills and addressed host country's need for Information Technology and skilled workforce.
- Created alternative and original fund-raising activities to increase financial resources.
- Directly obtained additional funds for local village garden and water conservation project from Canada Fund.
- Designed and conducted training workshops for community center members.
- Conceived and administered three-tier English language class for 20 workers of local nature reserve to expand staff/tourist communications.

Teacher of English as Foreign Language (10/01 – 10/02)
Taught English to students in grades four through eight at Secondary School for Girls.
- Improved instruction level and curriculum and facilitated transfer of skills to teachers of host community.
- Coordinated pen pal program for extracurricular English class, expanding student knowledge of geographical history and fostering use of English skills.
- Founded initial area summer camp for 25 female students to increase English skills through various communication activities.
- Established additional summer camp in neighboring village due to success of original program.

EDUCATION

Master of Arts, School of Diplomacy and International Relations
University of Florida, Gainesville, FL, 2001

Bachelor of Arts, Middle Eastern Religions, Dickinson College, Carlisle, PA

SKILLS

Intermediate–High Arabic language proficiency
Windows, Microsoft Office, Internet browsers

KEYWORDS: program coordinator, grant manager, grant coordinator, grant writer, fund-raising, project management, activism, educational program coordinator, nongovernment, nonprofit organizations, international relations

JANICE T. RALFAMA

3211 Acorn Way • San Jose, CA 95117 • (800) 737-8637 • jralfama@resume.com

Detail-oriented college graduate with organizational skills seeks challenging position in Conference and Events Planning

SUMMARY OF QUALIFICATIONS

- Expertise in coordinating and supervising activities. Very punctual.
- Excellent decision-making ability.
- Work well with people of different backgrounds and ethnicities.
- Enjoy working in a fast-paced environment. Highly attentive to detail.
- Strong communication skills, both written and oral.
- Fast learner. Creative problem solver.
- Friendly team player with professional manner.
- Able to travel as needed

PROFESSIONAL ACHIEVEMENTS

ORGANIZATIONAL
- Plan educational and social activities for children before and after school at California Children's Community.
- Take initiative to correct problems that need immediate attention.
- As Head Teacher, hold weekly meetings with teachers in order to field ideas for new and better programs for students and to review center's expectations.
- Effectively communicate ideas and concepts to students, parents, and teachers.
- Arrange monthly educational bulletin boards, showcasing cultures, inventions, and ideas.
- Promote and provide a positive, active, and engaging environment for children.
- Successfully manage multiple activities simultaneously.

SUPERVISORY
- Oversee opening and shutdown operations of center.
- Assume management responsibilities of center in director's absence.

EMPLOYMENT HISTORY

ST. MARY'S HIGH SCHOOL, San Rafael, CA   6/97 – present
Head Teacher for an after school quality enrichment program for children.
- Promoted from Teacher to Head Teacher in one year.

EDUCATION

UNIVERSITY OF CALIFORNIA, SAN JOSE, San Jose, CA
Master of Education, 1997. Key courses: Communications, Psychology, Sociology

SAN JOSE STATE UNIVERSITY, San Jose, CA
Bachelor of Arts, 1995. Key courses: Communications, Psychology, Sociology

COMPUTER SKILLS

PC, Mac, MS Windows 95, MS Word, Internet Savvy

LANGUAGES

American Sign Language (ASL), Signing Exact English (SEE)

EMPLOYER COMMENT

 "Janice has many great qualities as an employee. She is very responsible and reliable in carrying out her duties…she has displayed great leadership skills. … Her motivation and creativity are great assets to her job skills and she is a joy to work with."
Rose Raymond, Principal, St. Mary's High School

Additional references furnished upon request

Keywords: instructor, educator, teacher, college, liberal arts

Henry Maglione

110 Copper Street, #3 • Rohnert Park, CA 94928 • 800-737-8637 • hmaglione@resume.com

HIGHLIGHTS OF QUALIFICATIONS

Accomplished career of over 10 years in **Theater Arts** includes **university-level teaching**, direction of more than 50 theatrical productions, and acting in various plays; complemented by **Masters of Arts Degree in Education.** Open **teaching style allows** maximum expression and learning of students; provide the learning tools, motivational support and commitment necessary for the advancement of student education. Demonstrate sensitivity and openness to **diverse students** of culture, age, gender, and learning styles; strategically take casting risks to **enhance experience of actor** and **audience** during theatrical productions.

AREAS OF EXPERIENCE

Adjunct Professor	Theatre, Dramatic Arts	Team Environment
Diverse Student Base	Children's Theater, Shakespeare	Acting Methods
Lesson Plans	Theater Productions – Directing, Acting	Interpersonal Skills

WORK HISTORY

Diablo Valley Community College, Pleasant Hill, CA   2002 – present
Adjunct Professor and Stage Director
Teach introduction to theater and beginning acting classes; student base composed of various cultures and ages.
- Develop and implement lesson plans; teach different acting theories catering to diverse learning styles.
- Directed major high-profile stage production with 45 actors and 164 attendees.
- Recognized by tenure staff for collaborative abilities.

St. Avery High School, San Rafael, CA   1996 – 2002
Drama Teacher
Oversaw three daily classes of over 35 students, teaching all aspects of drama and literature to elective students.
- Dramatic readings range from Homer to Arthur Miller and include analysis and comprehension training.
- Create curriculum, test, and homework assignments.
- Test students on monthly basis, including oral exams, written finals, and understanding of theory.

District of Santa Rosa, Santa Rosa, CA   1993 – 1996
Substitute Teacher
Taught high school student in all subjects, including English, Mathematics, and Science.

Sonoma Valley Shakespeare Festival, Sonoma, CA   1990 – 1993
Founder/Artistic & Executive Director
Relied on administrative and diplomatic skills to manage budget and production of festival and numerous theatrical productions.

THEATRICAL BACKGROUND

Odyssey Children's Theatre / Odyssey Stage, Sonoma and Santa Rosa, CA   1984 – present
Founder/Artistic & Executive Director
Santa Rosa Players, Santa Rosa, CA   2001 – present
Board Member
Sonoma Valley Shakespeare Festival, Sonoma, CA   1992 – 2001
Founder/Artistic & Executive Director
Sonoma County Theatre Alliance, Sonoma, CA   1987 – 1992
Cofounder/Member

EDUCATION

M.F.A   Master of Education, University of California at Davis, Davis, CA
B.A.   Bachelor of Arts Degree in Theater Arts, Sonoma State University, Rohnert Park, CA

Keywords: Instructor, Assistant Professor, Trainer, Mentor, Head Teacher, Fine Arts, Dramatic Arts

FELISA ROSARIO

69 Old Grandfather Way • Oahu, HI 96815 • 800-737-8637 • frosario@resume.com

***Award-winning telecommunications professional with record of achievement
in global technology***

SUMMARY OF QUALIFICATIONS

- Proven ability to manage complex, multi-million-dollar projects, including government contracts.
- Excellent crisis manager. Led corporate emergency response team after September 11 tragedy.
- Superior customer liaison; able to manage relationships for maximum productivity and success.
- Experienced team leader, motivator and mentor.
- Bright, creative strategic thinker as well as problem solver.

PROFESSIONAL EXPERIENCE

Silicon Alley Services, Oahu, HI   **09/99 – Present**

Customer Service Associate/FTS 2001 Business Office *(09/00 – Present)*
Create and implement strategies, programs and processes for $756 million telecommunications contract with federal General Services Administration (GSA).

- As liaison to GSA FTS 2001 program team, facilitate meetings and other communications between company and its government customers.
- Led emergency response team that partnered with GSA on technology management after September 11 tragedy. Represented company in accepting public recognition from GSA.
- Execute reporting and monthly trend analysis on problem-related customer interface.
- Conduct training programs for new employees.

Assistant Manager/Global Technical Service Center *(12/99 – 09/00)*
Managed team of professionals providing technical service and support to customers.

- Developed and implemented innovative troubleshooting procedures for FTS 2001 program.
- Facilitated successful working relationships between service teams and account managers.

Technical Service Specialist Team Coleader *(09/99 – 12/99)*
Coordinated activity within service operation to ensure seamless service delivery to customers.

- Provided customers with timely, complete and accurate updates of account status.

EDUCATION

University of San Francisco, San Francisco, CA
Bachelor of Science, 2000
Major: Communications

COMPUTER SKILLS

Microsoft Office, Access, Word, Excel, proprietary software, Internet, E-mail

LANGUAGES

Bilingual fluency in Spanish.

AWARDS AND ACTIVITIES

Government Markets Employee of the Quarter, 3Q 2001
First in Service, 1999
Circle of Honor, 3Q 1999
Women in Technology Protege Mentor Award

KEYWORDS

Technology, data management, telecommunications, customer service, program management, facilitation, telecom, wireless

ERIC R. SMITH

874 Colts Boulevard • Indianapolis, IN 46204 • 800-737-8637 • esmith@resume.com

---

Enthusiastic, highly motivated Telecommunications Technician with expertise in circuits and switches

Summary of Qualifications

- Over six years of experience in telecommunications with special focus on switches, hardware, software and transmission.
- Problem solver who persistently follows up until issue is resolved. Exceptional troubleshooter.
- Friendly with positive attitude. Proven team player.
- Ambitious and hardworking, with commitment to excellence.
- Effective communicator, both written and verbal.
- Highly attentive to detail. Effectively manage multiple tasks simultaneously.
- Good listener with outgoing, friendly demeanor and good sense of humor.

Technical Knowledge and Professional Accomplishments

- Circuit testing and Installing: DS-3 circuits with T-Berd 310; OC-3, OC-12, OC-48 and OC-192 circuits with Digital Lightwave; SDH with Hewlett Packard 717 OmniBerd; CAT-5 LAN lines with handheld testers; DS-1 with T-Berd 310 and 224; DS-3 coax and DS-1 wire cross-connects plus fiber for OC SDH level circuits and CAT-5 cable for LAN connections.
- Skilled in utilizing circuit layout reports to facilitate cable/fiber runs and testing.
- Coordinated with NOC and CLEC personnel in testing and circuit runs.
- Superior hardware maintenance ability in card swaps, power cabling and alarm wiring on various equipment, including Nortel OP Tera, Passport, OC-48 and OC-192 bays, Cisco (Cerent) 15454 boxes, Ciena Corestream, ADC DSX and VAM shelves, Cisco 3600, 7500 and 12000 series routers and 1900 and 5505 series switches, Juniper M40, Bay Networks, Redback and Cosine routers, Ascend and Nortel ATM switches.
- Effectively worked with generator and battery backup systems in military and commercial environments.
- Excellent understanding of breaker distribution bays and Nortel DC power plants.
- Successfully ran and tested two-wire phone connections (private line) off junction boxes connected to local switch.
- Coordinated trunk connections between local switch and POP site in flexible secure network.
- Hands-on experience with orderwire, encryption devices, multiplexers, phone number databases, packet switching.
- Successfully troubleshoot local phone problems, identify and take corrective course of action.

Work Experience

GPS SOLUTIONS, Indianapolis, IN *Field Engineer*	03/01 – present
NETWORK PRODUCTS AND SERVICES, Indianapolis, IN *POP Technician III*	07/99 – 12/00
UNITED STATES ARMY, Fort Hood, TX *Network Switching Systems Operator/Maintainer*	04/98 – 01/99
WIRELESS ENGINEERING INTELLIGENCE, INC., Austin, TX *Control Room Coordinator,* (04/97 – 04/98) *Cathode Ray Tube Operator (CRT),* (10/97 – 04/97)	10/97 – 04/98

Professional Training and Education

Cisco 15454 Training Program Certificate, Cisco Systems, 2000
Introduction to Cisco Router Configuration, Cisco Systems, 2000

Leadership Subjects, U.S. Army Training School, 1999
Electronic Switching Systems Operator Course, U.S. Army Training School, 1999
Network Switching Systems Operator/Maintainer, U.S. Army, 1998

CYBILL V. WASHINGTON

12G Halesite Lane • Detroit, MI 48910 • 800-737-8637 • cwashington@resume.com

Award-winning, highly experienced telecommunications technician trained in circuit testing and installation for nationwide wireless services

SUMMARY OF QUALIFICATIONS

Extensive and progressive experience in telecommunications, including wireless, optical fiber, and telephone communications. Possess strong analytical and troubleshooting skills with ability to quickly identify areas of weakness and implement comprehensive solutions. Easily adapt to new technologies and procedures; in-depth knowledge of cutting-edge tools. Able to interface with clients and technicians on all levels. Superior communication skills with unique capacity to translate complex jargon into easily understandable language.

PROFESSIONAL EXPERIENCE

SURVEYORS OF DETROIT, DETROIT, MI   1999 – 2003
Site Survey Technician
Conducted nationwide site surveys from Maine to California to assess efficiency and productivity of corporate services.
- Inventoried equipment and assessed overall circuiting utilization for 200 branch offices.
- Drafted diagrams and drawings for engineers and planners to determine equipment location.
- Received Employee of the Year Award in 2002.

Transition Technician
Replaced obsolete equipment with new technology; reoptioned routers, moved jumpers, and rewired circuits.
- Created and implemented administrative forms, increasing product awareness.
- Facilitated customer transition in service changeovers, using exemplary negotiation and communication skills.

TELECOM LIMITLESS, Detroit, MI   1990 – 1999
Technician
Performed extensive fieldwork at central office.
- Tested SS7 circuits and constructed seven-foot environments.
- Built comprehensive shelving system to organize and house data equipment.

LOCAL AREA NETWORK, Lansing, MI   1988 – 1990
Communications Technician
Processed trouble reports from customers and work centers, diagnosing problem circuits.
- Utilized React, N.M.A. to remotely test all digital circuits including 1.544-megabit, subrate 56KB/9.6KB, 4.8KB, 2.4, 911, frame relay, sonnet rings, ISDN, and other voice grade circuits.
- Generated reports based on collected data and dispatched to respective areas.

1A Craft Position
Oversaw daily work list, adapting to increasing database computer usage.
- Instrumental in testing and installing circuits.
- Scheduled testing and transfer of T1 circuits from copper cable facilities to fiber, successfully converting premier clients.

EDUCATION

A.A.S. in Engineering and Communications, Detroit Community College, Detroit, MI

COMPUTER SKILLS

Frame Relay, ISDN, T1, T-bert 211, 310, TPI 108-109, Sonnet Rings; MS Word, Excel; Visio

KEYWORDS: field technician, WAN/LAN, data communication systems, coding, fiber optic

12

The Information Technology Resume

The Information Technology (IT) resume is a highly specialized document that is quite different from the other resumes we've discussed. The IT resume uses specific technical language as its driving force, showing hirers how you can meet the needs of today's changing marketplace.

The IT industry has undergone radical changes over the last 20 years. From the beginning of widespread computer use by consumers in the 1980s to the dot-com craze in the late 1990s and beyond, IT has affected every aspect of the marketplace. More than ever employers are turning to IT specialists to help them automate positions, secure internal operations, streamline workflow processes, and maximize employees' productivity by training staff members on proprietary software.

Unfortunately, the end of the 1990s witnessed massive layoffs in the technical sector, with the telecommunications industry perhaps being the most heavily affected. As the competition among IT professionals is especially fierce, partly as a result of layoffs and partly because of an increasing level of qualified candidates in the marketplace, the need for a professional resume has become essential.

INDUSTRY DIVERSITY

The IT field is extremely diverse and vast, with specializations ranging from help-desk support and Web site design to network administration and coding.

Perhaps more than is the case in any other industry, IT's complexity and variety of positions makes resume writing a process that needs to be clear and efficient. IT professionals need to know what hiring managers are looking for in their unique resumes. This chapter is intended to help technical professionals create attractive, effective documents that stand out from the competition.

Hiring managers are looking for IT professionals who have extensive technical skills as well as demonstrable people skills. A common mistake IT professionals make is to underestimate the importance of noncomputer skills such as the ability to communicate effectively and collaborate with coworkers at all levels. The key to creating a successful IT resume is highlighting today's in-demand skills and understanding the needs of the marketplace. Including both hard skills and soft skills allows you to position yourself as a strong candidate, and building a twenty-first-century IT resume is the first step in this process.

CHOOSING THE RIGHT FORMAT

All successful resumes will sell your strongest skills and achievements within 10 seconds, and the IT resume is no different. Your strongest selling points must be organized clearly in the right format for a hirer to identify your talents and traits. There are few rules governing the correct format to use.

Use the chronological format if you

- Have had progressively responsible positions and promotions
- Are applying for jobs similar to your current or last job

Use the functional format if you

- Have multiple employment gaps in your work history
- Are a recent college graduate with no paid work experience
- Are switching industries or careers

Use the combination format if you

- Have extensive work experience as a consultant
- Can better display your project management experience in this style

---

To view different formats and styles, see Chapter 6.

Choosing the best format is the foundation of creating a professional resume. The next seven steps will guide you in selecting and organizing your strongest selling points to develop a winning resume.

STEP 1: THE HEADER

The header is the first section at the top of a resume, and it contains your name, address, phone number, and e-mail address. You also can include your cell phone, fax, or pager number in this section, but that information is optional. You can list one or two relevant certifications next to your name to highlight valuable certifications in your area of expertise, but make sure those certifications support your professional goal; if they do not, personalize each resume according to the position you are applying for or just list your certifications and degrees in the appropriate section on the resume. For example, if you are a systems engineer, your name may be presented as "John Doe, MCSE."

Separate your name from your contact information with a solid line, as we discussed in Chapter 6. Each component of your contact information should be separated with a symbol. For example, your header may look like this:

John Doe, MCSE

225 Adams Drive • New York, NY 10013 • H: (212) 222-2222 • C: (917) 222 2222 • jdoe@resume.com

Double- and triple-check that your contact information is spelled correctly. If your e-mail address is incorrect, a prospective employer will not spend time and energy tracking you down no matter how skilled you appear on paper.

For additional tips on creating effective headers, refer to Chapter 6.

STEP 2: THE HEADLINE

A headline sells your greatest assets in one to two sentences. It appears at the top of the resume, just below the header, and acts as the main advertisement for what you can offer an employer. This can include years of experience, awards, certifications, and technical expertise and is usually the first area a prospective employer will examine when reviewing your resume. It's here where you have to hook them and motivate them to keep reading.

IT Headline Examples

➤ A highly analytical, certified network administrator with eight years of expertise and extensive skills in QA, technical support, and systems repair

➤ Creative, motivated Java programmer with five-year proven track record developing cutting-edge programs for dynamic software products

➤ Dedicated technical support specialist with solid background in troubleshooting systems, updating networks, and providing on- and off-site support for over 500 end users

A great way to start a headline is to begin with an adjective modifying your professional objective or job title:

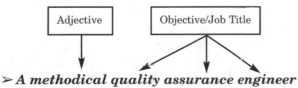

➤ *A methodical quality assurance engineer*

Next, you can add your strongest selling points, including years of experience or relevant certifications:

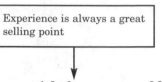

Experience is always a great selling point

> *A methodical quality assurance engineer with four years of hands-on experience*

Although the headline above is quite strong and could stand alone, you can bolster a headline with additional strengths and traits, including areas of expertise or skill:

Additional information can be a benefit to your headline

> *A methodical quality assurance engineer with four years of hands-on experience and proven expertise testing and debugging complex telecommunications systems*

Do not place a period at the end of the headline.

STEP 3: THE SUMMARY OF QUALIFICATIONS

The Summary of Qualifications section follows the headline and highlights your top five to eight selling points in bulleted statements. This section can include years of experience, number of employees you manage, industry awards and recognition, special training, technical skills, network users you support, and "soft skills" (communication skills, organizational skills, etc.).

As most hirers spend only 10 seconds reviewing a resume, your resume stands a good chance of being rejected if it does not impress them. Therefore, a strong Summary of Qualifications must encapsulate your most attractive traits and accomplishments.

What to Include in the Summary of Qualifications

For IT professionals the Summary of Qualifications should contain a mix of technical knowledge and soft skills, providing a hirer with a well-rounded picture of an applicant's qualifications. To convey to an employer that you're too valuable to pass by, show precisely how your previous experience affected the company's bottom line, using quantifiable results if possible. Some areas to emphasize can include the following:

✓ Specific industry expertise:
   Exceptional background in diverse facets of IT and MIS, including software development, database administration, and application development.

✓ Certifications and training:

Extensive professional development includes Microsoft Certified Systems Engineer (MCSE) and Microsoft Certified Professional (MCP).

✓ Projects you've completed:

Created and implemented database to catalog and track evidence for Atlanta Police Department, virtually eliminating lost and stolen items.

✓ Planning and implementation results:

Developed migration plan to move over 100 databases from FoxPro to SQL Server 6.5, improving SQL architecture capacity and increasing available current records.

✓ Systems or applications you've developed to streamline operations:

Developed automated real-time pricing tools for sales force, creating centralized system with no downtime from remote sites.

✓ Employee training:

Taught staff dBase and Visual FoxPro during company acquisition.

For an in-depth explanation of the Summary of Qualifications, review Chapter 6.

The following are a few ground rules to follow in developing your Summary of Qualifications:

- **Prioritize your selling points in order of importance.** Specific and quantifiable skills (10 years of experience) and certifications should precede soft skills (communication skills).
- **Always end your bullets with periods.** Although fragments are acceptable in a resume, a period at the end of the bullet helps contain the information you are highlighting. If your spell checker indicates that your bullets are fragments, don't worry: Using fragments is a common way to write professional resumes.

Summary of Qualification Examples

SUMMARY OF QUALIFICATIONS

- Over 12 years of quality assurance experience, specializing in telecommunications industry.
- Significant troubleshooting and debugging background.
- Possess extensive Java development experience. Skilled in Linux and HTML.
- Expert knowledge of developing and implementing patches to ensure seamless operation for company and end users.
- Highly successful background in testing extensive databases and writing new code to execute daily fixes.
- Excellent communication, interpersonal, and presentation skills.

SUMMARY OF QUALIFICATIONS

❑ More than 14 years of progressive experience in software development.

❑ Solid understanding of all aspects of management information systems, obtained through aggressive formal and independent studies.

❑ In-depth comprehension of cutting-edge technologies and methodologies, implementing business, scientific, and technical applications on private, corporate, and global levels.

❑ Recognized for outstanding analytical abilities in resolving complex issues, exhibiting sharp aptitude for "out-of-box" theories, as well as unprecedented vision and foresight in seeing completed project from conception to completion.

❑ Able to build strong, working relationships with clientele, managers, and employees.

❑ Fluent in German, with basic comprehension of French.

❑ Results-oriented with superb interpersonal, organizational, and communication skills.

SUMMARY OF QUALIFICATIONS

- Five years of experience in networking systems and infrastructure management.

- Diverse professional development in systems setup, administration, support and training.

- Strong troubleshooting, installation and configuration skills.

- Strategic thinker and planner; adept at effectively overseeing the design and execution of systems, projects and solutions.

- Exceptional focus and follow-through abilities, with track record of efficiency and productivity.

- Detail-oriented multitasker, with strong organizational and managerial abilities.

STEP 4: TECHNICAL SKILLS AND CERTIFICATIONS

In the IT industry your computer skills will play a dominant role in the decision-making process. Your languages, applications, networking tools, and platforms are great assets, and we recommend listing them in a clear location on your resume after the Summary of Qualifications or Professional Experience section.

Prioritizing Your Computer Skills

Extensive computer skills should always be categorized and prioritized according to the specialty or field you are pursuing. For example, if you are a programmer, you should list your programming languages at the top of your computer skills list. Popular ways to prioritize technical skills include listing separate categories for hardware, software, programming languages, and operating systems. Depending on your expertise, you may want to merge categories or include more distinct sections.

> The most important aspect of the technical skills section is to delineate your proficiencies in a manner immediately recognizable to prospective employers.

Be sure to spell your technical proficiencies correctly. You would be surprised how often this section is overlooked by IT professionals. Typos are one of the most common mistakes people make when writing resumes, and spelling errors are a primary reason why employers reject resumes. Double-check the spelling of all technical proficiencies; if you are not certain about the spelling, there are many online resources that can provide the right answer in seconds. We recommend www.RefDesk.com for spelling and definitions; it is especially helpful if you are unsure about which category you should use to list a specific computer skill.

Computer Skills Examples

COMPUTER SKILLS

Operating Systems:	Novell Network, MS DOS, MS Windows 95/98/ME/2000/NT Workstation/NT Server/XP Home/XP Pro/CE, Pocket PC 2000/2002, Palm, UNIX
Networking:	Token Ring Ethernet, TCP/IP, IPX/SPX, PPP, T1/T3/DS3, SS7, ISUP
Hardware:	Processors/RAM/HDD/FDD/Interface Cards /Modems/SCSI, PC, Printers, Scanners, Zip Driver, Motherboards
Software:	NMS, PC Anywhere, Telegence (Wireless Billing System), CARE (Wireless Billing System), Microsoft Office, Word Perfect Suite, Corel Draw, Adobe Photoshop, Harvard Graphics, Oracle

TECHNICAL EXPERTISE

OPERATING SYSTEMS:
- MS-DOS
- Windows 3.X, 9.X, NT 4.0 Workstation, 2000
- Windows NT 4.0 Server, 2000 Server, 2000 Advanced Server
- Novell Netware 5.0
- ZEN works

NETWORKING:
- Windows NT Administration
- Windows NT to Windows 2000 Migration (certified)
- Installation and configuration of multiple network hardware, including:
  - Routers, Hubs, Cat 5 Cable, Fiber Optics, Ethernet Cards
- Configuration troubleshooting and maintenance of:
  - TCP/IP, WINS/ DNS, IPX/SPX, NAT, ICS, RIP, OSPF, subnetting
- Routing & Remote Access Administration
- Remote Installation Services
- Knowledge of security protocols:
  - PPTP, L2TP, IPSec, MPE, MSCHAP

HARDWARE:

Repaired and upgraded numerous computers, replacing motherboards, HD, memory, video cards, network interface cards and drives.

- o X86i-based machines from 286 to Pentium IV, including Celeron and AMD CPUs
- o Installation and configuration of various wireless Ethercards, including:
  - ▪ 3com, Lynksys, SMC
- o Installation and configuration of various ISA/PCI/AGP cards
- o Cat 5 and fiber optic cabling
- o Print server configuration and maintenance

SOFTWARE:

- o Microsoft Office XP/2000/97
- o Microsoft Outlook XP/2000/98
- o Adobe PhotoShop 6

Certifications

Your certifications should be listed as a separate category, as it is vital to draw added attention to valuable selling points in a competitive industry. For all certifications, list the full name as well as the acronym and the date you received the certification.

Certifications Examples

CERTIFICATIONS
- Microsoft Certified Professional (MCP), 2002
- Cisco Systems Administrator (CSA), 2001
- Microsoft Certified System Administrator (MCSA), 2000

CERTIFICATIONS
- Microsoft Certified System Engineer (MCSE), 1997
- CompTIA A+, 1997
- Microsoft Certified System Administrator (MCSA), 1997
- Certified Novell Administrator (CAN), 1996

STEP 5: PROFESSIONAL EXPERIENCE

The Professional Experience section makes up the bulk of your resume and informs a potential employer about your accomplishments, capabilities, and professional duties. If you are using the chronological format, organize your background by employer and date. For functional resumes, your professional experience is divided into skill sets, followed by a work history section consisting of your employers, job titles, and dates of employment (see Chapter 3).

As with the Summary of Qualifications, the key to creating an effective Professional Experience section is to prioritize your bullets according to your most important skills and achievements.

As with all professional resumes, the Professional Experience section of an IT resume combines job responsibilities with accomplishment statements. The difference between the two is that a responsibility statement explains your day-to-day duties and an accomplishment statement describes the specific results you achieved. These results can be in the form of increased efficiency, productivity, and revenues or decreased expenditures, downtime, and waste. A good tip for creating effective responsibility statements is to begin your sentence with "Responsible for" and complete that statement with a list of your general duties. Another good way to distinguish the two is to write the responsibility statement in paragraph form and the accomplishment statements in the form of bullets, making those significant achievements stand out on your resume.

Start with quantifiable results, such as years of experience or number of employees managed, followed by less pertinent responsibilities and results.

Some areas to highlight in this section include the following:

✓ **Years of experience:** Over 10 years of experience creating diverse software applications and database designs.

✓ **Day-to-day responsibilities and tasks:** Responsible for resolving computer difficulties by analyzing and identifying errors and documenting operational procedures.

✓ **Innovations or improvements you were responsible for:** Implemented protocol translation task, converting transactions from proprietary bus protocol to SYMAX Ethernet.

✓ **People you interacted with and supported:** Routinely met with clients to define needs in order to create interface specifications.

✓ **Any awards based on performance:** Received "Employee of the Year Award," 1995.

Professional Experience Example (Chronological)

Wayne Electric, New York, NY   1997 – 1999

Project Analyst
Managed third-party development, implementing connection between SAP, Manufacturing Execution System/Enterprise Resource Planning (MES/ERP) system, and PLC to import and export data.

- Wrote Web-based Java Client to access Program Logic Controller (PLC) Device Descriptions through 16-bit COM server.
- Created custom decoder for Sniffer Pro Network Analyzer (C++), effectively reducing data packet analysis life cycle from 20 minutes to one second per packet.
- Constructed test strategy to verify functionality of third-party hubs, switches, and redundancy manager with Fred's Electric Ethernet products.
- Developed MFC and ATL C++ COM clients with GUI to test COM servers.
- Implemented protocol translation task (coded in C), converting transactions from proprietary bus protocol to SYMAX Ethernet.
- Documented application program interface to back plane driver software.
- Analyzed object-oriented Supervisory Control and Data Acquisition (SCADA) development framework to interface with namespace databases.

Professional Experience Example (Functional)

PROFESSIONAL EXPERIENCE

Technical Management

- Maximize overall business by leveraging traditional and innovative technologies based on client requirements.
- Create stable and scaleable e-business environments: communication, data intelligence, OLAP, Web, and client/server systems.
- Launched information technology department and performed staff training as founding MIS Director.
- Performed business requirements advisory, established partnerships, created operational initiatives, and prioritized user management requests.
- Revised overall disaster recovery plan by reducing system recovery time by 83%. Fine-tuned system to increase throughput more than 25% while reducing performance drain by over 90%.
- Redesigned retail price changes, increasing timesaving by 50% and improving accuracy 85%.
- Increased system availability hours while decreasing cost by reducing batch from eight to four hours.
- Improved data integrity using forensic investigation and audit techniques to identify security breaches, misuse, and fraud.

Business Management

- Develop and implement effective strategic initiatives to support management, budgets, and infrastructure.
- Recruit, motivate, and retain highly talented workforce.
- Solidify realization of business goals by defining and establishing enterprise-aligned goals, objectives, and processes.
- Maximize competitive edge through evaluation and implementation of business best practices.
- Create technology business processes, review emerging technologies, formulate infrastructure, and identify outstanding intellectual capital.

Client Management

- Establish and cultivate relationships with strategic partners, including raising $45 million in seed money.
- Simultaneously direct up to 50 technical engagements.
- Consistently exceed client goals and expectations.

STEP 6: EDUCATION

As with industry certifications, the Education section can be listed immediately beneath the Computer Skills section if your degree is relevant to your professional goals. For example, if you have a bachelor's degree in computer science from 1995, you can list your education section after your computer skills section because your education lends merit to your credentials.

However, if your education is in a field different from your professional goals, you can list it below your Professional Experience section. Include the name of the college or university you attended, your major, and your grade point average (GPA) if it was 3.0 or better. If you did not graduate, list the number of credits completed if 60 or above or the general coursework you took.

Education Example

EDUCATION
NEW YORK UNIVERSITY, STERN SCHOOL OF BUSINESS
Master of Business Administration, *Information Systems and Marketing*, 1996

HOFSTRA UNIVERSITY
Bachelor of Business Administration, *International Business*, 1994
GPA: 3.8/4.0, Magna Cum Laude

STEP 7: KEYWORDS

Keywords are a relatively new component of resumes that have appeared only over the last five years, but as technology has become an integral aspect of the hiring process, they are an essential element in every resume. If you're not handing your resume directly to a friend, make sure it has a keywords section (see Chapter 7).

Hirers gather nonelectronic resumes via fax and mail and receive electronic resumes via e-mail and job boards. These resumes are stored in a database where hiring personnel can use keywords to sort resumes and eliminate those which do not meet the criteria, potentially reducing a stack of 1000 applications to a select few. If your resume does not contain these keywords, there's a good chance you won't be called in for an interview.

You should include in the keywords section alternative job titles, key responsibilities, acronyms, technical knowledge, and industry jargon not already included in the resume.

Keywords Section Examples

Keywords: Junior Mechanical Engineer, Junior Maintenance Engineer, Assistant, Associate, Technician

KEYWORDS

Insurance, benefits specialist, general, executive secretary, human resources, medical, health care, dental, office management, office manager, branch manager, senior benefits administrator, payroll, business

FRANK K. JOHNS

24 Andover Way • Sonoma, CA 94947 • (800) 737-8637 • fjohns@resume.com

*Experienced and analytical IT professional with background
in systems administration and data center management*

SUMMARY OF QUALIFICATIONS

➢ Eleven years of Information Technology experience with current expertise in Windows 2000 Active Directory installation and management.

➢ Excellent business acumen with background developing and administering budgets, negotiating contracts, and managing vendors and contractors.

➢ Specialty in installing, monitoring, and troubleshooting Compaq and Dell servers.

➢ Successfully managed design and implementation of large fault-tolerant database servers.

➢ Extremely capable in fast-paced, chaotic business environments.

➢ Analytical, dependable, and willing to work long hours.

➢ Team player with excellent communications skills.

➢ Able to work well with large groups of people in face-to-face meeting environments as well as teleconferencing.

COMPUTER SKILLS

Hardware: Dell hardware, servers, laptops, desktops, SANs, EMC & Dell San Hardware
Servers: Compaq servers, SQL 7.0
Software: Dell Open Manage, HP OpenView, F5/Big IP Load Balancers, Microsoft Office; Microsoft Exchange
Networking: Network Appliance N.A.S., Advocent & Freevision KVM Switching, TCP/IP, LAN/WAN
Data Center Facilities: Generator, UPS, FM200, AC & Noc systems
Platforms: Windows 2000 Active Directory, IIS 5.0, Veritas Backup Exec

CERTIFICATIONS AND TRAINING

Microsoft Certified Systems Engineer (MCSE), NT 4.0
Microsoft Certified Professional (MCP)

Completed courses in: SQL Server 7.0/2000, Server Management and Backup software, PC LAN/WAN environments, Microsoft Exchange 5.0, Microsoft System Management Tools

PROFESSIONAL EXPERIENCE

HORNET TECHNOLOGY SOLUTIONS, Diablo, CA   2002 – Present
IT Consultant working on variety of full- and part-time consulting jobs during job search. Consulting jobs include serving as IT Manager for ABC Technology.

• Upgraded ABC's office to Windows 2000 Active Directory.

• Perform new LAN and WAN configurations.

• Consult on system upgrades and stability for small businesses.

MOUNT DIABLO COMPUTER EMPORIUM, North Diablo, CA   1994 – 2002
Data Center Operations Manager & Senior Systems Administrator. Oversaw management of 24/7 facilities and operations (HVAC, FM200, UPS, Generators). Hired personnel and performed annual reviews. Upgraded all server standards and configurations; devised change control standards.

• Directed design and construction of four data center facilities totaling 10,000 sq. ft.

• Managed staff of eight System Administrators and Server Technicians.

• Scheduled and managed deployment of 750 corporate servers.

• Planned and supervised implementation of equipment installation with facilities and operations.

• Strategized capacity planning for acquisition consolidations.

(Mount Diablo Computer Emporium, Continued)

- Designed, built, and maintained several Windows 2000/SQL 2000 database clusters.
- Upgraded entire farm from NT 4.0 to Windows 2000.
- Designed large-scale data mining operation for daily updates to Website.
- Directed complete move of Website to newer facilities.
- Negotiated purchase of over $9 million in Dell server equipment.
- Successfully installed Windows 2000 Active Directory structure.
- Awarded Employee of the Year for outstanding work.

PERSONAL COMPUTER SOLUTIONS, San Francisco, CA   1991 – 1994
Customer Service Manager. Troubleshot hardware problems for end users, providing excellent customer service. Designed test environments to duplicate problems and failures with customer hardware.

- Managed nationwide technical support call center and telephone support group of 46 technicians as Tech Lead.
- Oversaw team of hard drive specialists handling recovery and troubleshooting.
- Supervised relocation of Technical and Customer Support after 1994 Northridge earthquake destroyed three buildings.
- Prepared new customer service warehouse to be ready to ship 10 days after earthquake.
- Promoted to Customer Service Manager to manage 24/7 customer service group.

EDUCATION
WESTLAKE INSTITUTE OF TECHNOLOGY
Computer Science/Technology Technical Degree

SAN DIEGO STATE UNIVERSITY
Bachelor of Science in Business Administration

KEYWORDS
Programmer, Senior Programmer, Engineer, Consultant, Applications Developer, Technical Support, Help-Desk Coordinator, Technical Help Desk, Technical Computer Technician, Network Support, PC Technician, Systems Support Engineer, Systems Analyst, Network Administrator, Help-Desk Manager

REFERENCES AVAILABLE UPON REQUEST

FRANK K. JOHNS

24 Andover Way • Sonom[...] • fjohns@resume.com

Experienced and analytical IT professional with background in systems administration and data center management

SUMMARY OF QUALIFICATIONS

➤ Eleven years of Information Technology experience with current expertise in Windows 2000 Active Directory installation and management.

➤ Excellent business acumen with background developing and administering budgets, negotiating contracts, and managing vendors and contractors.

➤ Specialty in installing, monitoring, and troubleshooting Compaq and D[...]

➤ Successfully managed design and implementation of large fault-tolerar[...]

➤ Extremely capable in fast-paced, chaotic business environments.

➤ Analytical, dependable, and willing to work long hours.

➤ Team player with excellent communications skills.

➤ Able to work well with large groups of people in face-to-face meeting environments as well as teleconferencing.

COMPUTER SKILLS

Hardware: Dell hardware, servers, laptops, desktops, SANs, EMC & Dell San Hardware
Servers: Compaq servers, SQL 7.0
Software: Dell Open Manage, HP OpenView, F5/Big IP Load Ba[...] Microsoft Exchange
Networking: Network Appliance N.A.S., Advocent & Freevision K[...] LAN/WAN
Data Center Facilities: Generator, UPS, FM200, AC & Noc systems
Platforms: Windows 2000 Active Directory, IIS 5.0, Veritas Backup Exec

CERTIFICATIONS AND TRAINING

Microsoft Certified Systems Engineer (MCSE), NT 4.0
Microsoft Certified Professional (MCP)

Completed courses in: SQL Server 7.0/2000, Server Management and Backup software, PC LAN/WAN environments, Microsoft Exchange 5.0, Microsoft System Management Tools

PROFESSIONAL EXPERIENCE

HORNET TECHNOLOGY SOLUTIONS, Diablo, CA   2002 – Present
IT Consultant working on variety of full- and part-time consulting jobs during job search. Consulting jobs include serving as IT Manager for ABC Technology.

• Upgraded ABC's office to Windows 2000 Active Directory.

• Perform new LAN and WAN configurations.

• Consult on system upgrades and stability for small businesses.

MOUNT DIABLO COMPUTER EMPORIUM, North Diablo, CA
Data Center Operations Manager & Senior Systems Administrator. [...] facilities and operations (HVAC, FM200, UPS, Generators). Hired personnel and performed annual reviews. Upgraded all server standards and configurations; devised change control standards.

• Directed design and construction of four data center facilities totaling 10,000 sq. ft.

• Managed staff of eight System Administrators and Server Technicians.

• Scheduled and managed deployment of 750 corporate servers.

• Planned and supervised implementation of equipment installation with facilities and operations.

• Strategized capacity planning for acquisition consolidations.

(Mount Diablo Computer Emporium, Continued)

- Designed, built, and maintained several Windows 2000/SQL 2000 database clusters.
- Upgraded entire farm from NT 4.0 to Windows 2000.
- Designed large-scale data mining operation for daily updates to Website.
- Directed complete move of Website to newer facilities.
- Negotiated purchase of over $9 million in Dell server equipment.
- Successfully installed Windows 2000 Active Directory structure.
- Awarded Employee of the Year for outstanding work.

PERSONAL COMPUTER SOLUTIONS, San Francisco, CA   1991 – 1994
Customer Service Manager. Troubleshot hardware problems for end users, providing excellent customer service. Designed test environments to duplicate problems and failures with customer hardware.
- Managed nationwide technical support call center and telephone support group of 46 technicians as Tech Lead.
- Oversaw team of hard drive specialists handling recovery and troubleshooting.
- Supervised relocation of Technical and Customer Support after 1994 Northridge earthquake destroyed

> In the **Education** section list the name of the college or university you attended, the major, and GPA if 3.0 or better. If you did not graduate, you can list credits completed if 60 or above or list general coursework.

service warehouse to be ready to ship 10 days after earthquake.
Service Manager to manage 24/7 customer service group.

EDUCATION
WESTLAKE INSTITUTE OF TECHNOLOGY
Computer Science/Technology Technical Degree

SAN DIEGO STATE UNIVERSITY
Bachelor of Science in Business Administrati

> **Keywords** are an integral part of all IT resumes. Include alternative job titles, acronyms, and technical proficiencies.

KEYWORDS
Programmer, Senior Programmer, Engineer, Consultant, Applications D
Help-Desk Coordinator, Technical Help Desk, Technical Computer Tech
Technician, Systems Support Engineer, Systems Analyst, Network Administrator, Help-Desk Manager

REFERENCES AVAILABLE UPON REQUEST

Ryan Sanchez

248 W. 35th Street ♦ New York, NY 10001 ♦ (800) 737-8637 ♦ rsanchez@resume.com

A certified systems engineer with expertise in programming and database administration

SUMMARY OF QUALIFICATIONS

- ➢ Five years of experience analyzing, designing, installing, maintaining, and repairing systems, software, and networks.
- ➢ Superior troubleshooting and technical support abilities.
- ➢ Develop exceptional relationships with coworkers, management, and end users.
- ➢ Excellent oral and written communication skills. Fluent in Spanish.

COMPUTER SKILLS

Hardware:	Windows Workstation 4.0, Server 4.0
Software:	Microsoft Office Suite
Languages:	COBOL, Pascal, Assembly, C, C++, PL/SQL
Operating Systems:	Windows 98/2000/NT, DOS, UNIX, Linux
Database Platforms:	Oracle 8.0, Developer 2000, Microsoft Internet Information Server, Relational Database Management Systems (RDBMS)
Networking:	TCP/IP, LAN

CERTIFICATION

Microsoft Certified System Engineer (MCSE)

PROFESSIONAL EXPERIENCE

Computer and Electronics Warehouse, New York, NY   02/00 – Present
Systems Administrator
Perform all levels of technical support, using Enterprise Research Planning (ERP) applications, including inventory control, financial statistics, and electronic database interchange (EDI).

- Create proactive procedures for problem preventions and resolutions, interfacing with software developers, analyzing issues, and designing solutions.
- Outstanding team leadership skills exemplified through supervision, tasks assignments, and follow-up on quality of product.
- Provide superior product service, including hardware and software systems.
- Compose and assess documentation, appraising users and administrators of vital information.
- Skillfully administrator and maintain UNIX environment security.

First Database, Inc., New York, NY   09/98 – 02/00
Systems Administrator
Engineered all phases of computer installation, planning, and implementation.

- Designed, developed, and modified reporting processes in accordance with client specifications.
- Performed hands-on administration, monitoring, and troubleshooting of Local Area Network (LAN), resulting in optimum performance and minimum downtime.
- Coordinated with committees detailing enhancement specifications.

EDUCATION

Bachelor of Science in Computer Science and Information System, Upstate University, Albany, NY
Diploma in Software Technology, University of Phoenix

KEYWORDS: Database Administrator, Systems Administrator, Network Administrator, Supervisor, Programmer, Quality Control, Computer Technician

ROGER K. PETERSON

3 Essex Road • Boston, MA 01930 • (800) 737-8637 • petersonrk46@resume.com

A highly qualified and motivated IT graduate with extensive programming and troubleshooting skills seeks entry-level position

SUMMARY OF QUALIFICATIONS
- BS degree in Microcomputers, with concentration in programming.
- Exceptional focus and follow-through abilities, with record of efficiency and productivity.
- Excellent troubleshooting, debugging and problem-solving skills.
- Work effectively with colleagues at all levels; gifted communicator.
- A committed team player, with extensive organizational and interpersonal skills.
- Highly adaptable and trainable; fast learner.

EDUCATION
MANHATTAN COLLEGE OF COMPUTER TECHNOLOGY, New York, NY
BS, Computer Microcomputers, September 2002

Key Subjects: Java, Java2, Sybase, Javascript, HTML, C, C++

COMPUTER SKILLS
Programming Languages: Java, Java2, Sybase, Javascript, HTML, C, C++, Oracle
Operating Systems: Windows 95/98/2000/ME/XP, Windows NT 4.0
Software Applications: Microsoft Office Suite (Word, Excel, PowerPoint)

PROFESSIONAL EXPERIENCE
MANHATTAN PUBLIC SCHOOL, New York, NY   12/99 – 04/00
Computer Technician
Assisted Computer Department in integration of multiple computers.
- Worked closely with instructors to set up computers, install software, and perform upgrades.
- Tutored students in compilation of C++ programs.

IT PROJECTS
➢ Helped students complete various senior projects using C++, Oracle, Java, JavaScript, and Visual Basic.
➢ Provided comprehensive tutorials in various operating systems and software applications to enhance students' understanding of fundamental programs.
➢ Mentored students one-on-one in computer labs.
➢ Supported students in creating databases and learning diverse applications.

KEYWORDS
Entry-Level Programmer, Software Developer, Database Developer, Software Engineer, Web Developer, File System Developer, C++ Programmer, Java Programmer

13

The Student/Entry-Level Resume

The student/entry-level resume is built primarily on academics and skills, as the majority of candidates who use this format have little professional experience. The essential elements of this type of resume include relevant coursework, extracurricular activities, internships, and memberships, highlighting specialized information to emphasize an applicant's potential.

Whether you are completing high school, college, or graduate school or have only a few years of experience, this chapter will guide you through the process of creating a winning resume that translates classroom experience and entry-level skills into a successful job search.

GETTING STARTED

Although other job candidates use professional experiences and job-related information to create their resumes, recent graduates, current students, and entry-level professionals must emphasize their skills and academic coursework as their main selling points. The first step in creating a professional resume is to organize a list that includes your academic background and extracurricular activities, as well as your paid and unpaid work experience. Compiling this information will help you determine your professional objective and assist you in targeting suitable positions and industries. To expedite this process, consult the worksheet in Appendix A.

Once you have this information, the next step is to assemble the data into a cohesive document and determine which format is best for you: the chronological, functional, or combination format (see Appendix B). The construction of the student resume (see below) uses the basic chronological format.

STEP 1: THE HEADER

The first step in creating any professional resume is writing and formatting the contact information at the top of the page. Include your name, address, telephone numbers, and e-mail address. A fax or pager number can be included, but this information is optional. Remember, make sure to double- and triple-check this information, as a mistake in this section will result in elimination.

STEP 2: THE HEADLINE

An essential aspect of every successful resume is an effective headline or objective. This simple one- or two-line sentence at the top of the resume should be a concise, powerful statement that combines your professional objective with the talent and skill you can bring to a potential employer. This promise can take the form of a certain skill set, your major, or your degree. It may be easier to create a headline after you have written and formatted your resume.

Headline Examples

➢ *Business administration student with exemplary research, writing, and communication skills and strong financial internship experience*

➢ *Dynamic student with outstanding academic track record seeks entry-level position in pharmaceutical sales*

➢ *Results-oriented entry-level business professional with exceptional academic success in accounting, finance, and business management*

The headline should engage a hirer. Don't include a period at the end.

STEP 3: SUMMARY OF QUALIFICATIONS

As employers typically spend only 10 seconds reviewing a resume, your most attractive skills and accomplishments should be listed in the Summary of Qualifications section. Under a clear header create a list of five to eight bullets highlighting the experiences and abilities that would make you an ideal candidate in an employer's eyes. Use your work history, coursework, and extracurricular activities as a guide. Scholarships, awards, and any academic success or specialized courses of study also should be listed here. Keep this section brief, highlighting just the essential areas that will allow you to stand out in a crowd.

The Student/Entry-Level Resume

Summary of Qualifications Examples

SUMMARY OF QUALIFICATIONS

- ➤ BS in Engineering with strong technical background, including "real-world" mechanical engineering experience at leading cell phone manufacturing company.

- ➤ Lauded for keen design skills, earning American Society of Mechanical Engineering Award for senior design project in 2002.

- ➤ Skilled at utilizing mechanical engineering techniques in machinery development.

- ➤ Extensive knowledge and training in diverse computer tools and applications.

- ➤ Superior interpersonal and communication abilities. Bilingual in Spanish.

SUMMARY OF QUALIFICATIONS

- ❑ Successful marketing, sales, and account management experience, with focus on providing superior customer service.

- ❑ Adept at preparing and conducting individual and group presentations.

- ❑ Superior organizational, follow-through, and closing skills.

- ❑ Outstanding communicator; able to relate to all types of personalities.

- ❑ Talent for managing multiple accounts in high-volume atmosphere.

- ❑ Efficiently troubleshoot and resolve problems quickly and responsibly.

- ❑ Work well independently within teams; responsible, dependable, and loyal.

STEP 4: EDUCATION

The education section is usually the most substantial section in a student resume. Begin this section with the college, location, degrees, and GPA if 3.0 or better.

EDUCATION
University of Southern California, Los Angeles, CA
Bachelor of Arts, English Literature. GPA: 3.77

Next, in subcategories, list relevant coursework, scholarships, awards, activities, and memberships. For example, if you were a biology major and are seeking a position in research, you can list your coursework here (Biology 101, Elements of Human Life, etc.), but your paid/work-study lab experience, which should be considered employment even if it was for a scholarship, should be listed in your work history. This hands-on experience will be an attractive selling point to a potential employer and should be emphasized.

Education Examples

Include coursework relevant to the position and industry for which you are applying.

EDUCATION
California State University, Sacramento, CA
Bachelor of Science in Business Administration, 2004

Key Courses: Business Calculus, Business Law, Business Communication, Computer Information Systems for Management, Accounting Fundamentals

EDUCATION
University of New Brunswick, Fredericton Campus   2002
Bachelor of Business Administration
GPA 3.7; Dean's List

HONORS
- Received Dr. Hemlick Everetson Prize in Economics for best research paper.
- Awarded University of New Brunswick scholarship for 2000 – 2001 academic year.
- Achieved Honor Roll 4 consecutive semesters.

STEP 5: PAID/UNPAID PROFESSIONAL EXPERIENCE

List internships and professional jobs in this section, including company name, city and state, job title, and dates. If you worked during the summer, you can list the specific months or write "summer" followed by the year.

Write your daily job responsibilities in paragraph form below your job title. Next, write any achievements or honors you earned at this position in bullet form below the responsibility statement and discuss the skills you used to achieve a specific result. List hard facts and quantifiable results first (such as sales percentages or customers served) and then move on to other less pertinent accomplishments. If you do not have any professional or internship experience, you can skip this section and concentrate on strengthening your Education section as the primary selling point of your resume.

Professional Experience Examples

Work Experience
Logan James Mines, Cadillac, Quebec   Summers 2000 – 2002
Inventory Clerk
Served as acting Inventory Manager when necessary.
- Coordinated shipping and receiving of parts.
- Communicated with suppliers to ensure accuracy and timeliness of orders.
- Assisted employees with location of specific pieces.
- Managed inventory levels.

Thalassa Howard Architects   Spring 2002
Intern

- Played key role in client presentations by creating AutoCAD drawings and choosing samples.
- Prepared premeasurements at work location.
- Kept resource library systematic and up to date.
- Performed basic office duties, including faxing, filing, and photocopying.

American Society of Interior Designers   1999 – 2002
Helped designers gather materials and ship packages to clientele.

- Attended Member Conference held at Florida Southern College.
- Created kitchen and bathroom blueprints for $2 million home.
- Assisted in design and building of homes with Habitat for Humanity.

STEP 6: COMPUTER SKILLS

Every recent graduate has had some interaction with a computer during the course of his or her academic career. This includes experience with the Internet, e-mail, software programs, hardware, operating systems, and programming languages. Regardless of what position or industry you are targeting, always include your level of computer literacy, as this is a fundamental aspect of today's work environment. Even if you feel that "everyone" has the same computer skills you do, list them—it can only help you.

Computer Skills Examples

COMPUTER SKILLS
Macintosh and PC; AutoCAD, Microsoft Office Suite, MS Windows, Internet, e-mail

COMPUTER KNOWLEDGE
Microsoft Office Suite (Word, Excel, PowerPoint, Access, Outlook)

STEP 7: ADDITIONAL SECTIONS

Add additional sections if they relate directly to the position for which you are applying. If you know a foreign language, include your level of proficiency. For example, you can highlight your communication skills by creating a section dedicated to your foreign language skills.

FOREIGN LANGUAGE
Bilingual fluency in Spanish; Conversational proficiency in Italian.

STEP 8: KEYWORDS

Keywords are essential to Internet resumes as a way of listing alternative job titles or industry-specific words not already mentioned in the body of the resume. Medium- and large-size employers use computer scanning software to scan and file resumes according to certain essential buzzwords. For additional information on keywords, see Chapter 7.

Keyword Section Examples

KEYWORDS

Editorial Assistant, Publishing, New Media, Administrative Assistant, Office Assistant, Secretary

KEYWORDS

Retail Sales, Sales Associate, Cashier, Stocker, Night Shift, Clothing, Customer Service

Keyshana Emerson

66 Hook Avenue ♦ Upper Hill, NY 10564 ♦ (800) 737-8637 ♦ kemerson@resume.com

Highly focused Master's graduate with extensive background in multimedia production

SUMMARY OF QUALIFICATIONS
- Experienced in both on-air and behind-the-scenes aspects of producing radio shows.
- Excellent language and communication skills. Fluent in Greek.
- Strong organizational and administrative abilities and experience.
- Knowledgeable of film, literature and theater.
- Solid educational background degree includes Master's degree in Media Studies.

EDUCATION
New School University, New York, NY   May 2003
Master of Arts, Media Studies

Fordham University, Bronx, NY   May 2001
Bachelor of Arts, Communications and Media Studies

University of London, Pittsburgh, PA   Summer 2000
Semester at Sea Program

EXPERIENCE
VH1 Radio Network, New York, NY   6/02 – 8/02
Intern
Performed all administrative tasks, including organizing tapes and interviews.
- Worked with writers on planning interviews.

Fordham University, Bronx, NY   9/01 – 5/02
Research Assistant
Advised professors and faculty members on research methodology.
- Provided research data through participant interviews.
- Completed data entry of research results.

K-Cosmo FM, Brooklyn, NY   5/01 – 8/01
Editorial Internship
Spoke with listeners about various issues for "Man on the Street" program.
- Revised on-air material.

WFUV FM, Bronx, NY   9/00 – 5/01
Intern
Provided administrative support to disc jockeys during radio programs.

COMPUTER SKILLS
MS Word, Excel, PowerPoint, Outlook, Internet-savvy.

LANGUAGE SKILLS
Fluent in Greek. Basic knowledge of German.

KEYWORDS
Production Assistant, Media Assistant, Film Production, Assistant Editor, Administrative Assistant

Keyshana Emerson

66 Hook Avenue ♦ Upper Hill, NY 10564 ♦ (800) 737-8637 ♦ kemerson@resume.com

Highly focused Master's graduate with extensive background in multimedia production

SUMMARY OF QUALIFICATIONS

- Experienced in both on-air and behind-the-scenes aspects of producing radio sh
- Excellent language and communication skills. Fluent in Greek.
- Strong organizational and administrative abilities and experience.
- Knowledgeable of film, literature and theater.
- Solid educational background degree includes Master's degree in

EDUCATION

New School University, New York, NY   May 2003
Master of Arts, Media Studies

Fordham University, Bronx, NY   May 2001
Bachelor of Arts, Communications and Media Studies

University of London, Pittsburgh, PA   mer 2000
Semester at Sea Program

EXPERIENCE

VH1 Radio Network, New York, NY   6/02 – 8/02
Intern
Performed all administrative tasks, including organizing tapes and interviews.
- Worked with writers on planning interviews.

Fordham University, Bronx, NY   9/01 – 5/02
Research Assistant
Advised professors and faculty memb
- Provided research data throu
- Completed data entry of rese

K-Cosmo FM, Brooklyn, NY   5/01 – 8/01
Editorial Internship
Spoke with listeners about various issues for "Man on the Street" program.
- Revised on-air material.

WFUV FM, Bronx, NY   5/01
Intern
Provided administrative support to disc jockeys during radi

COMPUTER SKILLS
MS Word, Excel, PowerPoint, Outlook, Internet-savvy.

LANGUAGE SKILLS
Fluent in Greek. Basic knowledge of German.

KEYWORDS
Production Assistant, Media Assistant, Film Production, Assistant Edito

LUCILLE MASTERS

248 W. 35th Street ♦ New York, NY 10001 ♦ 800.737.8637 ♦ lmasters@resume.com

Successful and experienced professional with demonstrable skills to succeed in Pharmaceutical Sales

SUMMARY OF QUALIFICATIONS
- Three years' experience in sales with ability to use marketing strategies to increase profits and improve brand recognition.
- Apply in-depth product knowledge to present services and drive sales.
- Excellent communication and interpersonal skills; easily develop positive rapport with clients.
- Create and implement various marketing initiatives to prospect, grow, and maintain clientele.
- Proven record of exceeding goals and expectations.

SKILLS AND ACCOMPLISHMENTS
Sales and Marketing
- Consistently achieved high sales volume, increasing assets from $110 million to over $220 million.
- Created and implemented innovative sales campaigns using comprehensive market research.
- Designed numerous sales brochures and tools to boost company visibility and grow clientele.
- Retain and incorporate client histories to develop and maintain strong rapport.
- Launched successful direct mail campaign, which achieved 10% response rate.
- Performed telemarketing, qualified investors, conducted seminars, and assisted with informational seminars as Salomon Smith Barney.

> The use of skill sets defines your professional experience and allows you to apply for multiple positions in diverse fields.

Business Development
- Secured increased market share by instituting a new sales approach in department.
- Effectively interacted with all levels of business management, including top-level executives, utilizing professional, assertive approach.
- Improved client relations through development and presentation of in-depth financial seminars.
- Oversaw, supported, and trained staff of finance and marketing interns.

WORK HISTORY
ABC COMPANY, New York, NY   1999 – 2000
Outside Sales Representative

ABC COMPANY, Chicago, IL   1997 – 1999
Marketing Associate, Private Client Division (05/98 – 10/99)
Intern (12/97 – 05/98)

EDUCATION
NEW YORK STATE UNIVERSITY, New York, NY
Bachelor of Science in Business Administration, concentration in Marketing, 1998
Certification in Graphic Design, 2002 (GPA 3.25)

COMPUTER SKILLS
Microsoft Office (Word, Excel, and PowerPoint), ACT Database Manager, HTML, Java, Visual Basic, Illustrator 9, Photoshop 6, Quark 4, Director 6, Dreamweaver 4, GIF Builder

KEYWORDS: Pharmaceutical Specialist, Sales Representative, Sales Associate, Health-Care Sales, Account Management, Pharmaceutical/Biotech Sales, Outside Medical Sales Representative

14

The Executive Resume

Executive resumes are designed specifically for senior-level professionals who are pursuing high-ranking positions in both the corporate and noncorporate sectors. You can use numerous formats to market the extensive responsibilities, accomplishments, strengths, and skills that define you as a seasoned professional, but regardless of the style you choose, all executive resumes should emphasize accomplishments, accomplishments, and more accomplishments.

WHO SHOULD USE AN EXECUTIVE RESUME?

You should use an executive resume if you:

- Are applying for any junior management to senior-level professions
- Have management experience and are seeking an upper-management position
- Are working with executive recruiters

Executives and corporate officers are expected to have established reputations within their industries and therefore usually have two-page resumes with numerous sections defining their background. These sections include the executive profile (which is an enhanced Summary of Qualifications), work experience, education, affiliations, awards, computer skills, industry-specific proficiencies, professional licenses or credentials, technical training, and publications, presentations, patents, or all three. Obviously, these credentials will be predicated on your professional experience and background, and you should not feel obligated to include any section that does not pertain to either the position or you.

These resumes reflect long-term achievements that often date back more than 20 years and consistently emphasize why the target organization can depend on you for leadership and growth. Here are a few rules governing the creation of an executive resume:

- The format is usually chronological because executives generally have held progressively responsible positions in the same position or field. If you wish to highlight previous work more than your most recent experience, you may decide to use the functional skill sets within the combination format.
- An executive usually will have professional affiliations that complement his or her professional work, and these affiliations usually are included.
- Most executive resumes are two pages in length.

Achievements are the essential element of the executive resume, and when possible you should use quantifiable results, including dollar amounts or percentages. Hirers, however, also value strong character traits in an executive candidate, such as leadership and mentoring capabilities. Aim for a confluence of outstanding accomplishments and a variety of intangible talents. The following steps will walk you through the proper format, layout, and content to demonstrate why you're the perfect candidate for the position.

STEP 1: THE HEADER

The header provides prospective employers with your contact information. To create an eye-catching header, write your name on one line and your telephone numbers, street address, city, state, Zip Code, and e-mail address on the line below. Listing your pager or cell phone number is optional. Separate your name from your contact information by using a border. Here is an example:

STEVEN MASTERS

248 W. 35th Street – 12th Floor • New York, NY 10001 • (800) 737-8637 • smasters@resume.com

For a step-by-step tutorial on formatting your header, see Chapter 5.

STEP 2: THE PROFILE

Unlike other resumes, the executive resume does not have a headline but instead uses an introductory paragraph of up to 10 lines called a **profile** or **summary**. The introductory "profile" condenses your greatest selling points into paragraph form and is formatted to provide potential employers with a comprehensive overview of your career. A successful profile should describe your title and field, years of experience, key accomplishments, and unique abilities. Similar to the Summary of Qualifications in its subject matter, this section begins with your most attractive attributes and ends with soft skills or other intangible traits. Some key issues to address include the following:

- Years of experience (do not go back farther than 25 years in an executive resume).
- If you work for a Fortune 1000 company, list this information. If you're a manager for a unit of a "Fortune 1000 company with $350 billion in annual revenue and 2000 employees worldwide," let an employer know; it's an impressive credential.
- Number of employees you manage.
- Areas of expertise, such as general management, operations, or business development.
- Key achievements. In this area, stress their relevancy to the position opening.
- Soft skills such as negotiation, communication, and presentation abilities.

Your profile serves as a "hook" to hirers, motivating them to read further. Make sure that you don't write a book, as too much text can be intimidating. A general formula for success is to incorporate attractive numerals ($75 million, 285%), bottom-line results, and characteristics that distinguish you as a unique and ideal professional.

Executive Profile Examples

SUMMARY
Multifaceted business, finance, and IT professional with exceptional background building and implementing processes that increase revenue, reduce downtime, and allow for peak operations across multiple divisions. Exceptional research and analysis background, with a demonstrated ability to clearly assess fragmented information and create successful solutions. Extensive background leading and overseeing professional teams, including developing and mentoring coworkers and employees. Premier IT experience, including creating and managing computing platforms, data and voice networks, applications systems, and databases. Expertise in contract negotiation. Adept manager; experienced in overseeing budgets exceeding $25 million annually. Able to translate and explain complex technical and financial concepts to diverse audiences.

SUMMARY
More than 23 years of experience in marketing, business development, management, and product development. Skilled in market analysis, opportunity identification, and revenue production. Ten years of experience overseeing day-to-day operations for debt division of major credit card company. Strong management skills; able to motivate and lead professional teams to complete projects both on time and within budget. Key experience arranging proposals with vendors, partners, and clients. Excellent financial management abilities. Proficient at strategy implementation and project modeling. Outstanding presentation and communication skills.

If your spell check feature indicates that you are writing in fragments, don't worry. This is an accepted style for resume writing. Complete sentences are discouraged.

STEP 3: PROFESSIONAL EXPERIENCE

The Professional Experience section is similar to the nonexecutive Professional Experience section, but the number of bulleted accomplishment statements is generally greater to accommodate the lengthier career. While nonexecutives should not exceed eight bullets, an executive resume can list up to 11 extensive skills and achievements per job title.

Likewise, your professional history can extend to 25 years. By describing your accomplishments and professional development through the scope of a 25-year career, you provide the necessary framework that hirers want to see in qualified candidates.

Remember that hirers want to know your key accomplishments, and the Professional Experience section is the place to demonstrate why you're the best in your field. You should strive to explain how your strategic skills have affected the company's bottom line; that is the defining factor of an executive, regardless of industry. This includes motivating staff, organizing teams, implementing tasks, and ensuring that goals are met.

Here are some key areas to focus on in an executive resume:

- Your management skills, including your supervision of employees, departments, or both.

- Cost-saving measures, revenue growth, profit and loss responsibilities, and innovations—for example, "Increased production of canned goods 80%." Use the percent sign; don't spell it out.

- Policies and procedures you may have designed and implemented and the way those changes directly affected the bottom line.

- Partnerships and relationships you created and exposure you brought to the organization.

- Any new products or programs you developed.

- Responsibilities, soft skills, and technical proficiencies you possess.

Professional Experience Section Examples

PROFESSIONAL EXPERIENCE

ABC Company, New York, NY   2000 – 2002
Vice President of Sales
Oversaw sales operations for chain that achieved between $12 million and $15 million in annual sales each year.

- Hired sales staff, supervising 30 sales personnel and eight managers across multiple locations.

- Monitored sales performance by store and person, ensuring all goals were attained.

- Established program of setting and following weekly store goals to increase sales.

- Developed and implemented customer service policies. Carried out in-store monitoring of sales techniques, customer service, merchandise levels, and operations.

- Actively involved in planning and opening of new locations, performing staffing, training sales personnel, and assisting with merchandise layout.

ABC Company, New York, NY   1996 – 2000
Partner

Founded and operated interior design firm servicing upscale clientele. Hired and supervised interior designers.

- Selected building site; designed and supervised renovations.
- Grew company from start-up to $1.2 million in annual sales. Developed business strategies, conducted marketing, competitive analyses, and business development.
- Performed all buying by visiting trade shows and conferences.

ABC Company, New York, NY   1985 – 1996
Vice President of Sales

Directed sales operations for retail chain that grew to $75 million in revenue and from 24 stores to 42.

- Played key role in 16 store openings between 1994 and 1996, including flagship store on Broadway in New York. Planned interior layouts and displays; worked with contractors and performed staffing.
- Supervised team of district managers. Monitored sales on individual store and district basis.
- Developed selling techniques, set goals, and managed marketing and promotions
- Previously held position of District Manager; promoted after four years.

ABC Company, New York, NY   1980 – 1985
General Manager

Carried out sales of manufactured products to major retailers in New Jersey and parts of New York.

- Developed relationships, negotiated agreements, and worked with stores on product placement. Ensured proper delivery of all goods and resolved any customer issues.
- Grew territory from $800,000 to more than $2 million in annual sales.
- Previously held position of Warehouse Manager with company.

PROFESSIONAL BACKGROUND

1997 – Present   ABC COMPANY, New York, NY
Vice President of Distribution and Partnership Sales
for Internet Digital Music Service provider. Develop distribution channels and structure user acquisition models to complement strategic objectives for sophisticated digital music platform.

- Implemented innovative acquisition strategy with Wal-Mart stores within 120 days of Board of Directors' approval despite present economic downturn.
- Created investor confidence and momentum for product launch in December 2000 after negotiating and closing deal with Gateway Computers.
- Registered 100,000 new users in first 60 days of Gateway launch as most listened to Digital Music service on Internet.
- Instrumental in securing $8 million from Philips Consumer Electronics in B investment round.

1990 – 1997	ABC COMPANY, New York, NY

Vice President of Sales for highly complex software application company.

Built effective sales organization to launch company in Internet industry.

- Defined sales strategy for identifying and approaching new opportunities with existing customers and potential customers.
- Analyzed and developed new markets and channels beyond financial institutions.

1985 – 1990	ABC COMPANY, New York, NY

Director, OEM and Microsoft Sales for this national Internet Service Provider.

- Created sales environment to augment focus and product specialization.
- Hired and managed five national sales executives, exceeding plan revenues within first six months.

National Sales Executive

- Responsible for reinvigorated Prodigy brand image within PC channel.
- Grew OEM PC, Modem, and Software Channels, surpassing revenue goals 35%.
- Built partnerships with Gateway, HP, IBM, and Toshiba.

In the above examples the employment dates are left aligned. This adds emphasis to your career progression and is best applied to highlight a seamless work history.

STEP 4: AWARDS AND RECOGNITION

Nearly all executives have received promotions, professional recognition, or awards from their peers, industry groups, or other sources. These awards can help a hirer decide between two otherwise equally qualified candidates.

Although you can incorporate awards within the professional history sections, you also can emphasize these credentials in a separate category. List the title and year you received an award as well as any circumstances that clarify or add value to the accomplishment. Chapter 6 provides an in-depth discussion on constructing the Awards section.

Awards and Recognition Example

AWARDS AND RECOGNITIONS
Sales Manager of the Year, 2002
President's Circle, Award of Excellence, 2001
Humanitarian of the Year, The Human Society, 2001
Certificate of Appreciation, Chicago Community Recreation Club, 2000

STEP 5: PROFESSIONAL MEMBERSHIPS AND AFFILIATIONS

Professional affiliations can help hirers make a choice between two otherwise equally qualified candidates. Affiliations and memberships convey dedication to a particular industry and community, and this is a valuable trait in a career-oriented professional. List your affiliations to the degree that they pertain to your professional goals. If you are a volunteer at the Christmas food drive and are also the fund-raiser for Detroit's Women in Business Organization, you should list your standing in the Women in Business Organization first.

Professional Memberships and Affiliations Examples

PROFESSIONAL MEMBERSHIPS

American Society of Radiology Technologists
American Health Care Radiology Administrators
American Cancer Society
Los Angeles Medical Group Management Association

COMMUNITY ACTIVITIES AND OFFICES

Director - Parker-Davis Investment Board   2002 – Present

- Guide decisions of board endowed with $30 million budget and charged by the Governor's Office with developing employer and job seeker resources in Armstrong, Butler and Indiana counties.

Vice Chairman - Progressive Workshop of
Marin County   1999 – Present

- Manage $1 million budget and endowment fund, including strategic planning, profit and loss, and overall performance for this nonprofit dedicated to finding employment for the mentally handicapped.

Marin County Fiscal Preservation Committee   1998 – 1999

STEP 6: EDUCATION

Although an educational background can be an optional component of your resume, if you have done advanced college or graduate schoolwork, you should highlight your educational career as a strong element of your professional success.

Beginning with your most recent degree or certification, list the name of college or university, its location, and your major (if applicable to the position). You may list the year you received the degree, but this information is not necessary on an executive resume as it can date a candidate, especially if you received your degree more than five years ago. Additionally, your focus should be on career-related accomplishments, and executives should not stress the education section if it does not directly apply to the field or position sought.

In addition, you may list professional development or special training in this section if it superseded your educational career. Many professionals have an extensive amount of professional development, having attended numerous seminars or courses to augment their positions. If this is the case with you, create a "Professional Development" section in addition to an education section.

One note: Executives without diplomas should not be discouraged. If you've achieved a remarkable amount of success without a college degree, that speaks very highly of your abilities. Remember, Bill Gates dropped out of college.

Education Section Examples

EDUCATION
WESTERN MICHIGAN UNIVERSITY, KALAMAZOO, MI
Master's Degree in Business Administration 2000
Bachelor of Arts Degree in Economics

EDUCATION AND PROFESSIONAL DEVELOPMENT
TULANE UNIVERSITY, NEW ORLEANS, LA
B.S. IN FINANCE, 1990

STEP 7: COMPUTER SKILLS AND KEYWORDS

Most executive resumes do not include computer skills or keywords sections, but you may include both if they support your professional objective. For more information on constructing these sections, review Chapter 6 for step-by-step instructions on how to choose and format this information.

A WORD ON EXECUTIVE RECRUITERS AND HEADHUNTERS

Many executive professionals rely on executive recruiters and headhunters to help them identify opportunities and facilitate the interview process. But as with any career services provider, make sure that the headhunter or recruiter you are considering using has a proven track record of success placing professionals similar to you.

JACK M. WALTERS

248 W. 35TH STREET • NEW YORK, NY 10001 • (800) 737-8637 • JWALTERS@RESUME.COM

PROFILE

Analytical, innovative, and results-oriented Information Systems executive with demonstrated, hands-on experience optimizing IT infrastructures as well as integrating current systems across multiple platforms. Master's degree in Business Administration. Adept at combining business-driven objectives with technology, creating strategic and tactical direction with an eye on minimum investment and realistic solutions. Promote professional development of skilled, multitiered staff. Expertly plan and coordinate detailed tasks within quality standards, established deadlines, and budgetary requirements.

AREAS OF EXPERTISE

- ➢ Operations Management
- ➢ Business Process Improvement
- ➢ Design and Development
- ➢ Project Management
- ➢ Strategic Planning
- ➢ Analysis and Resolution

PROFESSIONAL EXPERIENCE

ABC COMPANY   2001 – 2002

Vice President of Operations

Provided strategic direction to two functional business units. Led development and implementation of $3.1 million customer relationship management contact/call center application and workflows. Spearheaded and coordinated outsourcing of $2.1 million imaging system.

- Created project plans based on approved charters, tracked key milestones, adjusted project plans, handled budget requests, and tracked resources to meet business unit needs.
- Streamlined staffing to achieve reduction of 14 FTEs, increasing productivity by 50 to 73% and consistently meeting and exceeding objectives.
- Improved application processing from 14 days to less than five days by establishing new SLA thresholds.
- Reorganized call center operational structure and staff, improving first call resolution to 60% and resolved within standards to 95%.
- Directed and facilitated JAR/JAD; provided standard methodologies for planning projects (SDLC).

ABC COMPANY   2000 – 2001

Director of Information Technology

Conceived, formulated, and proposed innovative strategies to expand market and products within IS group to support business direction. Accountable for P&L management, personnel management, vendor management, system design, and data center/infrastructure design.

- Reduced error rate 22% by identifying and executing comprehensive project management solutions for clinical, financial, and administrative functions of health-care delivery.
- Increased file transfers and retrieval by 45% after designing and implementing network topology deploying Frame Relay Architecture using hubs, bridges, routers, and firewall VPNs.
- Developed and administered enterprise imaging systems and e-commerce/e-business solutions on Internet and intranet, reducing commutation costs by 37% and telephony costs by 16%.
- Coordinated $2.3 million budget administration, as well as end-user support, business unit relations, and staff and contractors supervision servicing client base of 485 in 42 remote locations.
- Reviewed and implemented HIPAA Security Standards within health-care industry and developed IT disaster recovery and Business Continuity strategy.

ABC COMPANY   1999 – 2000

Managing Director, Business Development

Spearheaded team for newly consolidated project management office to support company's objectives and improve customer services with support staff of 10 direct reports. Monitored and reported on strategic projects to CEO and Board of Directors.

- Created strategic plans to develop and launch unique, end-to-end, integrated approach to critical business Project Portfolio Management (PPM) to minimize risk and maximize return.

(PROFESSIONAL EXPERIENCE CONTINUED)

- Managed future planning initiatives for worldwide operations and reengineering of e-business solutions.
- Supported senior management in design and execution of strategic, tactical and operating plans.
- Recommendations to president, department heads, and field stations resulted in $6.2 million savings.
- Provided proper visibility and understanding of PPM, facilitating focus on optimum portfolio of projects and enabling maximum value.

ABC COMPANY   1994 – 1999
Director, US Operations-Solutions Business Group
Oversaw policy and procedure development and documentation with emphasis on situation analysis, process improvement, and automation enhancement.
- Identified and implemented strategic direction for consulting corporation outsourcing project management, software solutions, and multiplatform and new systems architecture implementation.
- Managed outsourcing operations with $7.1 million annual budget; engaged in contact negotiations on behalf of parent company.
- Developed complex technical aspects of business operations while promoting effective and efficient delivery of service.
- Recruited, trained, and promoted professional development of IS managers and staff.
- Implemented disaster planning and recovery procedures for county and critical application systems.

Financial Consultant, Applied Technologies Group
Led design and execution of strategic automation systems that increased revenues, customer satisfaction, and productivity while streamlining staffing requirements.
- Provided support to sales and customer service functions related to Enterprise Resource Planning system.
- Coordinated $2.3 million in distribution, manufacturing software, and professional services sales revenue.
- Analyzed and implemented best practice methodology, ensuring efficient utilization of CA-BAAN software.
- Supervised technology team responsible for packaged application selection, implementation, integration, and ongoing maintenance.

ABC COMPANY   1977 – 1994
President and Founder
Developed, marketed, and supported applications for corporate customers, with core philosophy on service, trust and realistic solutions with minimum investment in ASP environment.
- Successfully increased revenues from zero base to over $1.4 million annually with 28% profit margin.
- Conducted market surveys, developed advertising, secured financing, and established loyal customer base.
- Built and implemented clinical information system and customized interactive computer applications for various industries.
- Supervised staff of 25 servicing 50 corporate clients.

EDUCATION
Masters in Business Administration, Southwest University
Bachelor of Business Administration, University of Texas

TECHNICAL AND PRODUCTIVITY TOOLS
Mainframe, Midrange, Client/Server, Windows NT, Frame Relay, LAN/WAN, VPN, Voice over IP, Telecom communications network architecture (hubs, bridges, routers, firewalls, frame relays), Financial, Health Care, Manufacturing, PeopleSoft, MS Office, MS Project, MS VISIO, Niku

MARLENE ATKINS

248 W. 35th Street • New York, NY 10001 • (800) 737-8637 • matkins@rcsume.com

SUMMARY

Award-winning communications executive and talented team leader with demonstrated track record developing highly successful, client-oriented programs that continually increase both profits and customer retention rates. Extensive background implementing effective communication processes at both the national and global levels, including directing 160-member market-leading division with $150 million in annual revenues. Adept at designing, developing, and implementing innovative strategic programs across diverse fields, including marketing and market research, customer loyalty, public relations, corporate/financial relations, and media relations. Successful motivator, team leader, and coach.

PROFESSIONAL EXPERIENCE

A+ Computer Centers, Inc., New York, NY   1998 – Present
Manager, Market Intelligence for Fortune 500 Company providing communication solutions.
Created company's first customer loyalty and retention program aimed at enhancing revenue and client satisfaction by encouraging repeat business.
- Designed and implemented "customer listening post" transaction analysis programs that gather feedback at all key points of company/client contact.
- Developed annual customer loyalty measurement system.
- Implemented customer service/customer loyalty training programs for employees.
- Manage team conducting market sizing, opportunity assessment, and competitive tracking.
- Present market research findings and recommendations to corporate executive committee.

Diverse Media, Ltd., New York, NY   1994 – 1998
Vice President of communications management consulting agency with 15 Fortune 100 clients.
Counseled organizations undergoing technological improvements, including directing all technology acquisitions and internal operations development.
- Created and implemented strategic solutions in public affairs management.
- Designed strategies for applying leading-edge technologies to marketing communications.

Ramirez Communications, Inc., Detroit, MI   1989 – 1994
Senior Leader in $70 million public relations firm providing professional counsel and strategic communications for clients worldwide.

President and General Manager of 11-person, $44 million regional headquarters. (1991 – 1994)
Implemented programs that resulted in office assuming market leadership within three years.
- Office achieved annual increase in profitability and client satisfaction scores.
- Served on Hevlo Communications, Inc., Board of Directors.
- Increased market share 64% by implementing new technologies and offering stronger services at competitive rates.

Executive Vice President of seven-person team with $11 million annualized billings. (1989 – 1991)
- Accountable for group proving corporate image and advanced technology communications.
- Led successful new business teams in winning major new accounts, including MR Productions, Cape Element Township, Heart-McDale Enterprises, and Solar Cola.
- Managed key client relationships, such as Solar Cola, Pen Branding Corporation, and Hollywood-California Malls and Housing Complex.

(Continued…)

Kakelnikov Public Relations, Inc., Troy, MI   1984 – 1989
Vice President directing $500,000 in annualized billings. (1986 – 1989)
Executed trade/professional association communications, public affairs campaigns, and corporate image programs.
- Led teams in winning competitive accounts. including Raceway Motor and Bike, Inc.
- Developed communications/media training workshops attended by 850 executives from international Fortune 1000 companies.

Account Executive (1984 – 1986)
For American Academy of Etymologists, developed program that tripled public awareness of etymologists, linguists, and lexicographers, raising $295,000 in donations.
- Created and delivered communications/media training workshops preparing 350 lexicographers for positions in media companies worldwide.
- Developed public relations support for worldwide launch of Spellaid for L.J. International.

EDUCATION
The Wharton School of the University of Pennsylvania, Philadelphia, PA
Advanced business management training

University of Illinois, Beloit College, Springfield, IL
Bachelor's Degree, English Literature

KEYWORDS: executive, communications management, strategic communications, public relations, marketing, market research, public affairs, corporate relations, customer loyalty and retention, account management

15

The Career Change Resume

A career change resume is a highly functional and flexible document that facilitates an applicant's ability to move from one industry to another. Whereas a chronological resume emphasizes accomplishments at specific companies, a career change resume follows the functional format (see Chapter 3) and is a skill-oriented document that highlights your transferable abilities so that you can adjust easily to a new position in a new industry by using skills you already possess.

The career change resume is ideal if you

- Are switching professions and would like to enter a new line of work
- Are reentering the workforce and are pursuing a new field
- Are a recent graduate applying for a position unrelated to your major

---

THE CAREER CHANGE RESUME

There are three areas of the career change resume that are vital for success: the headline, the Summary of Qualifications, and the professional skill sets sections. The headline introduces you and your expertise as well as the position for which you are applying. The summary should demonstrate your success and give an overview of your transferable skills, whereas the skill sets section will delve further into those transferable skills to emphasize how these traits will transfer to a new field. By using the combination of targeted headline, summary of qualifications, and skill sets, you can highlight your case when transferring from one function to another.

Additional components of the career change resume are similar to those of the functional resume, including the work history, computer skills, education, keywords, and any additional miscellaneous sections (awards, affiliations, foreign languages). We will discuss each of these sections in greater detail as we walk you step-by-step through the creation of an effective career change resume. To identify and organize the information you'll need to create your resume, use the worksheets in Appendix B.

STEP 1: THE HEADER

Start the resume with an eye-catching header containing your name, complete address, telephone numbers, and e-mail address. Write your name on one line and include the rest of your contact information below it, using a border to differentiate the information. You may include your fax, pager, or cell phone number, but this is optional. Here is an example:

PETER SMITH

77 Wayne Drive • New York, NY 10013 • (800) 737-8637 • psmith@resume.com

For additional pointers on creating attractive headers, review Chapter 6. After you have created the header, you are ready to start constructing the resume, beginning with one of the most essential parts of the career change resume: the headline.

STEP 2: THE HEADLINE

The headline is a fundamental part of the career change resume. In one to two sentences it introduces who you are and what skills and talents you can bring to the table. Most hirers spend only 10 seconds reading a resume, and this section can help you stand out from the competition and compel prospective employers to call you for interviews.

The headline serves multiple purposes, including

- Describing you in terms of job title or years of experience (most career changers will highlight an applicable skill)
- Explaining the abilities you are able to contribute
- Emphasizing the career or industry you are pursuing

The key to changing careers is showcasing the transferable skills and outstanding experiences that will convince a hirer that you are the right candidate for the position. Construct an effective headline by beginning with an introduction and description of who you are:

- *A talented professional*

Then, working from your introduction, introduce two or three skills from your previous work history that can be applied to a new career you would love to have.

We recommend not placing your last job title in the headline and instead using the word "professional" to allow for maximum flexibility in applying for new careers and industries.

- *A talented professional skilled in marketing, communications, and management*

Once you've incorporated your strongest skills into the headline, finish with the position or professional objective you are pursuing to create a targeted resume for the industry or position for which you are applying:

- *A talented professional skilled in marketing, communications, and management seeks supervisory position in advertising*

We recommend always tailoring the headline to the specific position or industry for which you are applying. Also, **never end the headline with a period**. The purpose of this sentence is to hook the hirer into wanting to read your entire resume, so omit any ending punctuation here. For additional examples of headlines, review the 30 examples in Chapter 6.

STEP 3: THE SUMMARY OF QUALIFICATIONS

The Summary of Qualifications furthers the intensive interest that you must foster in a prospective employer's mind beginning with the headline. This section encompasses the top five to eight selling points that reflect your greatest accomplishments and transferable skills, basically creating a very strong overview of the abilities you can bring to a future employer. For example, if you managed a sales team of 10 people, many of those skills—motivating them, ensuring that they were acting in the company's best interest, scheduling, and talking with them—are all transferable to a manager at a bookstore. Areas you can highlight in this section should focus primarily on your soft skills (which are nonquantifiable skills) that transfer easily from one position to another. These skills may include the following:

- Management experience, including operations, departments, or people
- Communication skills, including improving interdepartmental communications as a result of processes you created or instituted
- Special awards or commendations that reflect exceptional work performance

- Organization, administration, scheduling, presentation, or negotiation abilities
- Willingness to travel or relocate

As with all bullets, incorporate powerful action words to augment your talents and abilities.

Summary of Qualifications Example

<u>**SUMMARY OF QUALIFICATIONS**</u>
- Skilled background in new business development, marketing, communications and client services.
- Solid presentation skills with personable, effective communication talents.
- Proven track record for improving company profits while remaining adaptable in fluctuating consumer environments.
- Practiced in administration, event coordination, and information management.
- Willing to relocate.

If you are having a difficult time discerning your strongest skills and achievements, you may want to delay writing the Summary of Qualifications until after you have completed the resume. For guidance and ideas, see Appendix B.

STEP 4: SKILLS AND ABILITIES

In the skills and abilities section your professional background should include two to four skill sets that will demonstrate why you are the best candidate for the position. Unlike the linear, company-specific professional experience section of a chronological resume, this skills and abilities section (which can be titled "Skills and Accomplishments" or titled as you see fit) plays an integral role in demonstrating specific, transferable talents and capabilities. **You also can incorporate into this section achievements and abilities that have no direct relationship with your professional history, allowing your skills to apply to your new professional goal.** For example, if you are attempting to return to the field of sales after many years in interior design, you can touch on the interpersonal, prospecting, and communication skills you use in your current field and in everyday life. You then can apply those skills to a vast array of sales-oriented positions not limited to your last job. Creating a section of skill sets, along with your Summary of Qualifications and headline, will highlight these areas of transferable skills. Some key areas to discuss in this section include

- Quantifiable results as a result of your demonstrable skills, such as cost-cutting achievements, sales numbers, or number of employees you've managed
- Awards and honors you've received for exceptional performance
- Soft skills such as strong communication and interpersonal abilities
- Projects or processes you have proactively developed and/or implemented
- Your ability to learn new tasks quickly and "go the extra mile"

Skills and Abilities Section Example

<u>SKILLS AND ABILITIES</u>

Management and Team Development

- Founded and managed regional territory, identifying and acquiring new customers, negotiating agreements, and managing department finances.
- Interviewed, hired, and supervised personnel. Trained employees in diverse facets of industry, including sales, marketing, customer service, and technical support.
- Developed training strategies and materials, writing comprehensive guide and tutorials.
- Managed all financials, including budgets, sales, forecasting, ROI, labor costs, and inventory.
- Created and implemented Excel spreadsheets for budget, P&L, and labor cost tracking.

Technical Support

- Provided hardware, software, and product support for customers.
- Researched technical issues, identified causes, and formulated solutions.
- Supported proprietary software as well as Microsoft and Apple systems and applications. Assisted clients with product selection. Earned 10 Customer Recognition Awards during tenure.
- Telephone support expert for home/small business laptop customers.
- Provided hardware/software setup, configuration, usage, and troubleshooting assistance.
- Received appreciation award for job performance; recognized for outstanding service by several customers in letters to executive management.

Marketing and Sales

- Produced $36,000 in first month as number one salesman out of 50-plus representatives.
- Improved sales 250% in two previously stagnant markets within 45 days as marketing manager.
- Acquired over 100 new customers in first six months.
- Increased franchise sales 11% in less than seven months; reduced employee turnover 95%.
- Created and managed telemarketing and direct sales programs.
- Formulated local marketing strategies for several branches.

STEP 5: WORK HISTORY

The work history or employment history section contains a list of your employment going back up to 25 years, including company name, location, dates of employment, and job titles. This is the section of the resume that should be deemphasized and should be the polar opposite of the chronological resume's Professional History section. The following are a few ground rules to follow in creating and formatting the Work History section:

- If you have gaps in your employment, do not list the months (mm/yy); instead, list only the years you worked (yyyy – yyyy).

- Use an en dash to separate dates by selecting Insert, Symbol, Special Characters, En Dash. The en dash is longer and visually more attractive than a hyphen.

- You may include a short description of your responsibilities within the Work History section, but this is optional.

Sample Work History Section

<u>**EMPLOYMENT HISTORY**</u>

Sales Representative, Wayne-Gotham Industries, New York, NY	2001 – Present
Assistant General Manager, Logan Industries, Newark, NY	1998 – 2000
Assistant General Manager, Rogers Metals, Greenwich, CT	1997 – 1998
Senior Manager, Kent Papers, Newark, NJ	1995 – 1997
Managing Partner, Kidd Running Supplies, Astoria, NY	1994 – 1995

STEP 6: EDUCATION

If you have college or graduate school experience, it should be included in the Education section of your resume. Hirers are interested in your school name, course of study, and grade point average (GPA) if it is 3.0 or higher. Here are some important points to remember:

- **The more relevant and recent the education, the more it should be played up.** Major, minor, relevant coursework, honors, academic awards, achievements, and extracurricular activities should all be listed *to the degree to which they are relevant*. For example, if your college courses and major have nothing to do with your new career, list the school, the graduation year, and the degree you earned.

- **If you went to college but did not graduate,** list years attended and credits earned (if over 60).

- **Avoid listing high school education unless it is your highest education level and is called for specifically in the job announcement.**

Education Section Example

<u>**EDUCATION**</u>
Manhattan College, Manhattan, NY
Bachelor of Arts, 1993. GPA: 3.5

Key Courses: Business Information Systems, Business Administration, Accounting, Management I-II

STEP 7: COMPUTER SKILLS

There is a need for professionals with strong computer skills in almost every industry, and technical skills may give you a competitive edge in the application process. We recommend listing all computer programs you are proficient in, including operating systems, hardware, and Internet and e-mail programs.

Technical skills are an essential part of the IT resume. Computer skills should be listed clearly in a prominent section. For more information on IT resumes, see Chapter 12.

Computer Skills Section Example

COMPUTER SKILLS

Microsoft Office Suite, Outlook, Explorer, Adobe Acrobat, AS400, BOSS billing system, E-mail

---

Include miscellaneous sections after computer skills, such as memberships and affiliations (if they are relevant to your professional goals). The purpose of this resume is to define your transferable skills, so don't include data that will trap you in your current field.

STEP 8: KEYWORDS

A keywords section is a vital way to ensure that your resume will not be eliminated by computer scanning software. This is software that is used by many human resources personnel at large companies to eliminate a resume before a person reviews it. Here's how the process works: Hirers gather nonelectronic resumes via fax and mail and receive electronic resumes via e-mail and job boards. These resumes are stored in a database where hiring personnel can use individual keywords to sort resumes and eliminate those which do not meet the criteria, reducing a potential stack of 1000 applications to a select few. If your resume does not contain these keywords, you probably will be eliminated from consideration.

Effective keywords include job titles, industry-specific jargon, and acronyms not already found in your resume. A career change keywords section can be modified according to every position you are applying for to maximize your success, but the areas suggested by keywords should be supported by resume content. This section is purely functional and does not have to follow the formatting of the previous sections. Keywords can be listed as a string of words at the bottom of the resume or formatted similarly to the other sections.

To find the most effective keywords to include in your resume, do a quick job search in a major newspaper or job board. The resulting job descriptions will provide a list of alternative job titles, industry jargon, and buzzwords that you can add to your keywords section. An effective career change keywords section for a communications professional might look like this:

KEYWORDS
Associate Producer, Production Assistant, Editor, Associate Editor, Editorial
Assistant, Personal Assistant, Television, Video, Media

A FINAL NOTE ON CAREER CHANGE RESUMES

Switching careers and industries can be a daunting goal in a job search. Before
jumping in feet first, research the marketplace to find out who's hiring, what
jobs are in demand, and, more important, what jobs and fields would be a good
fit for your background and interests. If you feel that now is the time, however, don't let anything hold you back.

LAWRENCE FAUNA

248 w. 35th Street – 12th Floor ♦ New York, NY 10001 ♦ (800) 737-8637 ♦ lfauna@resume.com

*A highly successful and motivated professional with expertise in
management and administration*

PROFESSIONAL SUMMARY

➢ Over 10 years of exceptional management and production experience.
➢ Adept at organizing teams of people to focus on corporate goals and complete tasks on time.
➢ Exemplary written and oral communication skills; effective negotiator and mediator.
➢ Able to handle multiple projects simultaneously within deadline-oriented environment.
➢ Proven track record in developing and implementing processes that remarkably increase both efficiency and productivity.

SKILLS & ACCOMPLISHMENTS

ADMINISTRATION

- Ten years of fast-track management experience in demanding environments.
- Spearhead corporate communications, including speeches, online newsletters, and Websites.
- Extensive background in recruiting, developing, and maintaining both large and small teams.
- Assess organizational needs, develop strategies, and implement proactive solutions.
- Proven record in planning events, meetings, and travel arrangements.
- "Hands-on" leadership style, with ability to motivate staff.
- Create and manage organizational programs and special events, including annual incentive trips, training programs, meetings, and corporate team-building events.
- Develop and maintain vendor and trainer relationships.
- Balance billing and payroll timesheets.

MANAGEMENT

- Five years of experience supervising all phases of operations, including staff, billing, vendor relationships, and office administration, in multiple venues across the United States.
- Develop and implement operational procedures to increase workplace efficiency.
- Hire staff, create budgets, negotiate contracts, and schedule hours.
- Bachelor of Arts in Corporate Management.

PROFESSIONAL EXPERIENCE

Operations Manager
Pinewood Financial Services, New York, NY   1996 – Present

Outsourcing Manager
Clark & Johnson, New York, NY   1991 – 1996

Assistant Engineering Manager
Broadway Circuitry, New York, NY   1989 – 1991

Administrative Assistant
Yorkshire Andelway TV, New York, NY   1987 – 1989

COMPUTER SKILLS

Microsoft Word, Excel, Publisher; WordPerfect, Lotus 1-2-3, PrintMaster Gold, ABRA

EDUCATION

Bachelor of Arts in Corporate Management, New York College, New York, NY, 1986

Keywords: Corporate Development, Organizational Development, Program Administration, Office Manager, Office Supervisor, P/L

16

Must-Have List for an Effective Job Search

Although a professional resume is the backbone of any successful job search, it is only one of many documents that must be sent to a prospective employer. Additional materials that are vital to the success of a job search include a custom-tailored cover letter, a follow-up letter for the job application, and a postinterview thank-you letter. A list of references often is required as well.

Beginning with the cover letter, this chapter will take you step-by-step through the process of creating and sending effective correspondence, including what information to include and exclude, why you shouldn't send a cover letter as an attachment, and how to address special—and sometimes sensitive—topics such as work status, visas, salary requirements, and relocation.

THE COVER LETTER

A cover letter is your introduction to a potential employer. It should be concise and clearly written, and it has a single purpose: to persuade the hiring manager to pick up your resume. Your ability to market yourself effectively begins the instant a hiring manager reads your cover letter. Although there's no distinct format that makes a cover letter a success, there are key points that should be followed to ensure that your application avoids the rejection pile.

An effective cover letter should target the position you're applying for. A form letter in which only the company's contact information changes is a mistake and should be avoided. A smart step is to include the name of company you are applying to in the body of the letter, not just in the "address to" section at the top. Even if it's just in one sentence ("I am confident that my visual editing skills would be a great asset to Tralfama Films"), composing a cover letter that targets one company, not every company, is an important key. It also lets the employer know that you're pursuing *this* position, not *any* position.

Here are some helpful guidelines to keep in mind in creating cover letters:

- Keep the cover letter concise. Your letter should have up to four paragraphs of single-spaced 11- or 12-point type and should not exceed one page.
- The header should appear at the top the page and should be identical to the header on your resume. Include your name, address, telephone numbers, and e-mail address.
- Focus on including key accomplishments and skills that fit the position's requirements. This is where you need to entice the reader to move to the resume.
- Close your cover letter with a thank you. Most hiring managers are asked to do too much with too little; let them know that you appreciate their time and consideration.
- Spell check your cover letter. Many hiring professionals will not review a resume if the cover letter has a typo in it. Have a friend or relative proofread it. Then read it again.

Although the cover letter won't secure you a position, it's a necessary step in the process. If done well, it can increase your chances of finding a great job exponentially.

WHAT TO INCLUDE

The cover letter should explain who you are, what you have to offer the employer, why what you have to offer is valuable, and what you hope to gain from the position. Pay special attention to the job description of the position for which you are applying. Just as your resume needs to cover all the points discussed in the job description, your cover letter also should touch on those areas. Introduce your professional qualifications and address any special requirements the hirer has in mind for the perfect candidate, including certifications, years of experience, knowledge of particular procedures or applications, and educational degrees. If your letter doesn't address the employer's advertised needs, your resume may be rejected.

You should never discuss personal information such as age, nationality, and religion in a cover letter. The focus of the cover letter must be positive, and the tone should show why you would be an invaluable asset to a potential employer because of your specific talents and credentials.

First Paragraph: Reason for Writing the Company

The opening paragraph of an effective cover letter addresses the employer's needs and wants and either identifies a need the employer has and shows how you will fill that need or promises a benefit that you will bring to the employer.

This paragraph introduces you to a hirer and usually highlights your job title, years of experience, and **key selling points relevant to the position being sought**. To incorporate the most relevant skills and accomplishments, closely read the job description. Basically, you're making a promise to fill the void the company currently has. How are you going to do this? A good tip is to touch on the things that you currently do or have done for a previous or current employer and how the skills you used for past successes will translate seamlessly to your new position. Additionally, you can focus on your greatest achievement, but basically this is the setup to keep the reader moving into the second paragraph.

Paragraph 1 Example

As a highly successful senior management professional with over nine years of experience in marketing and product development, I am confident that I would be an ideal candidate for the Marketing Manager position that Evergreen Industries currently has posted on the Careers page of the company Website. I have developed and implemented highly profitable marketing campaigns for a diverse range of products, and I feel that I would bring the same prosperity to your organization.

By focusing on key achievements, you immediately establish your value as well as your role as a strong manager capable of improving a company's bottom line—clearly an asset to a company seeking a marketing manager.

Second Paragraph: Addressing Your Skills to an Employer

The second paragraph provides the potential employer with a list of reasons why you will be able to fill the position's needs and thrive at the company. Using your greatest skills, accomplishments, or education highlights, describe the abilities you currently have that would enable you to fill this position better than any other candidate could.

Areas to focus on include your responsibilities for a previous or current employer *and how those responsibilities translated to powerful results*. A great way to impress hirers is to describe how your assets profited an employer in terms of cost-cutting measures, increased productivity, greater revenues, additional clientele—basically, how and why you can meet the position's needs and/or deliver a benefit.

Paragraph 2 Example

My background working with distributors, graphic artists, and consumer analysts to create and execute highly successful promotional campaigns has provided me with a broad knowledge of marketing strategies, and I have closely followed the launch of your new product, the XL 8799. Having served at numerous Fortune 100 companies in the telecommunications industry, I am able to thrive in fast-paced environments where working within tight time constraints is the norm. My keen business acumen, coupled with my proven record of success overseeing marketing operations, would allow me to thrive at Evergreen Industries.

> You can use bullets in the cover letter to draw added attention to your key achievements. Bullets are a great way to personalize cover letters.

Paragraph 2 Bulleted Example

As you can see from the attached resume, my background working in the telecommunication industry is robust and is measured by one success after another. Some of the benefits that I will bring to your company include:

- Experience working with distributors, graphic artists, and consumer analysts to create and execute highly successful promotional campaign.
- Broad knowledge of marketing strategies.
- A background in Fortune 100 company environments and the ability to thrive in fast-paced atmospheres where tight time constraints are the norm.
- Keen business acumen coupled with a proven record of success overseeing marketing operations.

Third Paragraph: Addressing Special Issues and Closing

The third paragraph provides additional supporting details about your key abilities or can be used to cite additional benefits you have to offer. It also can reference your resume's attachment (if mailed or faxed) or placement (if e-mailed). This is also the place to address any special circumstances regarding your application. This might include salary requirements, work samples or your portfolio, and your ability to work in the United States.

Start this paragraph with a strong closing statement such as "The accompanying resume provides an overview of my skills and accomplishments." You now can address special issues such as **salary requirements.**

Salary Requirements

Salary requirements are one of the most common kinds of information employers ask of job applicants. If you give a figure either above or below the hirer's planned salary range, you probably will be eliminated from consideration. We recommend stating a flexible salary range that takes into account your background, the job title, the industry, and the company's size. Many hirers will reject candidates with unrealistic requirements; don't end up in the "rejected" pile by aiming too high or too low. The best way to avoid doing that is by remaining flexible: "Based on my background and expertise, my flexible salary requirements are $X to $X."

Paragraph 3 Example

The accompanying resume provides an overview of my skills and accomplishments. While it represents a summary of my work history, I am confident that a face-to-face meeting will provide the best opportunity for me to learn more about your objectives and convey the many ways I can help you reach them.

Fourth Paragraph: Follow-Up and Close

The last paragraph states how you will follow up and thanks the hirer for his or her time; this should be a concise two- to three-line paragraph. You should be the one to initiate the follow-up, saying, for example, "I'll contact your office to see when we might be able to meet." If the letter is to be used in response to ads, also indicate that you will follow up, designating a time frame in which you will do so ("I will e-mail you next week to arrange the possibility of a meeting.").

Always try to follow up even if all the contact information is *not* listed in the job ad. For example, if you are responding to an ad by fax, send a follow-up fax letter a few days after you send your resume. The same rule holds true for e-mailed submissions and mailed resumes. We recommend always indicating in your cover letter that you will follow up. This demonstrates your interest, and your intent should be included in the last paragraph.

Being persistent in your job search is one key to success.

You should always close the cover letter by thanking the hirer for his or her consideration. A little courtesy from the job seeker can do wonders in creating a strong and lasting impression.

Paragraph 4 Example

I will contact your office next week to arrange a time when we might be able to speak by phone. I look forward to talking with you, and I thank you for your time and consideration.

Sincerely,

Lawrence Pearle

How to Send a Cover Letter

If you are mailing your cover letter, it should be printed on the same type of paper you use for your resume. If you are e-mailing your cover letter, paste it directly above your resume and insert both documents into the body of the e-mail. Use a solid line or a row of asterisks to differentiate the information. A hirer shouldn't have to scan your e-mail closely to differentiate the information; remove all obstacles from the resume and cover letter. As we discussed in Chapter 8, never include your cover letter as an attachment to an e-mail, because it may be deleted automatically. Review the following cover letter samples for further ideas and ways to create powerful cover letters.

Greg Robinson

56 East 42nd Street, Apt. 11H • Chicago, IL 62811 • (800) 737-8637 • grobinson@resume.com

Date

Mr. John Smith
Hiring Manager
Cape Industries
678 Main Street
New York, NY 10001

> If possible, include the name and address of the person reading your resume. If you don't have this information, address your letter in a gender-neutral form; don't assume that a man or woman will be reading it. "Dear Hiring Manager" or "Dear Human Resources Associate" is a great start.

Dear Mr. Smith:

As an experienced sales representative with a Bachelor of Science degree in management, I am confident that I would be able to contribute to the profitability and success of your business. I have expertise in developing sales relationships with key decision makers in hospital and clinical management settings across the nation, and I am interested in bringing my skills, talents, and experience to your company.

Currently, as the top-ranked sales representative for The Saving Lives Corporation, I am responsible for selling pacemakers in a four-state territory while also overseeing a seven-member sales force. In this position, I promote products and services by developing relationships with physicians and hospital personnel while also mentoring and training junior sales members.

My history of success in sales is evident from the accompanying resume, which attests to my solid achievements in medical sales, including ranking fourth nationally in medical sales in 2001 and in the top 3% of the largest cardiovascular sales force in the United States.

I would welcome the opportunity to meet with you to discuss your company's goals and how I can help you achieve them. I will call your office in a few days to inquire about such a meeting. I thank you for your time and consideration.

Sincerely,

> End your cover letter with a professional and courteous greeting, such as "Sincerely." Do not use personal endings such as "Warmest Regards" unless you are acquainted with the reader.

Greg Robinson

> Use three to four line spaces before your name.

MAUREEN LEE

601 Flagship Avenue • Birmingham, AL 36101 • (800) 737-8637 • mlee@resume.com

October 8, 2003

Hiring Manager
Always Ready Shipping
55 Waterfront Drive
New York, NY 10001

Dear Hiring Manager:

As a highly trained purchasing agent with over 10 years of experience, I believe that my background and strong accomplishments would be valuable additions to Always Ready Shipping. My outstanding work ethic has earned me numerous promotions during my career, and my ability to build relationships with key vendors has been a tremendous asset to my current employer.

Some of my greatest qualifications include:

- Ability to work with diverse departments, such as purchasing, finance, accounting, shipping, and maintenance.
- Superior vendor negotiations relating to annual contracts involving pricing and delivery.
- Extraordinary professional reputation with vendors throughout the northeastern United States, with contacts in New York, New Jersey, Pennsylvania, and Delaware.
- Expert computer use and programming skills.
- Ability to coordinate and implement new policies and procedures.

Given the combination of these factors, I feel confident that I would quickly be considered a contributing and vital member of your company. I am an employee who offers exceptional purchasing knowledge, system integration experience, and supervision talent. Additionally, I enjoy exceeding expected goals through effective project management and cost savings.

I welcome the opportunity to meet with you or a representative of your organization to further discuss your specific needs. I have enclosed my resume to give you a comprehensive account of my qualifications. Thank you for your time and consideration, and I look forward to speaking with you.

Sincerely,

Maureen Lee

LIST OF REFERENCES

Prospective employers often ask for a list of references during or after an interview, and you should have a printed list of your contacts available before walking in the door for an interview. Sometimes a prospective employer will request references before an interview, but this process usually occurs after the first meeting. You can include both work and personal contacts on your reference list, but make sure that at least three professional contacts are listed. As a rule, call all the references you want to use and verify that it is okay for a prospective employer to contact them.

When creating your list of references, you only need to list the basics: name and title, the companies they work for, and the telephone numbers and e-mail addresses where they can be contacted.

Print out your references using the same letterhead you use for your resume and cover letter. The following chart will help organize your contacts:

Name	Organization and Title	Telephone Number/E-mail
1.		
2.		
3.		
4.		
5.		

Philip Eckstein

248 West 135th Street • Brooklyn, NY 11215 • (800) 737-8637 • peckstein@resume.com

REFERENCES

Arnold Lee
President
JOHNSON AND HEWLETT CLOTHING COMPANY
(800) 737-8637
alee@clocompany.com

Sandra Bellows
President
FINE SILK IMPORTS
(800) 737-8637
sbellows@finesilk.com

Roberto LeBlanc
Senior Manager
PAISLEY POP DANCE ACCESSORIES
(800) 737-8637
rleblanc@paisleydance.com

George Simpson
Vice President
TMC LIFE, INC.
(800) 737-8637
gsimpson@tmclife.com

LETTERS OF RECOMMENDATION

Although the resume and the cover letter are the two most important documents in a job search, the letter of recommendation can play a significant role in a hiring decision.

Also known as a letter of reference, a letter of recommendation emphasizes your skills and achievements from a previous employer's point of view, bringing to light your personality as well as your job experience.

The letter of reference is usually one page long and is written by a manager or personal associate. It should discuss your overall performance, including sound communication skills, proven intellect, and a strong sense of responsibility. Qualifications like these will stand out in a letter even if the tone of the entire piece seems overly generous.

Your reference writer may ask you to construct a letter that he or she will then edit; this is considered a common practice. If this is not the case, however, make sure to remind the person writing the reference of your accomplishments and achievements when you worked together.

It's important to use a reference who will respond favorably to your request. A half-hearted or poorly written letter of reference can have an extremely negative impact on your application.

FOLLOW-UP LETTER

Follow-up letters are e-mailed, faxed, or mailed to a hirer after you submit your resume and cover letter. These letters remind the hiring manager of your qualifications and reiterate your interest in the position.

You should always send a follow-up letter a few days after submitting your application and every few days for at least two weeks or until you receive a response. In one or two paragraphs your follow up letter should include

- The position you are pursuing and the date you submitted your resume
- Two or three key qualifications you have for the position
- Your interest in meeting the hiring manager to discuss this position in person
- Your intention to follow up again in a few days
- The telephone numbers and e-mail address where you can be reached

Being persistent in applying for any position will set you apart from the competition and will leave a strong impression with the potential employer that you are seriously interested in the job.

Philip Eckstein

248 West 135th Street • Brooklyn, NY 11215 • (800) 737-8637 • peckstein@resume.com

Date

Hiring Agent Name, Title
Company Name
Address
City, State, Zip Code

Dear Hiring Manager:

I submitted my resume for your review on August 14 and would like to follow up with you to ensure that you received my application and reiterate my great interest in the Project Leader position at Omega Company.

As I mentioned in my last e-mail, I am an experienced team leader with extensive computer skills and multiple certifications. I believe that my well-rounded technical proficiencies and management abilities would fit very well with your business, as would my certifications in systems administration and various programming languages.

I believe it would be mutually beneficial for us to meet to discuss the many ways I can positively impact your IT group. I will follow up with you in a few days to inquire about scheduling a meeting, or you can reach me at (800) 737-8637 or peckstein@resume.com.

Thank you for your consideration, and I hope to hear from you soon.

Sincerely,

Philip Eckstein

THANK-YOU LETTER

The postinterview thank-you letter is an important but often overlooked component of a successful job search. When you are competing against a pool of equally qualified candidates, it is vital to continue to sell yourself at every stage of the job search.

In one or two paragraphs the thank-you letter should remind the interviewer of some key qualifications you discussed during your meeting. You don't have to go into minute detail, but you want to remind the hirer of your personality and the qualifications that make you a memorable candidate.

You letter should always begin by thanking the hirer for taking the time to meet with you. Then discuss two or three points you spoke about during your interview, such as with whom you would work, projects you would be responsible for, or how a specific aspect of your past employment would be a perfect match with a potential job duty. Conclude the letter by thanking the interviewer again and indicating when you next will follow up.

Try to e-mail or mail the thank-you letter as soon as you return home from the interview.

Must-Have List for an Effective Job Search

Franny Richardson

497 Willow Creek • Jackson, MS 39205 • (800) 737-8637 • frichardson@resume.com

January 30, 2003

Ms. Simone Heverson
Project Manager
South Park Solutions
23 Gold Avenue
New York, NY 10001

Dear Ms. Heverson:

Thank you for taking time out of your schedule to meet with me today. I trust you will agree it was time well spent, as I sensed that we connected on the points discussed.

I found your company's objectives exciting and your enthusiasm for the organization contagious. I appreciate the diverse, team-oriented and innovative environment of South Park Solutions. I believe my ability to identify and solve problems creatively and effectively, as well as my understanding of Web development, programming and database systems, would be valuable to your company and its goals.

As I mentioned in the interview, I am comfortable with and capable of working in a challenging environment. I also have the ability to manage multiple tasks and projects simultaneously while maintaining clarity and setting priorities. I am results-oriented and able to meet the needs of an ever changing and growing industry, and I work well with people at all levels.

I am very interested in the position and look forward to hearing from you. I will follow up with you next week. Thank you again for your time and consideration.

Sincerely,

Franny Richardson

Choosing the Right Resume Format

To choose the ideal resume format to use, take this quick quiz. If you select more of the chronological scenarios, that is probably the best format for you. You can review Chapters 2, 3, and 4 for a more detailed discussion of the proper format to use. Keep this quick quiz handy and check it against your future job search goals.

Scenario	Chronological	Functional
Continuous work history over the last 4 years or more	✓	
Applying for same position as your current/last job	✓	
Applying after a gap in employment of 2 years or more		✓
Changing careers or changing industries		✓
Executive or senior manager	✓	
Professional history of 15 years or more	✓	
Mostly community/volunteer service		✓
Multiple switches in industries		✓
Multiple positions in unrelated fields		✓
Prestigious or Fortune 500 companies	✓	
Postmilitary	✓	
Numerous job relocations	✓	✓
Performed same job duties during career	✓	✓
Recent graduate	✓	✓
TOTAL: Count the number of chronological or functional items applicable to you and use the format that receives the most marks.		

SPECIALTY RESUMES

Consultant or Freelance Project Manager	Combination	

Choosing the Right Resume Format

Professional Resume Builder Worksheets

C<small>ONTACT</small> I<small>NFORMATION</small>

Name:_____

Address: _____

Home Phone/Cell Phone:_____

E-mail: _____

1. What type of position are you looking for?

_____

_____

_____

2. Do you have any previous experience in this field? If so, what were some of your duties?

_____

_____

2a. If not, have you used similar skills in your other jobs/education, and what were they?

_____

_____

3. What sets you apart from other candidates applying for this position?

_____

_____

4. Are you willing to travel or relocate?

_____

5. What do your friends or coworkers say are your strongest traits?

_____

_____

6. Have you won any honors or awards in your professional or academic career?

_____

_____

WORK EXPERIENCE: CURRENT OR LAST POSITION

Last Employer (Name, City, State): _____

_____

Type of Business: _____

Size of Firm (annual revenue and/or number of employees):

_____

Worked from _____ **to** _____

Your Job Title: _____

What were your responsibilities? _____

_____

Did you solve any problems on the job? If so, what were they and how did you do it?

_____

_____

Describe any new systems or processes you suggested or instituted.

_____

_____

What did you accomplish that you are very proud of?

_____

_____

How did the company benefit from your performance? (Example: Did you hire or train coworkers or implement systems? How did you add to the company's bottom line? Did you do anything to increase productivity in the company?)

_____

_____

Did you improve communications in the firm? How? What was outcome?

_____

_____

ADDITIONAL INFORMATION

Have you done volunteer or community-related activities related to the position sought? _____

_____

Did you receive honors or awards related to the position? _____

_____

Date/Description of Award or Honor: _____

_____

(REPEAT THE SAME QUESTIONS FOR PREVIOUS POSITIONS, STARTING WITH YOUR LAST JOB FIRST)

EDUCATION: GRADUATE SCHOOL OR HIGHER

Name of college or university and city and state: _____

_____

Dates attended: _____

Year graduated/GPA:_____

Degree/major:_____

Honors, awards, prizes, scholarships? _____
_____

Key courses, programs: _____
_____

COLLEGE/UNDERGRADUATE SCHOOL

Name of college or university and city and state:_____
_____

Dates attended: _____

Year graduated/GPA:_____

Degree/major:_____

Honors, awards, prizes, scholarships? _____
_____

Key courses, programs: _____
_____

Extracurricular activities, offices held, or additional achievements:
_____

VOCATIONAL/TRADE SCHOOL

Name of school/organization and city and state:_____

Dates attended: _____

Year graduated/GPA:_____

Degree/license/certifications: _____

Major/concentration: _____

Skills learned: _____

Key courses, programs: _____

Continuing Education/Professional Development

Name of school/organization and city and state: _____

Dates attended: _____

Year graduated/GPA: _____

Degree/license/certifications: _____

Major/concentration: _____

Skills learned: _____

_____

Key courses, programs: _____

_____

Professional Associations/Community Activities

Name of group/offices held: _____

Dates of membership: _____

Military Service

Branch: _____

_____

Dates served: _____

Highest rank achieved: _____

Type of discharge: _____

Achievements: _____

_____

COMPUTER SKILLS

PC or Mac/operating systems: _____

Software/hardware applications: _____

Programming languages: _____

Networking tools: _____

FOREIGN LANGUAGES

Language/proficiency: _____

Resume.com's List of Action Verbs

IN ALPHABETICAL ORDER

A–B
accompanied
accomplished
achieved
acquired
acted
activated
adapted
added
addressed
adhered
adjusted
administered
adopted
advanced
advertised
advised
advocated
aided
affected
allocated
altered

amended
amplified
analyzed
anticipated
appointed
appraised
approached
approved
arbitrated
arranged
ascertained
assembled
assessed
assigned
assumed
assisted
audited
augmented
authored
authorized
automated
awarded

balanced
bargained
bought
broadened
budgeted
built

C
calculated
capitalized
captured
carried out
cataloged
centralized
challenged
chaired
checked
chose
circulated
clarified
cleared

closed
cold called
collaborated
collected
combined
commissioned
committed
communicated
compared
compiled
complied
completed
composed
computed
conceived
conceptualized
concluded
condensed
conducted
conferred
consolidated
constructed

consulted
contracted
contributed
controlled
converted
convinced
coordinated
corrected
corresponded
counseled
created
critiqued
cultivated
cut

D
debugged
decided
decentralized
decreased
defined
delegated
delivered
demonstrated
depreciated
described
designated
designed
determined
developed
devised
diagrammed
directed
disclosed
discounted
discovered
dispatched
displayed
dissembled
distinguished
distributed
diversified
divested
documented
doubled
drafted

E
earned
eased
edited
effected
elected
eliminated
employed

enabled
encouraged
endorsed
enforced
engaged
engineered
enhanced
enlarged
enriched
entered
entertained
established
estimated
evaluated
examined
exceeded
exchanged
executed
exercised
expanded
expedited
explained
exposed
extended
extracted

F–H
facilitated
familiarized
fashioned
fielded
figured
financed
focused
forecasted
formalized
formed
formulated
fortified
found
founded
fulfilled
functioned
furnished
gained
gathered
gauged
gave
generated
governed
graded
granted
greeted
grouped
guided
handled

headed
hired
hosted

I
identified
illustrated
implemented
improved
improvised
inaugurated
indoctrinated
increased
incurred
induced
influenced
informed
initiated
innovated
inquired
inspected
inspired
installed
instilled
instituted
instructed
insured
interfaced
interpreted
interviewed
introduced
invented
inventoried
invested
investigated
invited
involved
isolated
issued

J–M
joined
judged
launched
lectured
led
liaised
liquidated
litigated
lobbied
localized
located
maintained
managed
mapped

marketed
maximized
measured
mediated
merchandised
merged
minimized
modeled
moderated
modernized
modified
monitored
motivated
multiplied

N–O
named
narrated
negotiated
nurtured
observed
obtained
offered
offset
opened
operated
orchestrated
ordered
organized
originated
overhauled
oversaw

P
paid
participated
passed
patterned
penalized
perceived
performed
permitted
persuaded
phased out
pinpointed
pioneered
placed
planned
prepared
presented
preserved
presided
prevented
priced
printed

prioritized
probed
processed
procured
produced
profiled
programmed
projected
promoted
prompted
proposed
proved
provided
publicized
published
purchased
pursued

Q–R
quantified
quoted
raised
ranked
rated
reacted
read
received
recommended
reconciled
recorded
recovered
recruited
rectified
redesigned
reduced
referred
refined
regained
regulated
rehabilitated

reinforced
reinstated
rejected
related
remedied
remodeled
renegotiated
reorganized
replaced
repaired
reported
represented
requested
researched
resolved
responded
restored
restructured
resulted
retained
retrieved
revamped
revealed
reversed
reviewed
revised
revitalized
rewarded
routed

S
saved
scheduled
screened
secured
selected
sent
separated
served
serviced

settled
shaped
shortened
showed
shrank
signed
simplified
sold
solved
spearheaded
specified
speculated
spoke
spread
stabilized
staffed
staged
standardized
steered
stimulated
strategized
streamlined
strengthened
stressed
structured
studied
submitted
substantiated
substituted
suggested
summarized
superseded
supervised
supplied
supported
surpassed
surveyed
synchronized
synergy
synthesized
systematized

T–W
tabulated
tailored
targeted
taught
terminated
tested
testified
tightened
took
traced
traded
trained
transacted
transferred
transformed
translated
transported
traveled
treated
tripled
uncovered
undertook
unified
united
updated
upgraded
used
utilized
validated
valued
verified
viewed
visited
weighed
welcomed
widened
witnessed
won
worked
wrote

Index

ABOUT THE AUTHORS

Rose Curtis, CPRW, and **Warren Simons, CPRW,** served as Senior Managing Editors of Resume.com, the nation's leader in Web-based career services, with more than 100 professional resume writers and career consultants across the nation.